Perspectives on Cormac McCarthy

Perspectives on Cormac McCarthy

REVISED EDITION

EDITED BY

EDWIN T. ARNOLD

AND

DIANNE C. LUCE

UNIVERSITY PRESS OF MISSISSIPPI
Jackson

http://www.upress.state.ms.us

Southern Quarterly Series

Copyright © 1999 by *The Southern Quarterly*
Manufactured in the United States of America

Print-on-Demand Edition

The paper in this book meets the guidelines for permanence and durability of the Committee on Production Guidelines for Book Longevity of the Council on Library Resources.

Library of Congress Cataloging-in-Publication Data

Perspectives on Cormac McCarthy / edited by Edwin T. Arnold and Dianne
   C. Luce. — Rev. ed.
      p. cm. — (Southern quarterly series)
   Includes bibliographical references and index.
   ISBN 1-57806-104-0 (cloth : alk. paper). — ISBN 1-57806-105-9
(paper : alk. paper)
   1. McCarthy, Cormac, 1933-   — Criticism and interpretation.
2. Mexican-American Border Region — In literature.   3. Tennessee,
East — In literature.   4. Southern States — In literature.
I. Arnold, Edwin T.   II. Luce, Dianne C.   III. Series.
PS3563.C337Z82   1999
813'.54—dc21   98-36319
                                             CIP

British Library Cataloging-in-Publication Data available

Contents

Introduction

In his 1974 *New Yorker* review of Cormac McCarthy's third novel, *Child of God,* Robert Coles wrote, "Cormac McCarthy is a forty-year-old American novelist who lives in the high country of Tennessee. His first and second novels, *The Orchard Keeper* and *Outer Dark,* earned him awards and fellowships. His *Child of God* . . . will further enhance his reputation. . . . Mr. McCarthy might easily have obtained a fortune with this novel, but he was not intent upon a psychiatrist's best-seller, and one begins to wonder whether he must reach many Americans through the long, circuitous route Faulkner took: a limited recognition here, increasing response from Europeans to his strange and brooding novels, and only later the broader acknowledgment of his own countrymen" ("The Stranger" 87). Coles's question was an appropriate one and was still worth considering twenty years later, when we first compiled this collection, even though McCarthy's time of recognition finally seemed to be at hand. From the publication of *The Orchard Keeper* in 1965 up to the arrival of *All the Pretty Horses* in 1992, McCarthy worked largely in obscurity. Although published by a prestigious company, Random House, the books before *All the Pretty Horses* sold poorly, despite often impressive, not to say impassioned, reviews. First examined primarily as a southern writer—Orville Prescott's *New York Times* review of *The Orchard Keeper,* for example, was entitled "Still Another Disciple of William Faulkner"— McCarthy came to confound those who attempted thus to categorize him. While he employed southern locales and folkways, his stories reverberated beyond them. His subsequent movement from the hills and towns of Tennessee in his first four novels to the borderlands and deserts of the Southwest in the next two further challenged any easy assumptions previously made. In addition, McCarthy's adamant refusal to publicize either himself or his work—as Madison Smartt Bell wittily put it, "[H]e shunned publicity so effectively that he wasn't even famous for it" ("The Man Who Understood

Horses," *New York Times Book Review* 9) reinforced his reputation as a reclusive, brilliant, but dark and difficult cult writer. He was tagged by Vereen M. Bell as the "best unknown major writer by many measures" (*Achievement* xii), a line that was often repeated in subsequent profiles.

Although McCarthy has guarded the details of his personal life, he is by no means the brooding, solitary figure sometimes conjured up by rumor and tale. He is third oldest of six children (he has two brothers and three sisters) born to Charles Joseph and Gladys Christina McGrail McCarthy. The family moved from Providence, Rhode Island, in 1937, when Cormac was four, to Knoxville, Tennessee, where Charles McCarthy served on the legal staff of the Tennessee Valley Authority from 1934 to 1967 (as chief counsel from 1958–67). He and his wife then moved to Washington, DC, where he was principal attorney in a private law partnership until his retirement ("McCarthy, Charles Joseph").

The McCarthys lived in Knox County just outside Knoxville. Cormac (as eldest son, he was originally named for his father but later legally changed his name to the Gaelic equivalent of "son of Charles") attended Catholic High School in Knoxville and entered the University of Tennessee in 1951–52 as a liberal arts major. In 1953 he joined the US Air Force and served for four years, spending half of that time stationed in Alaska where he hosted a radio show. In 1957–60 he returned to the university, where he published two stories in the student literary publication *The Phoenix* (under the name C. J. McCarthy, Jr.) and won the Ingram-Merrill Award for creative writing in 1959 and 1960. In 1961 he married a fellow student, Lee Holleman, with whom he had a son, Cullen. Leaving the university without a degree, McCarthy and family moved to Chicago where Cormac worked, reportedly as a salesman in an auto parts store, while writing his first novel. After they returned to Sevier County, Tennessee, his marriage to Lee McCarthy ended. (Lee McCarthy would later write about their marriage in her book of poetry *Desire's Door* [1991].) Leaving home, McCarthy lived in Asheville and then New Orleans, continuing work on his first book. *The Orchard Keeper* was accepted by Random House—his editor there was Albert Erskine, who had been William Faulkner's long-time editor until Faulkner's death in 1962—and published in May of 1965.

The Orchard Keeper won the William Faulkner Foundation Award for the best first novel by an American and received a number of positive, though sometimes cautious, reviews in the national media. Most included, perhaps inevitably, a comparison with Faulkner. Thus, Orville Prescott wrote of McCarthy, "In his *The Orchard Keeper* he has his own story to tell; but he tells it with so many of Faulkner's literary devices and mannerisms that he half submerges his own talents beneath a flood of imitation. . . . All these factors insure that *The Orchard Keeper* is an exasperating book. But the wonder is that in spite of them it is also an impressive book" ("Still Another Disciple" 49). Others, however, saw it as illustrating a new approach to writing about the South. James G. Murray noted in *America*, "This is an interesting first novel by a young Southerner: interesting in part because it does not seem to be autobiographical, and in part because it almost (but not entirely) rejects the influence, more bad than good, of the Southern *mystique* . . . . [I]t is quite exceptional for young writers to be so objective" (866). Granville Hicks concluded in *Saturday Review*, "Although the novel as a whole develops erratically, particular episodes have narrative power. With his gift for vivid description and his strength in creating characters, McCarthy is another man to watch" ("Six Firsts for Summer" 36).

Even before the publication of *The Orchard Keeper*, McCarthy had received a traveling fellowship from the American Academy of Arts and Letters. With this support, in the summer of 1965 he shipped out on the liner *Sylvania* intending to visit Ireland, the home of his ancestors (the historic Cormac McCarthy is the king who built Blarney Castle). On board he met Anne DeLisle, a young English singer/dancer working on the ship bound home after entertaining in the States. Cormac and Anne married in England in 1966. That same year, McCarthy received a Rockefeller Foundation Grant (1966–68), and together he and Anne traveled by car through southern England, France, Switzerland, Italy and Spain before residing for a time on the island of Ibiza. There McCarthy finished revisions of his second novel *Outer Dark*. Anne DeLisle later recalled, "That was a time when Ebiza [sic] was all writers and musicians and it really was a bohemian time and everybody was avant garde, and I think it was like peopl. were trying to recapture a feeling of '20s Paris with Hemingway. . . . It never quite made it, but still it was an exciting time. We never should have left, but I, by that time, was very eager to come to America. I couldn't wait to see where he came from and how he lived" (Williams, "Annie DeLisle," E2). Returning to America on the *Queen Elizabeth* in 1967, the McCarthys settled in Rockford, Tennessee, outside Knoxville. "I was still young and this was the other side of [the] world to me," Anne DeLisle remembered. "He had five brothers and sisters and lots of nieces and nephews who were especially kind to me. We lived in a little house for $50 a month, a little pig farm. Just outrageous" ("Annie DeLisle" E2). In 1968 Random House published *Outer Dark*, again to generally strong reviews. Thomas Lask, in the *New York Times*, wrote, "Cormac McCarthy's second novel, *Outer Dark*, combines the mythic and the actual in a perfectly executed work of the imagination. He has made the fabulous real, the ordinary mysterious. It is as if Elizabeth Madox Roberts's *The Time of Man*, with its earthbound folkways and inarticulate people, had been

mated with one of Isak Dineson's gothic tales" ("Southern Gothic" 33). Guy
Davenport, in his *New York Times Book Review* article, also drew the connection to Dineson, adding, "Nor does Mr. McCarthy waste a single word on
his characters' thoughts. With total objectivity he describes what they do and
records their speech. Such discipline comes not only from mastery over
words but from an understanding wise enough and compassionate enough to
dare tell so abysmally dark a story" ("Appalachian Gothic" 4). Walter Sullivan, another early supporter but also a consistently demanding critic of Mc-
Carthy, noted in *Sewanee Review*, "There is no way to overstate the power,
the absolute literary virtuosity, with which McCarthy draws his scenes. He
writes about the finite world with an accuracy so absolute that his characters
give the impression of a universality which they have no right to claim. . . .
It is the way of the good writer to find the universal in the particular, for finally it is the universal that he seeks. McCarthy, on the other hand, seems to
love the singular for its own sake: he appears to seek out those devices and
people and situations that will engage us by their very strangeness." He concluded, "There is no way to avoid grappling with the intractable reality that
surrounds us. Even someone as extraordinarily gifted as McCarthy must pay
the full price that his art demands" ("Where Have All the Flowers Gone?"
661, 662). Other critics faulted McCarthy for his increasingly dense style
and sometimes arcane vocabulary, which many of them continued to see as
a bad imitation of Faulkner.

In 1969, McCarthy was awarded a Guggenheim Fellowship for creative writing. He and Anne moved into a small barn near Louisville, Tennessee, which
McCarthy renovated, adding a stone room and chimneys. "He did every bit of
that work himself," Anne remembered, "the stone work. All the rocks that you
see, we used to pick them up on the side of the road and from fields. He got
wood that he had cut, kiln-dried at a lumber mill in Townsend" (Williams,
"Annie DeLisle" E2). Reportedly McCarthy also salvaged bricks from the childhood house of James Agee, which was being torn down for the urban renewal in
downtown Knoxville, and used them to construct a wall in his own home.

McCarthy's next book was his most shocking and controversial to date.
Child of God, published in 1973, was inspired by actual events. A dispassion-
ate examination of a man driven by isolation and loneliness to murder and
necrophilia, the story challenged its readers to look beyond the sensational and
sometimes weirdly comic morbidity of its plot and into the heart of a crazed,
lost soul. Some were unable to do so, declaring the book depraved or even de-
spicable, a terrible misuse of McCarthy's obvious talent. "[T]he carefully cold,
sour diction of this book—whose hostility toward the reader surpasses even that
of the world toward Lester [Ballard]—does not often let us see beyond its nasty

'writing' into moments we can see for themselves, rendered. And such moments, authentic though they feel, do not much help a novel so lacking in human momentum or point," Richard Brickner wrote in the *New York Times Book Review* ("A hero cast out" 7). But *Child of God* also elicited the most thoughtful considerations of McCarthy thus far in his career. In addition to Robert Coles's lengthy essay in *New Yorker,* reviews by Anatole Broyard, Peter Prescott, Jonathan Yardley and Doris Grumbach all struggled with McCarthy's masterful portrayal of ghastly actions. "Whenever a theory of esthetics enters into the discussion of a novel it tends to distract somewhat from the point, that the *experience* of the book is the real thing, that there are varieties of such experience, and that some of them, a few of them, are so intense, so, well, *religious,* as to elude description by the critic attempting to communicate what he has felt," Grumbach wrote in *The New Republic.* "This is the long way into *Child of God,* a reading experience so impressive, so 'new,' so clearly made well that it seems almost to defy the easy esthetic categories and at the same time to cause me to thrash about for some help with the necessary description of my enthusiasm" ("Practitioner of Ghastliness" 26). Yardley declared in the *Washington Post Book World* that "McCarthy is perhaps the closest we have to a genuine heir to the Faulkner tradition. Yet he is not merely a skilled imitator. His novels have a stark, mythic quality that is very much their own. . . . The sordid material of Lester Ballard's tale becomes more than an exercise in southern grotesque because of McCarthy's artistry. . . . *Child of God* is an extraordinary book" ("Alone, Alone" 1).

In 1975, McCarthy turned his talents to screenwriting. He had long had an interest in drama, having himself acted in high school and while in the Air Force in Alaska. Largely because of the unconventional cinematic qualities of *Child of God*, independent producer-director Richard Pearce sought McCarthy out to script "The Gardener's Son" for public television's "Visions" series. Pearce was impressed that in *Child of God*, "By never presuming an author's license to enter the mind of his protagonist, McCarthy had been able to insure the almost complete inscrutability of his subject and subject matter, while at the same time thoroughly investigating it. Here was 'Negative Capability' of a very high order" ("Foreword" [v]). McCarthy and Pearce spent some time in South Carolina researching the historical event on which the film is based, then returned to McCarthy's home, where Pearce was on hand while McCarthy did the writing ("Foreword" [vi]). The resulting film was first aired in January of 1977. It was also shown at the Berlin and Edinburgh Film Festivals and received two Emmy Award nominations ("Foreword" [vi]).

McCarthy separated from Anne DeLisle in 1976 (there were no children), and moved shortly thereafter to El Paso, Texas, where he had already begun to work, and where he has continued to live. He and Anne were divorced several years later. In 1979, he published his fourth novel *Suttree,* on which he had worked intermittently for almost twenty years. This was McCarthy's "big" book, the one many consider the best of his southern novels. Set primarily in Knoxville in the early 1950s, the book details the events in the life of Cornelius Suttree, a young man from a prominent family who has chosen to live with the down-and-out in the McAnally Flats area of the city. While the story is based in experience—the characters, events and places often identifiable by local Knoxvillians—the extent of its autobiographical nature is difficult to determine. As Guy Davenport wrote in the *National Review,* "there is something of a portrait of the artist as a young man about this book. Coming after three objective novels with no trace of a self-portrait, there is nothing here of the author digesting his adolescence. Instead, it would seem that the author has projected himself into a character he might have been were circumstances otherwise, or that he is being autobiographical in an obliquely symbolic way" ("Silurian Southern" 369). The book hit close to home, resulting, according to the Knoxville *News-Sentinel,* in "more talk about town than any novel since James Agee's *A Death in the Family*" (Williams, "Cormac McCarthy's bibliography" E2). The *Memphis Press-Scimitar* ran an angry review, "'A Masterpiece of Filth': Portrait of Knoxville Forgets to Be Fair," to which the historian and novelist Shelby Foote, a long-time admirer of McCarthy, responded with a letter passionately defending the book. Other reviewers drew apt comparisons between McCarthy and Joyce, comparisons *Suttree* both invited and sustained. The majority commented on the sprawling structure of the lengthy story, which spans a period of six years (1950–55), noting an overabundance of episodes and characters and sensations. "One gets the impression that McCarthy walks through the world cramming his brain with experience both actual and vicarious and then goes to work and gives everything back, scene upon scene, the devil take the hindmost," Walter Sullivan wrote in *Sewanee Review.* "McCarthy is certainly the most talented novelist of his generation. He is the only writer to emerge since World War II who can bear comparison to Faulkner. . . . But I, for one, can also deplore what seems to me to be a limited use of an enormous talent. In his almost exclusive concern with the grotesque McCarthy offers a distorted view of creation, fragmented and debauched though that creation now may be. I hope he will read Faulkner again and learn how to broaden his scope and enlarge his image" ("Model Citizens and Marginal Cases" 341, 343). Still others celebrated that very scope and achievement. "The book comes at us like a horrifying flood. The language licks, batters, wounds—a poetic, troubled rush of debris. It is personal and tough, without that boring neatness and desire for resolution that you can get in any well-made novel," Jerome Charyn stated in the *New York Times Book Review* ("Doomed Huck" 15), while the novelist Nelson Algren proclaimed in the *Chicago Tribune Book World,* "This is a big, beautiful book, the best work of fiction to come along in years. It is as unique as the work of Dylan Thomas or Thomas Wolfe. It will be around for a long, long time" ("A memorable American comedy" 1).

In 1981, during a trip home to Tennessee from El Paso, McCarthy was notified (while staying in a Knoxville motel run by a friend) that he had been awarded a MacArthur Fellowship, also known as the "genius" grant. This money supported him during the writing of his next novel, an historical western set in the 1840s. While he worked on *Blood Meridian, or the Evening Redness in the West,* his first three novels (none of which, along with *Suttree,* had sold more than several thousand copies apiece) were reissued in paperback by Ecco Press in their "Neglected Books of the Twentieth Century" series. (*Blood Meridian* would also be reissued in paperback by Ecco in 1986; *Suttree* by Vintage, again in 1986, as one of the "Vintage Contemporaries.") Based on extensive research and first-hand knowledge of the locales (McCarthy retraced the journeys described in the book), *Blood Meridian* details the exploits of a band of scalp hunters as they murder, pillage, rape and desecrate throughout the border lands of the Southwest. For all of its repellent violence and gore, the book has haunted those who stayed with it. Although it has struck many readers initially as devoid of moral or even meaning, it has nevertheless compelled its readers to attempt an understanding. *Blood Meridian* received few major reviews at the time of publication, but it has since become one of the touchstones by which McCarthy readers define themselves. Some admirers of his "southern" novels disapproved of his new subject, his "metaphysical western." "This novel, despite its chronicling of appalling horrors and its straining for apocalyptic effects, is boring," Terence Moran declared in *The New Republic.* "McCarthy should go home, and take another, closer look. He'll find the real devil soon enough there" ("The Wired West" 38). Others saw more. "Any page of his work reveals his originality, a passionate voice given equally to ugliness and lyricism," wrote Caryn James in the *New York Times Book Review.* "This latest book is his most important, for it puts in perspective the Faulknerian language and unprovoked violence running through the previous works, which were often viewed as exercises in style or studies of evil. *Blood Meridian* makes it clear that all along Mr. McCarthy has asked us to witness evil not in order to understand it but to affirm its inexplicable reality; his elaborate language invents a world hinged between the real and surreal, jolting us out of complacency ("Is Everybody Dead Around Here?" 31). In the *Los Angeles Times Book Review* (where it appeared on the same page as a review of Larry McMurtry's romantic and nostalgic western *Lonesome Dove*), the assessment by Tom Nolan decreed *Blood Meridian* "a theological purgative, an allegory on the nature of evil as timeless as Goya's hallucinations on war, monomaniacal in its conceptions and execution" (B2). Slowly, this book above others (with *Suttree* as a close second) developed a dedicated readership. Studied and discussed as an historical novel, as a philosophical or theological treatise, or as a major achievement of postmodern fiction, *Blood Meridian* remains for many McCarthy's most problematic and extraordinary work to date.

By 1990, with five acclaimed novels to his name, with each novel carving out its own significant place in our national literature, yet with each novel going largely unread except by a small group of admirers, McCarthy seemed no closer to public recognition than when Robert Coles pondered the state of McCarthy's reputation some sixteen years earlier. In fact, he was so little known that when the Arena Stage in Washington DC was selected for a 1991 grant from the American Express/John F. Kennedy Center Fund for New American Plays to support the theatre's development of McCarthy's play *The Stonemason* for production, Arena Stage principals were surprised to discover that McCarthy was not a young black playwright. McCarthy went to Washington in March 1992 to participate in a workshop on the play, but the difficulties of the play itself, the conflicting expectations among the director and actors and the playwright, political concerns on the part of some connected with Arena Stage, and communication problems that prevented the collaboration process from working led to the production's being canceled under very awkward circumstances (Arnold, 117, 120–126). However, McCarthy's anonymity was soon to change. Following Albert Erskine's retirement (*Blood Meridian* is dedicated to him), McCarthy worked with editor Gary Fisketjon at Knopf, known for the selectivity of its publications and the high-profile publicity given them. Scholarly articles on McCarthy began to appear with some regularity, especially after the publication in 1988 of Vereen M. Bell's *The Achievement of Cormac McCarthy,* the first published book-length study of McCarthy's work. Our own special McCarthy issue of *The Southern Quarterly,* the first such collection of essays devoted to McCarthy, appeared in Summer 1992. It was in that same year that, almost thirty years after writing his first novel, McCarthy was at last discovered by the general reading public following Knopf's publication of *All the Pretty Horses,* the first volume of McCarthy's Border Trilogy. It tells the story of the idealistic sixteen-year-old Texan John Grady Cole, who ventures into Mexico to try to recover the kind of ranching life he has lost at home when his grandfather dies and his mother sells the family property, and whose venture is a confrontation with the intractability of the world. Combining a love story, an action plot, and a coming-of-age narrative, the book sold over 100,000 copies in less than a year's time. In December of 1992 it won the National Book Award for fiction, and in March 1993 it won the National Book Critics Circle Award for fiction (it was considered a favorite for the Pulitzer Prize as well, but lost to *A Good Scent From a Strange Mountain* by Robert Olen Butler). Vintage International paperbacks began reprinting all the earlier novels starting with *Suttree* and *Blood Meridian*, and McCarthy's books have remained in print throughout the 1990's. Articles on McCarthy appeared in such diverse publications as *Newsweek, Mirabella* and *Texas Monthly*, and McCarthy himself consented to his first substantial interview, published in *The New York Times Magazine*. It was reported that Mike Nichols had bought the screen rights to *All the Pretty Horses*. The publication of the second volume of the Border Trilogy was eagerly anticipated and was projected (over-optimistically, it proved) for January 1994.

Such a convergence of well-coordinated events kept McCarthy before the public as never before, insuring that his days of obscurity were now behind him. In the midst of the uproar of publicity some reviewers took the occasion to reassess the writer's achievement, to note that in the comparatively genial and inviting story of *All the Pretty Horses* are thematic and narrative concerns which link it to the dramatically darker and more disturbing books which preceded it. In the *Chicago Tribune*, Christopher Zenowich wrote "This is a prayer in prose fiction, a homage to the world. It has been for nearly 30 years present in McCarthy's work. His sentences, his vision are unique" ("Coming of age" sec. 14: 10). Madison Smartt Bell also stressed McCarthy's completely original vision: "His project is unlike that of any other writer: to make artifacts composed of human language but detached from a human reference point. That sense of evil that seems to suffuse his novels is illusory; it comes from our discomfort in the presence of a system that is not scaled to ourselves, within which our civilizations may be as ephemeral as flowers. The deity that presides over Mr. McCarthy's world has not modeled itself on humanity; its voice most resembles the one that addressed Job out of the whirlwind" ("The Man Who Understood Horses" 11). But for the most part the reviews of *All the Pretty Horses* contributed more to media show than to understanding. The book, despite substantial praise, received less thoughtful consideration than most of McCarthy's earlier novels. Its place in the canon had yet to be fully appreciated.

All the Pretty Horses still constitutes McCarthy's most popular success. By

June 1994 it had sold 180,000 hardcover copies and 300,000 in paperback, justifying an astonishing first printing of 200,000 copies for *The Crossing*, the second volume of the Border Trilogy (Jones, "Brightening" 54). Sales of *All the Pretty Horses* in paperback continued strong for months after the publication of *The Crossing*. *All the Pretty Horses* remained on the *Publishers Weekly* trade paperback bestseller list for forty-three weeks, through November 7, 1994.

The *Crossing* was published in June 1994. The novel had been eagerly awaited as the sequel to *All the Pretty Horses*, and advance publication of excerpts from the novel in *Esquire* and *Sports Afield* further whetted readers' appetites. *The Crossing* appeared on the *Publishers Weekly* hardcover bestseller list for eleven weeks from 20 June through 29 August 1994 (when *All the Pretty Horses* was still number four on the paperback bestseller list), and it was widely reviewed. But this longer, philosophically weightier novel puzzled those reviewers who expected the further adventures of John Grady Cole, and it failed to achieve the same degree of success as the first volume. *The Crossing* introduced a new set of characters in the years just before World War II, and while sixteen-year-old Billy Parham and his fated younger brother Boyd journey into Mexico on quests that parallel John Grady's, their experiences are more devastating. While some reviewers offered little more than perfunctory plot summaries, *The Crossing* elicited high praise and sharp insight from a few. Bruce Allen wrote in the *Chicago Tribune*, "This novel's intricate view of human travail embraces both blunt fatalism . . . and the stoical conviction that we do not, after all, wander in a meaningless void. . . . [T]his ambitious novel offers a masterly display of tonal control and some of the most pitch-perfect rapturous prose being written these days" ("The land of wounded men" 5). In the *New York Times Book Review*, Robert Hass labelled *The Crossing* "a miracle in prose, an American original . . . [that] deserves to sit on the same shelf certainly with 'Beloved' and 'As I Lay Dying,' 'Pudd'nhead Wilson' and 'The Confidence-Man'." He predicted that while it would remind readers of Faulkner, Twain, Melville, Shakespeare, Hemingway, O'Connor, Cervantes, Beckett, and Conrad, as well as John Ford, Sam Peckinpah and Sergio Leone, " 'The Crossing' is a tale so riveting—it immerses the reader so entirely in its violent and stunningly beautiful, inconsolable landscapes—that there is hardly time to reflect on its many literary and cinematic echoes or on the fact that Mr. McCarthy is a writer who can plunder almost any source and make it his own" ("Travels With A She-Wolf" 1). Sven Birkerts' lengthy review in *The New Republic* commented that even more than *All the Pretty Horses*, *The Crossing* "achieves resonance." Birkerts continued, "By structuring the narrative as he has, by writing with such unflagging lyrical power, McCarthy displaces our focus from the outer events to the primal archetypes that underlie them. The novel shifts us constantly from the physical to the metaphysical, creating a recursiveness of action in which we suddenly catch the ozone whiff of human souls eking their way forward under an indifferent sky" ("The Lone Soul State" 40). And Alan Ryan wrote for the Atlanta *Journal-Constitution*, "Despite the sunshine of his settings, McCarthy's vision is dark and dreadful, and 'The Crossing' is an exhausting book. It forces the reader to linger, to ponder its images and intent, to look away from the page and remember to breathe. This *noir* neo-western epic of the soul in search of a home is, by any definition, a great, great work of art" ("A soul in search of a home" N10).

In May 1994, just weeks before the publication of *The Crossing* by Knopf, Ecco Press released McCarthy's still unproduced five-act stage play, *The Stonemason*, about a family of black masons in Louisville, Kentucky—a play that embodies McCarthy's ideas about craftsmanship and the way the world itself is made, about human pride and compassion. In its published form, the play was moderately successful. The book's modest first printing of 10,000 copies sold out by August and was followed by a second printing. A limited signed edition, priced at $125 per copy, had sold out within two hours (Arnold 118). *The Stonemason* received very little notice in the popular press, but Bruce Allen, who reviewed the play together with *The Crossing* in the *Chicago Tribune*, wrote: "Expertly constructed and limpidly written, the play offers several incisive brief characterizations, and it triumphs in its presenta-tion of Papaw, whose earthy wisdom McCarthy makes altogether credible. . . . Like all McCarthy's work, 'The Stonemason' is a mixture of vividly rendered conflict and complex discursive commentary. Compared to his novels, it's minor work but seems to this reader both skillfuly [sic] fashioned and emi-nently playable" ("The land of wounded men" 5). In his brief notice for *Li-brary Journal*, actor-playwright Peter Josyph credited the work with "some wonderful scenes" but questioned its playability, stating that the play "places McCarthy—arguably America's best living novelist—in the long tradition of novelists who have tried the dramatic form and failed to meet its elusive de-mands" (76). Richard Ryan, who briefly considered *The Stonemason* in his review of *The Crossing*, noticed that it "shows, perhaps more strongly than any of McCarthy's writings to date, a deeply Christian sensibility, with Bib-lical nuances rippling across and through it" (13).

Ecco followed its publication of *The Stonemason* with *The Gardener's Son*, McCarthy's screenplay from the 1970's, in September of 1996. The book received almost no attention from reviewers, but in a brief notice for

Booklist, Bonnie Smothers wrote, "This is a monumental small work for Mc-Carthy, lesser in scope and impact than his *All the Pretty Horses* . . . or *The Crossing* . . . but bearing in full measure his gift—that ability to fit complex and universal emotions into ordinary lives and still preserve all of their power and significance" (200).

Although McCarthy has lived an inconspicuous life in El Paso, continuing to preserve his time and energy for writing, local newspapers and literary organizations gradually became aware of the remarkable writer they had in their transplanted citizen. Even before the publication of *All the Pretty Horses*, McCarthy was inducted into the *El Paso Herald-Post* Writers Hall of Fame in May 1991 (Martin, A1). The Texas Institute of Letters awarded McCarthy the Jesse H. Jones Award for *All the Pretty Horses* ("Texas Institute" B1) and the Lon Tinkle lifetime achievement award in April of 1997 ("El Paso writers" F1).

In March of 1998, announcements were finally made for the production of the film version of *All the Pretty Horses*. Based on a screenplay by Ted Tally and directed by Billy Bob Thornton, the film casts Matt Damon in the role of John Grady Cole. In May, publication of *Cities of the Plain*, the concluding volume of the Border Trilogy, occurred with a simultaneous release of an abridged audio-book read by Brad Pitt. The first printing of the novel was 200,000 copies, matching that of *The Crossing*; and like *The Crossing*, *Cities of the Plain* was selected as a Book-of-the-Month Club alternate ("Forecasts" 58). The novel unites John Grady Cole and Billy Parham on a ranch in New Mexico near El Paso in 1952, when John Grady is nineteen and Billy is twenty-eight. The plot of the novel had been substantially worked out in a screenplay of the same name, which McCarthy wrote in the early 1980's (Woodward 40). Billy introduces John Grady to the brothels of Juárez, where he falls in love with a young prostitute, tries to rescue her from bondage there so that they can marry, and is killed by her pimp in a knife fight that recalls his contest with the *cuchillero* in the Saltillo prison in *All the Pretty Horses*. Billy, whose friendship with the young John Grady has prompted him to cease his wandering, tries to warn and protect his friend but is unsuccessful. He can only witness his death and carry his body back across the border, recalling his history with Boyd in *The Crossing*. The novel proper is spare of the overt metaphysical considerations that are so prominent in *The Crossing*, but its epilogue, in which a stranger tells an aged Billy yet another parable, returns to them in its metaphors of the journey, maps, images, the teller and the tale, the dream, the world. Early reviews of *Cities of the Plain* were respectful but unenthusiastic and often uncomprehending, but by May 31 the novel was ninth on the

New York Times bestseller list for hardback fiction, and third in the *Los Angeles Times* ranking for Southern California. Reviewers who had read McCarthy's earlier novels were most able to appreciate his achievement in *Cities of the Plain*. In *Newsweek*, Malcolm Jones, Jr. followed his earlier review of *The Crossing* with the assessment that *Cities of the Plain* is "a splendid Western romance, full of death and heartbreak. . . . Nobody living writes about friendship better than McCarthy, nobody writes better about animals, or the land, the desert especially. With each book, he expands the territory of American fiction" ("Writing Into the Sunset" 75). Michael Dirda, who reviewed *The Crossing* thoughtfully for the *Washington Post Book World*, reassessed McCarthy's western novels in his review of *Cities of the Plain*: "Of Cormac McCarthy's four Western novels I think *Blood Meridian* and *All the Pretty Horses*—as different as they are—deserve their reputations as masterpieces of postwar American literature. To my mind and ear, *The Crossing* is overburdened by its philosophical divagations, and *Cities of the Plain* feels too light with its thinner texture and familiar storyline. . . . Like the novelists he admires—Melville, Dostoyevsky, Faulkner—Cormac McCarthy has created an imaginative oeuvre greater and deeper than any single book. Such writers wrestle with the gods themselves" ("The Last Roundup" 5).

On May 24, 1998, El Paso journalist Betty Ligon reported that McCarthy was rumored to have married Jennifer Winkley, a young woman who had attended the University of Texas at El Paso in the early 1990's, "focusing on English and creative writing"—and whom McCarthy had known for at least three years. Ligon wrote, "It's been confirmed that the couple bought a house in the upscale Coronado Country Club and friends say they are nesting" ("Looks like Cormac" 2b).

Scholarly attention to McCarthy has grown steadily since the early 1990's. The Cormac McCarthy Society, formed at the McCarthy Conference at Bellarmine College in 1993, held summer and fall conferences in 1996 and 1997, and as of this writing is planning its first colloquy in Europe for June 1998 and the first International Cormac McCarthy Colloquy for October 1998 in El Paso. The Society was accepted as a member of the American Literature Association, and the first session devoted to McCarthy took place at the national conference in San Diego in May 1998. Marty Priola created the first Cormac McCarthy Homepage <www.cormacmccarthy.com> in 1995 and in January 1997 it became the host for the Cormac McCarthy Society on the internet. It is an active site with the new *Cormac McCarthy Journal*, bibliographies of scholarship in English, French, and German, translations of the Spanish in McCarthy's novels, a forum for discussion of his work, and news about conferences and publications. 1996 also saw the publication of the first article on McCarthy in *American Literature*. Articles regularly appear now in such journals as *Southern Quarterly*, *Mississippi Quarterly*, *Western American Literature*, and *Southwestern American Literature*. A second collection of articles, *Sacred Violence: A Reader's Companion to Cormac McCarthy* (made up of selected essays from the First Cormac McCarthy Conference) was published in 1995, and other collections are currently being prepared for publication. In 1997, McCarthy was included in the Twayne United States Authors Series. And sessions or papers devoted to McCarthy are appearing at many regional conventions of MLA affiliates and smaller conferences, especially in the south and southwest. Perhaps most important for the future is that McCarthy's work is being increasingly chosen as a thesis or dissertation topic by graduate students.

The preceding chronicle provides context for the following essays. Most of them were written before the appearance or success of *All the Pretty Horses*, although surrounded by the rumors of its imminent publication. All of them came out of their writers' shared convictions that McCarthy was an underread and underappreciated writer of stunning talents. Our intention was to cover all of McCarthy's available work and to represent a variety of critical readings of that work. (*The Stonemason* is the single exception. Published in 1994, it was not included in the first edition of *Perspectives*, and receives no separate treatment in the second edition, not because it is unworthy of attention, but because of certain constraints of the publication process. For consideration of that play, we refer interested readers to Edwin T. Arnold's "Cormac McCarthy's *The Stonemason*: The Unmaking of a Play.") While some of the pieces compiled here approach McCarthy as a regional writer, we have also included essays that transcend the distinction between his southern and western novels or that suggest a framework for studies of McCarthy's career as a whole or of individual works within the context of the whole. Indeed, in these articles we have attempted to document and illuminate the full range and scope of McCarthy's accomplishment as a novelist, from his first novel to his most recent. Several of the essays concentrate on a single work: David Paul Ragan on *The Orchard Keeper*, Dianne C. Luce on McCarthy's one filmed screenplay "The Gardener's Son," Thomas D. Young, Jr. on *Suttree*, Gail M. Morrison on *All the Pretty Horses*, Dianne C. Luce on *The Crossing*, and Edwin T. Arnold on *Cities of the Plain*. Three critics—John Emil Sepich, Steven Shaviro and Leo Daugherty—examine *Blood Meridian*, each from a different stance, illustrating the multiplicity of possible studies. John M. Grammer and Edwin T. Arnold follow themes and images across several of McCarthy's books, including, in addition to those already mentioned, *Outer Dark* and *Child of God*.

It was not our purpose that these essays should emphasize any specific unifying theme other than an appreciation of McCarthy's art. Our main concern was then, and is now, to draw continued thoughtful attention to McCarthy, to encourage others to read and debate and further participate in the ongoing critical discussion.

Edwin T. Arnold   *Dianne C. Luce*   June, 1998

WORKS CITED

Algren, Nelson. "A memorable American comedy by an original storyteller." *Chicago Tribune Book World*   28 Jan. 1979, sec. 7:1.

Allen, Bruce. "The land of wounded men: A novel and a play from Cormac McCarthy, author of 'All the Pretty Horses'." *Chicago Tribune* 26 June 1994, sec. 14:5.

Arnold, Edwin T. "Cormac McCarthy's *The Stonemason*: The Unmaking of a Play." *Southern Quarterly* 33.2–3 (Winter-Spring 1995): 117–129.

Bell, Madison Smartt. "The Man Who Understood Horses." *New York Times Book Review* 17 May 1992, sec. 7: 9+.

Bell, Vereen M. *The Achievement of Cormac McCarthy*. Baton Rouge: Louisiana State UP, 1988.

Birkerts, Sven. "The Lone Soul State." *New Republic* (11 July 1994): 38–41.

Brickner, Richard P. "A hero cast out, even by tragedy." *New York Times Book Review* 13 Jan. 1974, sec. 7: 6–7.

Charyn, Jerome. "Doomed Huck." *New York Times Book Review* 18 Feb. 1979, sec. 7:14–15.

Coles, Robert. "The Stranger." *New Yorker* 26 Aug. 1974: 87–90.

Davenport, Guy. "Appalachian Gothic." *New York Times Book Review* 29 Sept. 1968, sec. 7: 4.

_____. "Silurian Southern." *National Review* 31 (16 Mar. 1979): 368–69.

Dirda, Michael. "The Last Roundup." *Washington Post Book World* 24 May 1998: 5.

"El Paso writers awarded." *El Paso Times* 18 May 1997: F1.

"Forecasts." *Publishers Weekly* 245 (6 Apr. 1998): 58.

Grumbach, Doris. "Practitioner of Ghastliness." *New Republic* 170 (9 Feb. 1974): 26–28.

Hass, Robert. "Travels With A She-Wolf." *New York Times Book Review* 12 June 1994, sec. 7: 1, 39–40.

Hicks, Granville. "Six Firsts for Summer." *Saturday Review* 48 (12 June 1965): 35–36.

James, Caryn. "Is Everybody Dead Around Here?" *New York Times Book Review* 28 Apr. 1985, sec. 7: 31.

Jones, Malcolm, Jr. "Brightening Western Star." *Newsweek* 123 (13 June 1994): 54.

_____. "Writing Into the Sunset." *Newsweek* 127 (18 May 1998): 75.

Josyph, Peter. Review of *The Stonemason*. *Library Journal* 119 (15 Apr. 1994): 76.

Lask, Thomas. "Southern Gothic." *New York Times* 23 Sept. 1968: 33.

Ligon, Betty. "Looks like Cormac is settling down." *El Paso Inc.* 24 May 1998: 2b.

Martin, Michelle. "Five writers selected for local hall of fame." *El Paso Herald-Post* 6 Apr. 1991: A1, 5.

"McCarthy, Charles Joseph." *Who's Who in America* 44th ed. (1986–87), vol. 2. Chicago: A. N. Marquis Company, 1987.

Moran, Terence. "The Wired West." *New Republic* 192 (6 May 1985): 37–38.

Murray, James G. *America* 112 (12 June 1965): 866.

Nolan, Tom. *Los Angeles Times Book Review* 9 June 1985: B2.

Pearce, Richard. "Foreword." In Cormac McCarthy, *The Gardener's Son: A Screenplay*. Hopewell, NJ: Ecco, 1996.

Prescott, Orville. "Still Another Disciple of William Faulkner." *New York Times* 12 May 1965: 49m.

Ryan, Alan. "A soul in search of a home: The American experience is at core of McCarthy's 'Crossing'." *Atlanta Journal-Constitution* 26 June 1994: N10.

Ryan, Richard. "McCarthy Bridges Gap To Mainstream Readers." *Christian Science Monitor* 7 July 1994: 13.

Smothers, Bonnie. Review of *The Gardener's Son*. *Booklist* 93 (15 Sept. 1996): 200.

Sullivan, Walter. "Model Citizens and Marginal Cases: Heroes of the Day." *Sewanee Review* 87 (Apr. 1979): 337–44.

_____. " 'Where Have All the Flowers Gone?' Part II: The Novel in the Gnostic Twilight." *Sewanee Review* 78 (Oct. 1970): 654–64.

"Texas Institute honors McCarthy." *El Paso Herald-Post* 22 Mar. 1993: B1.

Williams, Don. "Annie DeLisle: Cormac McCarthy's ex-wife prefers to recall the romance." *News-Sentinel* [Knoxville, TN] 10 June 1990: E1–2.

_____. "Cormac McCarthy's bibliography." *News-Sentinel* [Knoxville, TN] 10 June 1990: E2.

Woodward, Richard B. "Cormac McCarthy's Venomous Fiction." *New York Times Magazine* (19 April 1992): 28–31+.

Yardley, Jonathan. "Alone, Alone, All, All Alone . . ." *Washington Post Book World* 13 Jan. 1974: 1.

Zenowich, Christopher. "Coming of age: A lyrical tale of the Southwest from Cormac McCarthy." *Chicago Tribune* 10 May 1992, sec. 14: 5+.

Values and Structure in *The Orchard Keeper*

DAVID PAUL RAGAN

The crucial challenge in approaching Cormac McCarthy's demanding first novel, *The Orchard Keeper*, lies in the reader's locating a center of value, a source of moral authority. The novel's wandering structure, its shifting points of view, its refusal to invest any characters with either greater reliability or more acute perceptions all intensify the challenge and in part derive from it. Vereen M. Bell attributes the apparent lack of a coherent value system to the book's concern with "the irrelevance of the human in the impersonal scheme of things" and contrasts the actions of its characters with the natural designs against which they operate (10).[1] McCarthy depicts a world in which traditional embodiments of value—religion, community relationships, agrarian connections with the earth—have deteriorated as a result of the increasing pressure of urban culture, commercial interests and governmental intrusions upon the lives of the novel's essentially rural characters. This deterioration is a central issue in all of McCarthy's novels with Appalachian mountain settings, but it seems particularly prominent in *The Orchard Keeper*.[2]

The dislocation resulting from McCarthy's reluctance to provide an overt system of values in the novel has led some readers to misinterpret it, to decry an absence of any real values at all. Thomas Daniel Young, for instance, draws the conclusion that *The Orchard Keeper* presents "too much sin without redemption, too much horror that has no function but to furnish the reader a gratuitous emotional response" (101).[3] Such a reading ignores those areas of meaningful connection characters cultivate among themselves and in nature, and as a result the larger significance of many of the novel's seemingly random incidents evaporates. When disintegrating cultural values are understood as informing not only McCarthy's themes but his narrative method, however, the episodes reveal a fully controlled, deliberately structured examination of the intrinsic human need to order, or at least to interpret, the world of nature and to understand the motivations of men.

That these motivations are so frequently cryptic underlies the novel's structural method: the reader must piece together a serviceable apprehension of shifting cultural norms through the calculated juxtaposition of characters and incidents. McCarthy orders his material into four numbered sections which present standards of personal conduct in three generations of characters: Arthur Ownby, the old man whose traditional lifestyle enables an almost mystical connection to the cycles of nature; Marion Sylder and Kenneth Rattner, representatives of contrasting responses to the new social order; and the boy John Wesley Rattner, who attempts unsuccessfully to find a compromise between the old dispensation and the new. The sections introduce, develop and, finally, overtly define the standards by which the actions of individual characters are to be judged. Social disruption occurs, at least in part, because dialogue proves an inadequate means of asserting cultural values and instilling them in younger generations. As societal institutions begin to reflect this breakdown, they become indifferent, misguided and, finally, destructive.

Clearly, though, understanding and affirmation of values are possible in McCarthy's world, despite the prevalence of confused, misguided or willfully perverted actions. Frequently a character's integrity is manifested by the extent to which his motivations are uncorrupted by selfishness or personal delusions. John Wesley's mother, Mildred, for instance, is patently incorrect about the character and resources of her husband, Kenneth, whom Sylder has killed in self-defense. She attempts to instill in her son a sense of vindictive rage, urging him to "find the man that took away your daddy" (66). In contrast, Sylder later attempts to protect John Wesley, whom he has befriended, by offering him a simplistic interpretation of sin and retribution as practiced by the local law enforcement officials, though the

boy is rightfully suspicious of this neat package. McCarthy indicates that
the two characters serve diametrically opposing ends in these two scenes
in which the youth receives "moral" instruction: Sylder's interests are
altruistic, fatherly, protective; Mildred's are selfish, vindictive, serving no
needs but her own.

When John Wesley returns to her grave at the conclusion of the novel,
his perceptions clarify how he has responded to the figures who had most
influenced him as a child:

> He reached out and patted the stone softly, a gesture, as if perhaps to
> conjure up some image, evoke again some allegiance with a name, a
> place, hallucinated recollections in which faces merged inextricably, and
> yet true and fixed; touched it, a carved stone less real than the smell
> of woodsmoke or the taste of an old man's wine. (245)

The images he conjures are revelatory: feeling no special identification
with the watery memories of his mother, he focuses with greater clarity
on associations with his two older mentors. The woodsmoke recalls the
occasion when he had rescued Marion's hound from the icy creek and had
been warmed by a fire built in the woods; the old man who had earlier
served the boy wine is Ownby, Uncle Ather, the orchard keeper of the title,
who has told him stories and shared the wisdom distilled from his long
experience in the wilderness. These are the men whose values he has
embraced as an adult, whose view of the world determines the direction
the young man must take at the close of the book.

John Wesley heads west, away from the scenes of his youth to which
he has briefly returned for a visit noticeably lacking in nostalgia. By leaving, he rejects the locale, though not the sensibilities he has learned in
the hill country of eastern Tennessee. Ironically, these very sensibilities
contribute to his alienation from his contemporary surroundings. As
usual in *The Orchard Keeper*, the point is merely suggested through a
brief encounter. From his mother's cemetery plot, John Wesley sees a man
and woman in a car paused at a traffic light. He waves, twice, but the figures
merely continue to stare as the car pulls away. There is no response to his
gesture of acknowledgment, as if he were one of the novel's frequently
invoked relics of a prehistoric past, or one of the dead, as the iconography
of cemetery and sunset so strongly suggest. Though John Wesley is not
himself dead, his outlooks derive from figures whose names are now only
"myth, legend, dust" (246). The values he has inherited from them have
become arcane, outmoded, impractical.

John Wesley's visit to his boyhood home is the final such instance in this novel of homecomings and departures, and comparison of this one with earlier examples is instructive of McCarthy's indirect method of signifying meaning. Typically, the writer develops structural and thematic connections through parallels, contrasts and elaborations, rather than through more conventional devices.

Section I contrasts the return to the Red Branch community of both John Wesley's father, Kenneth, and the man who will become his father surrogate, Sylder. The former merely seeks a refuge until he can accumulate financial resources sufficient to escape again—through absence absolving himself of responsibility for his wife and son. He achieves this goal when the porch of the Green Fly Inn collapses and he robs the victims of the disaster. Juxtaposition of scenes suggests, though by no means certifies, that he is returning penniless from this excursion when he attacks Sylder, who kills him and dumps his body in the orchard's abandoned spray pit. Sylder's is, of course, the contrasting homecoming in this part, opposite in both circumstances and purpose from Rattner's. Sylder comes back because he has acquired money, not because he has run out. And he treats the men at the inn to drinks rather than exploiting their misfortune.

The centrality of the inn to this section reveals opposing views of community standards on an individual level. Rattner's arrival underlines both the comradeship felt by the regulars and the newcomer's alienation from them: Rattner "*lifted the bottle to his mouth, his eyes shifting among them or when they looked closing or seeking again that being in the outer dark with whom only he held communion, smiling a little to himself, the onlooker, the stranger*" (24). Though Rattner does not participate in the social structure, he understands its values and exploits them for his benefit alone. Indeed, he relies upon the ties of locale—the assumption that anyone from "back home" will be glad to offer him assistance—to wheedle his ride in Sylder's car. Sylder's reluctance to oblige stems from his desire for solitude, having just lost his job, and from Rattner's failure to observe polite form, entering the car before securing permission. Both men assume Sylder's willingness to help someone from the same region.

Uncle Ather is briefly glimpsed in section I as a solitary watcher of the night who notices Marion's car the evening of one of his sexual escapades and again the night he disposes of Rattner's body. Ownby assumes his role as the primary avatar of traditional mountain values only in part II, in which John Wesley begins to acquire the skills of woodcraft which the old man has mastered. Both Ownby and the boy are solitary largely because of their interests in the woods, the changing seasons, wild animals.[4] Trapping as a livelihood identifies them with earlier generations of woodsmen, those present before large stretches of land were cleared for farming and while game was plentiful. The difficulties the boy faces in following the old patterns of life reflect the new economic order, in which outsiders exert a growing influence upon the region which had formerly existed "beyond the dominion of laws either civil or spiritual" (16). The overbearing constable Gifford, the ludicrous humane officer Legwater and the nameless men who tend the mysterious government tank on a mountaintop represent the intrusion of institutional and bureaucratic authority upon age-old lifestyles. The values these figures project are faceless, exploitative and aligned with powers accountable to neither individual responsibility nor community standards.

The second section offers the response of the independent mountain people to this new order: Uncle Ather rejects it categorically by shooting his crude X on the government tank. Both Sylder and John Wesley attempt to adapt the new ways to their own needs: Sylder by picking up his loads of whiskey from the compound near the tank, John Wesley by claiming a hawk bounty. But all three are compromised by the imposition of the world beyond the mountains. Marion's wreck occasions his befriending John Wesley, but it affords Gifford's entrance into the community as well, foreshadowing Marion's downfall and the jeopardy the new order will place John Wesley in, should he not accede to its demands. John Wesley's courageous aid of Sylder after the car crash implicates him as an enemy of the new order, a fact the boy understands when he meets Gifford inquiring into the accident. Section III makes the danger more obvious when Gifford threatens him with incarceration and takes his traps, symbols of John Wesley's connection with the earlier modes of livelihood.

Largely, however, section III represents a diminishment in the forward progress of the novel, incorporating a paean to the values, sensibilities and passage of the older order. The dominating presence of a heavy snow induces a meditative atmosphere, slowing down the entire community. John Wesley and his friends hunt, talk about Indians (an earlier vanished race) and trapping and listen to Uncle Ather's reminiscences. Only Gifford's attempt to intimidate John Wesley and Sylder's night attack to avenge his young ward extend the action. But the personalities of the three central characters are significantly enhanced: those of Uncle Ather and Sylder by suggesting their backgrounds through fragmented memories, that of John Wesley by picturing him among boys his own age and by connecting him with Ownby, whom he questions about game animals and the legendary past.

Ownby is an appropriate source of information for the boy. The old man's face is "composed in wisdom" (148); the setting sun, anticipating that at the end of the novel, illuminates "his white hair with a prophetic translucence," and he and the boys who visit him drink the wine he serves "with the solemnity of communicants" (150). Uncle Ather provides the novel's clearest moral example: he lives alone, but his isolation is not the result of alienation from regional standards (as is Rattner's) or an attempt to circumvent the authority of the new order (such as Sylder's). Ownby accepts his obligations to the community, though he places a high premium on independence. He thinks how if he were younger he would retreat into the mountains, build his own snug cabin and "care for no man"; but he is careful to add, "Then I wouldn't be unneighborly neither" (55). He fulfills these obligations through his handling of the children who find Rattner's body, through his contributions to the boys' natural education and through his curious commitment to keeping watch over the human remains in the spray pit.

The clearest indication of Uncle Ather's adherence to standards of personal and community responsibility occurs when he is questioned by the social worker after his arrest in the novel's first section. When the young man defines the role of the welfare agency as "you see, we help people," Uncle Ather assumes he is being asked for a contribution: "Well, I ain't got nothin. I don't reckon I can hep yins any" (219). His answer, ironically humorous, clearly signals Ownby's willingness to be of assistance had he any resources; he recognizes an obligation to others in need.

Uncle Ather's values derive in part from his vital connection with the natural world. As his community links diminish, his dependence upon the wilderness intensifies. He is at peace in blizzard and flood; indeed, he is called "a lover of storms" (51). He remembers baiting younger men who could not distinguish between the screams of a "painter" and an owl, and he correctly suggests that a common house cat had damaged the fur of the mink John Wesley had trapped. He survives by gathering roots which he barters for staples, and his senses are remarkably attuned to the small details of the spring woods: "With his cane the old man felled regiments of Indian Pipe, poked the green puffballs to see the smoke erupt in a poisonous verdant cloud. The woods were damp with the early morning and now and again he could hear the swish of a limb where a squirrel jumped and the beaded patter of water-drops in the leaves" (200).

But Uncle Ather relies as well on his ability to read visionary signs. He seems generally associated with pre-Christian religious traditions,[5] a figure recalling Merlin and Prospero as well as the aging Leatherstocking. He carves a sort of wand, covered with cryptic symbols, and he is ostensibly a savant, identifying the exact day of the week on which the social worker had been born. His mystical knowledge bridges the gap between the areas in which Uncle Ather grounds his understanding of life's purpose and meaning—the web of human life and the mountain wilderness—and provides the rationale for his most significant actions: "keeping" the remains of Kenneth Rattner in the orchard and assaulting the government tank. Wreathing the skeleton annually with a green cedar, as he does during the snowstorm which begins on 21 December, the winter solstice, suggests service to a pagan celebration of the seasonal cycle.[6] His vigil continues until by his understanding the spirit of both killer and killed are free from accountability. (On the night when Sylder dumps the body in the spray pit, Ownby is coonhunting. He uses his horn to call in his hounds, but because of the juxtaposition of incidents, the call also pronounces a benediction upon Rattner's disposal and an absolution upon Sylder, who avoids a burden of guilt for the justifiable homicide.) The intrusion of the new, alien authority jeopardizes both sources of Ownby's wisdom, and he naturally assumes his actions will not be comprehensible to its agents.

The effects of section III are calculated and potent: they offer the novel's most attractive account of the patterns of the former age, though these lifestyles are not romanticized: they were harsh, violent and uncompromising. The snowy landscape is frozen, immobile, though hardly sterile or lifeless. The episodes insist that new circumstances, sweeping away the past, await. The young boys will soon leave adolescent pursuits behind, accepting adult problems and responsibilities, and Ownby must eventually confront the extinction of death. Section III closes with Sylder's "bile-sharp foretaste of disaster" (168) as he wonders why the old man had shot holes in the tank—a portent which includes Sylder among those whose lives will soon be radically transformed by confrontations with the civil authorities.

That foretaste becomes reality in the novel's final section, in which both Uncle Ather and Sylder are victimized by the new order John Wesley pointedly rejects, first by returning the hawk bounty and shortly thereafter by leaving the area entirely. Once more, structural juxtaposition provides McCarthy's method as the boy visits and receives "instruction" from both his mentors.

Sylder understands that his position as a representative of ethical probity is dubious, and his advice to John Wesley is designed to protect him from the inimical forces of which Gifford is the primary local instrument. Sensing that John Wesley is reluctant to accept the skewed view of moral account- ability Sylder fashions, he lashes out at the boy in assumed truculence:

> Anyway I never done nothin on your account like you said. I don't do nothin I don't want to. You want to do me a favor jest stay away from Gifford. Stay away from me too. You ought not to of come here. You'll get me charged with delinquency to a minor. Go on now. (214)

The ruse takes its toll on Sylder, who afterwards stares "at the emptiness before him" (214). Only after the boy leaves does he recant this view of the unjust order, branding Gifford a man who "*sells his own neighbors out for money*" (215), an offense which places him "*far beyond the pale*" of rogues such as Sylder himself, even of people like Kenneth Rattner. Shortly thereafter, John Wesley's accusation to the county clerk that the civil authorities "thow people in jail and beat up on em" (233) clearly reveals that he does not accept the value equation Sylder offers for his protection. He has learned more from judging people's behavior than from accepting their pronouncements.

John Wesley also indicts the new order with throwing "old men in the crazy house" (233), alluding to his visit with the venerable Uncle Ather, whose instruction is more forthright, if hardly more applicable for the boy in accommodating to the modern environment. Ownby advances his theory concerning cycles of growth and decay, which he explains to John Wesley come in seven-year intervals of plenty and deprivation.[7] This system accounts for Ownby's actions, and his comments provide the reader with an explanation:

> I worked near all my life and never had nothin. Seems like a old man'd be allowed his rest but then he comes to find they's things you have to do on account of nobody else wants to attend to em. Like that would make em go away. And maybe they don't look like much but then they lead you around like you might start a rabbit dog to hunt a fence-corner and get drug over half the county against nightfall. Which a old man ain't good at noway. . . . Most ever man loves peace, he said, and none better than a old man. (229)

The comment must seem cryptic to the boy, who knows nothing about the skeleton or the shooting of the tank, but the reader understands Uncle Ather's comment, extended by his thinking that he has acted his part selflessly, obeying his peculiar vision. He believes that spirits are capable of inhabiting the bodies of animals, "Specially somebody drownded or like that where they don't get buried proper" (227). Thus, he assumes that the cry of a cat carried away by an owl that Mr. Eller, the storekeeper, hears had been the departing spirit of the dead man. By his own reckoning, he has fulfilled his duty, despite the lapse of allowing the skeleton to be burned. Significantly, he offers the justification for his actions to John Wesley that he had refused to the police and the social worker. He expresses his intention to return home to his old cabin, should he ever be released, an event his vision is inadequate to foresee: "The ways of these people is strange to me" (230).

Little wonder that Uncle Ather has difficulty understanding the new order, or that his behavior is viewed as insane to its deputies. Indeed, his motivations must strike the reader as at least bizarre, if not crazy. But the values which he passes on to the boy are clear and uncompromising: personal responsibility and self-sacrifice. He finally requests that the boy keep an eye out for his dog, old and unable to fend for himself—a responsibility Uncle Ather is forced to abrogate when he is arrested. John Wesley promises to take care of the animal and to visit again. Both pledges affirm his acceptance of the old man's code, an acceptance underlined by his immediate return of the dollar hawk bounty.

The following incident, in which Legwater sifts the ashes of Rattner's skeleton to recover the platinum plate he supposedly had in his head, provides the novel's final, perhaps superfluous paradigm of the relationship between followers of the old ways and the exponents of the new. Legwater is beyond reason, feverish, like Henry Armstid at the close of Faulkner's *The Hamlet*. He continues his vain attempt to profit from someone else's calamity until wrenched away by Gifford, who presumably is not so much disgusted by the motive as by the incompetence with which the attempt has been undertaken. As a last gesture of needless destruction, Legwater shoots Ownby's dog, which has instinctively returned to the orchard in the absence of its master.

John Wesley is now clearly identified as an avatar of earlier values and ways of life. Gifford expresses to Mr. Eller his desire to have "a nice little talk" (236) with him, an expression which had earlier served as a euphemism for his cowardly beating of Sylder in jail. But the boy leaves the region before the presence of the charred skeleton in the pit is revealed to the authorities, and before the death of his mother, who is convinced that he is obeying her injunction to avenge his father. When he returns to Red Branch as an adult, distinct legacies of the two older men whose examples he has followed reveal the quality of the man John Wesley has become. As he visits his old house, the close attention he pays to the details of building and landscape recalls Uncle Ather's careful observations of the world throughout the episodes devoted to him. And the young man's removal of his shoes to check his socks for dampness parallels a character-istic gesture of Sylder's. Both his mentors are gone now, "Fled, banished in death or exile, lost, undone" (246), and nothing remains for him but to depart as well.

The Orchard Keeper closes with John Wesley pictured against a sunset, "as if the very air had gone to wine" (246). The *ubi sunt* theme is rendered poetically, but McCarthy is no sentimentalist. John Wesley is the man his past has made him, and that past condemns him to isolation in the modern world. The mention of the elm tree through which, according to the workmen, the iron fence surrounding the cemetery has "grown" re-minds the reader that John Wesley must adapt himself, like a living tree, to the iron will of the expanding new order. To the community in which he grew up he is a stranger, like his father had been before him.[8] He wan-ders off into a realm presided over by brutish constables, inept humane officers and governmental employees who follow nihilistic and futile policies they don't attempt to understand, like the social worker who ex-plains to Ownby that "we would like to have a record of your case for our, our, records, you see" (219). These figures reflect a world in which mean-ing is reduced to sterile formulas and the prevailing values are exploit-ative and self-serving. McCarthy's final and most chilling irony is that this is the world which the reader too must recognize as his own.

Notes

[1]Regarding McCarthy's work as a whole, Bell asserts that to attempt a summary of the writer's metaphysic is to conclude that he has "none, in effect—no first principles, no foundational truth, Heraclitus without Logos" (9).

[2]This theme has been recognized since the publication of *The Orchard Keeper*. The reviewer James G. Murray, for instance, identifies the novel's subject as "change in a rural area, and how the more or less noble savagery of three men confronts the more or less brutal civilization of a society in flux" ("The Orchard Keeper," *America* 12 June 1965: 866). Walter Sullivan defines its theme as "how old ways are doomed by the new" (*A Requiem for the Renascence: The State of Fiction in the Modern South* [Athens: U of Georgia P, 1976] 70). Dianne [Luce] Cox has stated the theme in terms of the opposition of the mountaineers' "individual

integrity" and "the societal obligations and strictures imposed by the community of men" ("Cormac McCarthy," *Dictionary of Literary Biography: American Novelists Since World War II*, ed. James E. Kibler, Jr. [Detroit: Gale Research, 1980] 225).

[3]Young's evaluation is perhaps extreme, but even so perceptive a reader as Bell seems to have difficulty deciphering the relationship between the novel's value system and its structure, asserting that readers "become ironic metaphysicians making order out of random data, though that order is as meaningless, finally, as the incoherence it supersedes . . . " (25).

[4]Other parallels connect the old man and John Wesley, including pious fundamentalist mothers, attachments to dogs who are removed from their care, love of stormy weather and tendencies to roam the woods during the night. John Wesley's throwing lettuce to a rabbit caught in a well shaft also anticipates Ownby's annual covering of Rattner's skeleton with a cedar tree.

[5]Bell traces the "tone and values" of the novel as a whole to a "distant Anglo-Saxon origin" (11).

[6]McCarthy underlines the significance of 21 December by also citing it as the date on which the Green Fly Inn burns at the close of section I (47).

[7]Ownby's theory is reminiscent of the Biblical story of Joseph, who capably interprets Pharoah's dream warning of seven years of plenty followed by seven years of famine. In Genesis, Joseph's ability to interpret this dream leads to his being given dominion over all of Egypt: visionary knowledge is related both to cultural values and to power.

[8]With typical subtlety, McCarthy draws the connection when the young man watches a wagon and team driven by a Negro disappear into the shimmering heat in precisely the manner that his father had watched a truck pass by on the novel's opening page.

WORKS CITED

Bell, Vereen M. *The Achievement of Cormac McCarthy*. Baton Rouge: Louisiana State UP, 1988.

McCarthy, Cormac. *The Orchard Keeper*. New York: Ecco, 1982.

Young, Thomas Daniel. *Tennessee Writers*. Knoxville: U of Tennessee P, 1981.

A Thing Against Which
Time Will Not Prevail

Pastoral and History in Cormac McCarthy's South

JOHN M. GRAMMER

Early on in *Suttree*, Cormac McCarthy's best novel, Cornelius Suttree—
drunken and disaffected scion of an old southern family—visits the ruins
of that family's plantation house. He wanders around, eyeing the "tall fluted
columns," the smashed chandelier, the ruined plaster, "the wallpaper hanging
in great deciduous fronds" and an old "Keep Out" sign, which "[s]omeone
must have turned . . . around because it posted the outer world." While
thus exploring he recalls a scene from childhood: he and an old man have
watched a racehorse run on a track; the old man gestures with his stopwatch and declares that they have seen a wonder, "a thing against which
time would not prevail." Something to remember, he means, but young
Suttree, already given to morbid speculation, thinks only of mortality and
time's inevitable way with all of us: he "had already begun to sicken at
the slow seeping of life" (135–36). Thus defined as a tension between the
permanence of memory and the power of time, the misunderstanding
between them remains unresolved, at least until Suttree, now grown but no
less obsessed with death, revisits the scene in his own ritual of memory
and raises the issue again. His efforts to resolve it will be, essentially, the
subject matter of his novel.

The plantation scene is notable for being one of the most flagrantly "southern" moments in McCarthy's work. Southern writing, from the antebellum period onward, has been full of ruined old houses, symbolizing the failure of southern order to preserve itself against time. One is a bit surprised to encounter such a symbol in McCarthy's work: he is a writer who studiously avoids cliches, for one thing, and a writer who—except perhaps for his allegedly Faulknerian prose style—seems to have very little to do with southern literary tradition. We will search his novels in vain for the great theme of "the past in the present," for the burden of southern history, for (excepting *The Orchard Keeper*) the conflict between tradition and modernity. And we will be hard pressed to wring from them the sort of humanistic content which, for all his gothicism, finally emerges from Faulkner's; it is hard to imagine McCarthy on some platform in Stockholm, assuring us that man will survive and prevail. "If this is the South," John Ditsky has said of McCarthy's characteristic landscape, "it is the South perceived by Vladimir and Estragon" (3).

Indeed one may be startled to discover, in one of McCarthy's notoriously inscrutable novels, not just "southern" symbols but any intelligible symbols at all. They suggest after all the presence of *theme* in a body of work which, as Vereen Bell has cogently argued, is essentially anti-thematic. What one takes from McCarthy's novels, Bell has taught us, is a "hyperrealistic" rendering of the physical world in all its dense, vivid specificity—and particularly the power of that world to upend whatever conceptual grids are imposed on it. To begin discovering themes and symbols in McCarthy's work is to risk the very delusive logocentrism that the novels themselves are meant to expose.

And yet there it is, a ruined mansion which might have been lifted from the pages of any southern pastoral lament since, say, George Tucker's *The Valley of Shenandoah* (1824). I have the feeling that McCarthy employs this symbol, and the cluster of thematic associations it evokes, quite deliberately, and that in doing so he is (among other things) asserting a particular sort of relationship to the southern literary tradition. And he is introducing a theme, though one so closely related to Bell's "anti-thematic" reading of McCarthy that distinguishing them will take some time.

We ought to begin by defining the tradition in question, which will require a bit of cultural history, some familiar, some perhaps less so. If in general terms the ruined mansion in *Suttree* represents the southern past, more specifically it refers to the failure of the pastoral dream with which the South has identified itself since the settlement of Virginia. This was a dream, essentially, of an escape from history. As Lewis Simpson has shown in *The Dispossessed Garden*, the South has from the very first represented itself as a refuge from all the ills to which European culture was heir—from politics, commerce, corruption, war and, ultimately, from time itself. The plantation, a quite deliberate symbolization of that dream of escape, was designed precisely as "a thing against which time would not prevail." It was indeed "posted"—it attempted to warn the outer world, the realm of time and change, to keep out. But the message was double, containing as well a warning to the plantation to attempt no entry into history, but rather to cling—hopelessly, it turned out—to the promise of changeless order offered by the pastoral realm.

Simpson, far and away our best guide to the pastoral impulse in the South, has characterized that impulse as a version of "gnosticism," as Eric Voegelin has glossed the term: a denial of history which becomes, at last, a denial of being; a desire to remake man and his world according to utopian theory. Recent research in the field of political philosophy sheds still more light on the phenomenon: J.G.A. Pocock, writing brilliantly about "the Atlantic Republican Tradition," has instructed us that republican cultures—of which the South, at least since Jefferson's day, has been a quintessential example—are characterized by their imprisonment within a "Machiavellian moment": the moment when the republic, conceived as a civic order created in defiance of history, begins to recognize its mortality. The response, almost invariably, is an attempt to theorize some social transformation which will effect an escape from history; the pastoral myth of the plantation has served this purpose admirably. The South, guided by pastoral and republican imperatives, has persistently attempted to portray itself as a region somehow outside of time and change, a permanent refuge of order in a chaotic world.

I think that we will discover in McCarthy's southern fiction a profoundly serious interrogation of this oldest cultural impulse of southern history. This is to say that McCarthy participates in the South's second-oldest intellectual tradition, that of the anti-pastoral. In common with, for example, William Byrd (who sought to expose the naive pastoral daydream of "Lubberland") and Robert Beverley (who discovered similar delusions among the early settlers of Virginia), McCarthy wants to question the old southern dream of escape from history. Like the humorists of the Old Southwest, the southern writers whom he most resembles, he would remind us of the wildness at the heart of nature, despite pastoral efforts to domesticate it, of the flux at the heart of experience, despite our attempts to stand athwart history, yelling stop: "Nothing ever stops moving," Suttree learns at the end of his novel. I believe McCarthy, like many modern southern writers, has been fascinated throughout his career with this characteristically southern delusion, the pastoral will to create a timeless order.

At one point in *The Orchard Keeper*, McCarthy's first published novel, Arthur Ownby offers this wistful reflection:

> If I was a younger man . . . I would move to them mountains. I would find me a clearwater branch and build me a log house with a fireplace. And my bees would make black mountain honey. And I wouldn't care for no man. (55)

For those who have learned to read McCarthy with an eye peeled for the buried literary allusion, this passage will set off alarms. Arthur's statement paraphrases the first stanza of "The Lake Isle of Innisfree," a poem which, with its own echoes of *Walden*, is already a kind of foster-child of the American pastoral myth:

> I will arise and go now, and go to Innisfree,
> And a small cabin build there, of clay and wattles made:
> Nine bean rows will I have there, a hive for the honey-bee,
> And live alone in the bee-loud glade.[1]

This allusion, put in the mouth of the admirable "Uncle Ather," is well chosen, and it hints at McCarthy's own powerful attraction to the pastoral impulse. One is not altogether surprised to discover this affinity, for it is a commonplace that anti-pastoral writing is a version of the pastoral, usually issuing from some disappointed or embittered engagement with the old pastoral dream. *The Orchard Keeper* is a more or less straightforward, elegiac celebration of a vanishing pastoral realm; the book is in the tradition of Virgil's *Eclogues*, Goldsmith's *Deserted Village* and the Agrarians' *I'll Take My Stand*. Unlike most of McCarthy's work in this vein, the novel offers a positive image of pastoral order, an image which we may employ as a kind of touchstone when reading McCarthy's later and bleaker examinations of the pastoral impulse.

Like many works in this tradition, *The Orchard Keeper* centers upon the fortunes not of a single protagonist but of a community—here, of a primitive community clinging tenaciously to existence in the mountains east of Knoxville, Tennessee:

> a dozen jerrybuilt shacks strewn about the valley in unlikely places, squatting over their gullied purlieus like great brooding animals rigid

with constipation, and yet endowed with an air transient and happen-stantial as if set there by the recession of floodwaters. Even the speed with which they were constructed could not outdistance the decay for which they held such affinity. Gangrenous molds took to the founda-tions before the roofs were fairly nailed down. (11)

Passages like this one lead Vereen Bell to read *The Orchard Keeper* as asserting the insubstantiality of human communities, their helplessness before encroaching wildness. I think that is only half the story, for the community of Red Branch, though perpetually in the advanced stages of decomposition, somehow does keep renewing itself; it has evidently maintained its armed truce with nature for a long time. I think that the great virtue of this community, as McCarthy presents it, is precisely that it has worked out such a truce, one which involves both tenacity and flexibility, an acceptance of the flux at the heart of things. Instead of trying to stand outside of time, Red Branch has somehow learned to swim comfortably in its currents.

The purest expression of this knowledge is the social center of Red Branch, a saloon known as the Green Fly Inn, built so as to hang precar-iously over a deep hollow, buffetted by the winds:

[T]he inn-goers trod floors that waltzed drunkenly beneath them, surged and buckled with huge groans. At times the whole building would career madly to one side as though headlong into collapse. The drinkers would pause, liquid tilting in their glasses, the structure would shudder violently, a broom would fall, a bottle, and the inn would slow-ly right itself and assume once more its normal reeling equipoise. The drinkers would raise their glasses, talk would begin again. Remarks alluding to the eccentricities of the inn were made only outside the building. To them the inn was animate as any old ship to her crew and it bred an atmosphere such as few could boast, a solidarity due largely to its very precariousness. (12–13)

The interdependence of "solidarity" and "precariousness" is an essen-tial idea for McCarthy; for him it seems that the only sort of permanence ultimately available to us is one based upon an intense awareness of impermanence; life is possible only in a continual and more or less cordial dialogue with death.

The main characters in *The Orchard Keeper* seem to have learned the lesson well. Thus Marion Sylder is violent enough to kill the murderous hitchhiker who attacks him, but humane enough to play the part of father to his victim's son. Arthur Ownby, an old man terrified of death, is able to domesticate that fear by ritualistically tending the corpse of that victim, which he has discovered in the woods. The dead man's son John Wesley Rattner, a boy deeply attracted to the dangerous wilderness around him, disciplines that attraction by learning woodcraft from his two elders; *Trapping the Fur Bearers of North America*, a book given him by Uncle Ather, becomes the bible of his homemade creed. That the three characters are unaware of the fact which really unites them—their shared connection to the dead Kenneth Rattner—emphasizes the communal and traditional nature of their relationships: they behave as they do not out of any sense of personal obligation, obedient to some Lockean social contract, but because their inherited modes of being instruct them to do so. The community of which these three are representative citizens seems quite real to me, and able to go on indefinitely keeping up its end of the tug of war with nature.

As in the *Eclogues* and nearly everything else in the tradition of elegiac pastoral, the more serious threat to this world comes from the other direction, from the city and what McCarthy will later call its "gnostic" impulses— impulses to impose stability, order and reason upon the fluid reality of existence at Red Branch. The central dilemmas of the story all concern the efforts of Red Branch and its representative citizens—Arthur, Marion and John Wesley—to resist these gnostic impulses and preserve something of their old-fashioned existence. Thus Arthur finds himself threatened not only by wildness and death (symbolized by the "painters" that haunt his dreams) but also by a mysterious government tank which has intruded upon the wilderness, and then by the lawmen who come to arrest him for damaging it. Marion Sylder must contend not only with Kenneth Rattner but also with the constable who seeks to end his bootlegging business and jail him. And John Wesley is confronted not only by the wild hound which peers in at him from the wilderness, but by the constable who bullies him, the government office which pays a bounty for the corpses of red tail hawks and his mother's insane demand that he avenge his father's death. This last threat typifies them all, for Mildred Rattner, invoking (as Bell points out [13]) an essentially literary cliché in order to rationalize the unexplained disappearance of her husband, is trying to impose on the situation precisely the sort of totalizing closure which Red Branch pre- serves itself by resisting. She wants, in effect, to involve her son in a plotted narrative, an involvement which he rightly shuns. Like the law- men, social workers and engineers who threaten Red Branch, she is ruled by the gnostic desire to remake a terrifyingly fluid reality by imposing stable order upon it.

Red Branch is thus poised between two threats, and it is this latter, "civilized" one which ultimately dooms the community. Uncle Ather ends his days in an insane asylum, harrassed by a social worker who "talk[s] like a God-damned yankee" and apparently makes his living by asking foolish questions (221). Marion is likewise jailed for bootlegging and then beaten up by the constable; in marked contrast to Mrs. Rattner, he dissuades John Wesley from taking vengeance on the lawman. John Wesley himself elects to leave Red Branch, dear as it has been for him; its value for him has been eliminated upon the arrest of his friends. The book ends tragically, that is to say, but affirmatively; we might think of it as an elegy for an older sort of pastoral community, nobly resisting but finally defeated by the gnostic will to deny history.

McCarthy's subsequent books depict a later stage in pastoral history, one in which the pastoral realm—terrified of mortality but lacking, say, Uncle Ather's means of facing that fear—surrenders to those gnostic impulses and defines itself a refuge from time. Certainly that is the case with *Outer Dark*, the author's second novel. Here the pastoral flight from history and its consequences are suggested quite vividly in an early scene, a description of the band of murderers who harry the community in which the main action occurs:

> *They entered the lot at a slow jog, the peaceful and ruminative stock coming erect, watchful, shifting with eyes sidled as they passed, the three of them paying no heed, seeming blind with purpose, passing through an ether of smartweed and stale ammonia steaming from the sunbleared chickenrun and on through the open doors of the barn and almost instantly out the other side marvelously armed with crude agrarian weapons, spade and brush-hook, emerging in an explosion of guineafowl and one screaming sow, unaltered in gait demeanor or speed, parodic figures transposed live and intact and violent out of a proletarian mural and set mobile upon the empty fields, advancing against the twilight, the droning bees and windtilted clover.* (35)

These menacing riders, armed with farming tools, are of course figures of *time*, reapers who move through the novel, leaving a trail of violent death behind them; the farm tools they carry will indeed become weapons as their spree commences. Thus they embody the deadly threat which history poses to the pastoral realm. And yet they are themselves pastoral figures, or at least parodic versions of such figures, bearing spades and brush hooks through a barnyard, frightening the stock. Whatever threat they represent, that is, emerges in some sense *from* the pastoral realm they scourge; they are that community's nightmare, the seed of destruction which lurks within the pastoral dream.

I believe that the novel as a whole bears out this reading. Its main action concerns a brother and sister, Culla and Rinthy Holme, their incestuous relationship and the surrealistically horrible consequences of this crime. Culla abandons the baby they produce in the woods; the baby is then taken by a mad tinker; Rinthy goes aimlessly in search of it; Culla goes in pursuit of Rinthy, finds himself continually accused of crimes large and small, pursued by lawmen and lynch mobs, often obliged to flee for his life, and at last, disturbingly, welcomed as a brother by the band of murderers: "Well, I see ye didn't have no trouble findin us," one says as Culla stumbles into their camp (232). The landscape through which they wander is full of robbed graves, mangled corpses, hanged men and a herd of Gadarene swine, transplanted directly from the New Testament. *Outer Dark*, like much of McCarthy's work, seems positively turgid with moral import, and yet it is difficult to say just what the moral issues involved might be. "It is almost as if these two poor souls, the brother and sister both, had let loose all the demons in the world by the fact of their fornication," says John Ditsky (6). Just so; yet why should this be? How is it that incest calls forth such dire retribution? And whence, in McCarthy's apparently godless universe, does this retribution come?

In answering these questions we might begin by taking account of an oddity which many readers of the novel have noticed, the vagueness of its temporal setting: sometime before the advent of the internal combustion engine, one gathers; beyond that it is difficult to say. The vagueness is appropriate, for *Outer Dark* concerns a pastoral community which has taken its retreat from history to pathological and eventually criminal lengths. It is a community outside of time; thus its citizens continually seem lost in time. At one point Culla travels to town, trying to purchase groceries, and needs to be told by the irate storekeeper that it is Sunday; somehow his isolated existence has not been subject to the calendar. "We still christians here," this same merchant growls, claiming membership in an apparently endangered remnant, left behind by history (26). A bit later, a family which has helped Rinthy are likened to "stone figures quarried from the architecture of an older time" (77). In fact the book's temporal setting is not only vague but contradictory: the band of marauders seem a kind of Murrell gang, figures from the antebellum days of frontier settlement; how can they coexist with a world equipped with coolboxes for "dope," store-bought meat and bread, and so on? The temporal setting is strange and surreal, emphasizing the novel's general sense of displacement in time.

Some have taken the book's temporal vagueness to suggest that specific historical references are insignificant, that the tale is in some sense timeless and universal. I think nearly the opposite is true; *Outer Dark* refers not to a vaguely defined moment but a fairly specific one—a Machiavellian moment, in Pocock's phrase: the moment when a community organized as a refuge from history is forced to confront it. And it is, therefore, about that confrontation, about time's revenge on a community which has attempted to deny its power: retribution, in this novel obsessed with retribution, comes not from God but from history.

We are given a number of clues that the community, even apart from the depredations of the murderers, is beginning to fall apart. Custom, neighborliness, even simple communication are nearly gone, replaced by fear, suspicion, estrangement. We encounter a woman who has made a lovely quilt, but complains of having to undertake this traditionally communal creation alone: "It's tedious to piece one for one person by herself" (67). Having made the quilt, she can think of nothing to do with it but sell it for three dollars. Rinthy, whose wanderings cannot have taken her very far from home, repeatedly meets neighbors who can't quite place her: I *ought* to know you, people keep saying to her. "They ain't a soul in this world but what is a stranger to me," she says at one point; it is a statement nearly any character in the book might make (29). Culla, trying to buy cheese and crackers in the local store, finds it nearly impossible to make the grocer understand how much he wants of each. Culla finds himself met with senseless suspicion and hostility everywhere he goes: he is pursued by a lynch mob, which for no apparent reason suspects him of robbing graves; later he is arrested on a flimsy charge of trespassing and set to work on "the Squire's" farm; when his sentence is up Culla asks to stay on, for room and board, and is turned away. A group of hog drovers, whose herd has stampeded and been lost, randomly assign the blame to Culla and prepare to lynch him. The whole social atmosphere of *Outer Dark* is one of near-total estrangement; we are shown a community, presumably once unified and solid, now shattered to atoms; such cohesion as remains becomes a destructive centripetal force.

The central event of the novel—which, like the adultery in *The Scarlet Letter*, occurs before the novel begins—is the clearest expression of this condition. Incest conventionally represents a social order which, in its anxiety to avoid contact with the corrupting outer world, ends by collapsing inward on itself—such an order as was dreamed by the pastoral visionaries of the South. Culla and Rinthy, that is, are the representative figures, in a sense the first citizens, of their dying pastoral world: one reason, perhaps, why everyone believes he knows Rinthy, and why everyone, including the band of killers whose path he inadvertently follows, seems to suspect Culla of some dire crime. Rinthy's aimless and hopeless quest for her child, the entire plot of her half of the novel, is an attempt to redeem the pastoral order. The powerfully maternal Rinthy, hunting her "chap" and lactating helplessly, is of course a figure of great natural fecundity, the earth-as-mother who lies at the heart of the pastoral myth. Bell has pointed out that Rinthy is McCarthy's version of Lena Grove, Faulkner's footloose embodiment of the maternal (and pastoral, as her name implies) life force. But Rinthy is a dark and hopeless version of Lena, just as *Outer Dark*—the very title suggests it—is a dark and hopeless version of *Light in August*. In Faulkner's work Lena's untouchable will to life balances Joe Christmas's death wish; but in this doomed pastoral community the death wish is nearly universal, and Rinthy's sad effort to redeem it is manifestly futile. Here the avengers, apparently summoned up by the community's, and particularly Culla and Rinthy's sins, end by killing their child and, perhaps more heartlessly, sparing the incestuous parents. The novel is a kind of *Paradise Lost*, but it ends with the sinful pair wandering hopelessly and separately through the ruins of their fallen garden—with all the world before them, perhaps, but not the faintest hint of providential guidance.

Child of God, McCarthy's third novel, is the one which most explicitly raises the issue of the pastoral, and particularly of the republican or Jeffersonian version of it which has dominated the southern imagination. This concern is revealed with astonishing clarity in the first scene, which depicts the sale at auction of Lester Ballard's farm, forfeited for nonpayment of taxes. As the sale progresses, Lester appears—a "[s]mall man, ill-shaven, now holding a rifle"—and quixotically attempts to interrupt the proceedings. "I want you to get your goddamn ass off my property," he says. "And take these fools with ye" (7). The auctioneer tries and fails to reason with him, and at last the dispossessed farmer is clubbed over the head with an axe and carried off by the high sheriff of Sevier County. "Lester Ballard never could hold his head right after that," explains an anonymous witness (9).

That judgment, as we see when Lester takes up his mad career as murderer and necrophiliac, turns out to be a considerable understatement. Thus we need to see just what is at stake in this early scene, somehow the beginning of Lester's descent into madness. Consider for instance the small detail of Lester's rifle. He is virtually never without it in the novel, the weapon apparently serving him as a powerful totem of some sort. He acquired it as a boy, we learn, and by now h: skills with it are the stuff of local legend: "He could by god shoot it," one neighbor recalls. "Hit anything he could see" (57). Early on Lester demonstrates this proficiency by winning several stuffed animals at a shooting gallery; later, taking up his career as a killer, he puts it to deadlier use.

What does the rifle mean to Lester? For one thing it identifies him as an anachronism, left behind by history: a Daniel Boone with only stuffed animals to shoot for. But there is more to it than that; in the mythology of the pastoral republic, with which *Child of God* is suffused, weapons like Lester's rifle carry enormous symbolic value. An armed man, prepared to defend the country and his own liberty and property, was for our ancestors the ideal republican citizen, the foundation of stable order: an idea which will seem most familiar to us, perhaps, as it is enshrined in the Second Amendment to the Constitution.

And so when Lester appears, rifle in hand, prepared to defend his property against the agents of tyrannical power (or so he perceives the situation), he is claiming a role for himself in one of the central dramas in the pastoral republican mythology. Raymond Williams has noted that almost invariably in pastoral literature "the contrast . . . is between the pleasures of rural settlement and the threat of loss and eviction" (17). The theme goes back all the way to Virgil's first *Eclogue*, but acquires additional force in America, where property-holding has been an important component of civic virtue, a guarantee of personal and social stability. The scene in which the yeoman farmer loses his property is the one which pastoral republics dread—the moment when death enters their world. It is Lester's personal Machiavellian moment. The sheriff and the auctioneer, with their talk of law, taxes and investment potential, are figures of modernity, of time; Lester casts himself as a reactionary, still hoping to resist the tides of history.

The scene is indeed the beginning of Lester's descent into madness— a madness which carries out, in horrifying ways, the essential impulses of the threatened pastoral republic. For, deprived of his land, he must now reconstitute the order which it represents. He begins, harmlessly enough, by trying to re-establish some conventional domestic arrangement: by setting up housekeeping in an abandoned cabin, and by paying court to several potential spouses, each more indifferent than the last. But finally, frustrated in these attempts, he begins killing women and collecting their corpses as lovers, eventually accumulating quite a supply in a remote cave. This gesture, as other readers have noted, is Lester's mad protest against history itself, against the passing of time. Among his corpses, there is a timeless order, immunity to change: the descriptions of them faintly echo the scene in *Outer Dark* in which rural folk sit like "stone figures quarried from the architecture of an older time." Here the figures really are motionless, outside of time. Lester's cave—which is discovered, with almost allegorical appropriateness, when a plowman's mules fall into it through a sinkhole—is the ultimate, deranged expression of the pastoral will to deny history.

McCarthy is fairly clear about Lester's gnostic version of the pastoral impulse: "Given charge," he explains, "Ballard would have made things more orderly in the woods and in men's souls" (136). In *Suttree*, the last of his southern novels, he shows us the logical end of this gnostic dreaming: the destructive urban landscape of Knoxville, where Lester Ballard's wish to "make things more orderly" has been realized with a vengeance. Cornelius Suttree's family, former inhabitants of the ruined mansion, have made a remarkably smooth transition from the old "plantation" version of the dream of changeless order to a new one, approved by the chamber of commerce. "If it is life that you feel you are missing," Suttree's father has instructed him, "I can tell you where to find it. In the law courts, in business, in government" (13–14). But Suttree has turned his back on that dream of order and, trying to discover some more authentic existence, now lives in the slum neighborhood of McAnally Flats, amid what his father calls "a dumbshow composed of the helpless and the impotent" (14). Here, living on a houseboat and fishing for a living, Suttree seems to divide his time about equally between a succession of mad prophets, from whom he seeks revelation, and the derelicts of the neighborhood, in whose company he pursues the temporary oblivion of drunkenness and the permanent one of death. Yet what he finds in this most optimistic of McCarthy's novels is neither deliverance nor death but a new awareness of the nature of life, of the solidarity which arises from precariousness.

Of the many literary allusions in McCarthy's work, one of the most important comes in the naming (really the nicknaming) of his protagonist in *Suttree*. "Sut," his Knoxville friends call him: instantly we are reminded of another famous East Tennesseean in our literature, George Washington Harris's Sut Lovingood. But at first the allusion seems a strange one, for Harris's Sut is an illiterate, anti-intellectual creature of instinct; he sums up his own epistemology by explaining that "plannin and studdyin"

. . . am ginerly no count. All pends, et las' on what yu dus an' how yu kerries yursef *at the moment ove ackshun*. Sarcumstances turn about pow'ful fas', an all yu kin du is tu think jis' es fas es they kin turn, an' jis' as they turn, an' ef yu du this, I'm durn'd ef yu don't git out sumhow. (67)

Now Cornelius Suttree, as everyone has noticed, is unique among McCarthy's protagonists in being reflective and articulate; he has been to college, is known to his friends as a smart fellow and is presumably more able than most when it comes to planning and studying. But he seems to have deliberately suppressed these gifts, out of a growing awareness of what his spiritual ancestors at the Green Fly Inn (and his literary ones in the pages of George Washington Harris) have always known about the interdependence of solidarity and precariousness. He learns to accept what the rest of Knoxville, barring McAnally Flats, is engaged in denying: the flux at the heart of existence, to which we must simply adjust ourselves. In McCarthy's world planning and studying never *are* any use; to resort to them is to slip into the gnostic fallacy of the southern pastoral dream in all its versions.

This notion is made plainest, perhaps, in the presentation of Suttree's friend Gene Harrogate, certainly the most memorable character in the book. We realize as soon as we meet him that Harrogate represents a particularly virulent strain of naive pastoralism: if modern environmentalists are "tree huggers," if Faulkner's Ike Snopes falls in love with a cow, then McCarthy goes them all one better in his comic presentation of the "moonlight melonmounter," whose erotic encounters in the garden patch land him in the workhouse with Suttree. Upon his release the former "country mouse" re-christens himself "city rat" and travels to Knoxville, full of schemes for success. He learns that the city, fearing an outbreak of rabies, will pay a bounty for dead bats, so he devises a method for poisoning the creatures and delivers an enormous sackful to the Health Department; he is astonished when his foolproof plan fails. He follows the caverns which lie under Knoxville until he reckons he is just beneath a bank vault, then sets off a charge of dynamite; again he is astonished to find himself almost blown up, then nearly drowned in the wash from the sewer main he has breached and finally lost in the caves for days. Prospering for a time with an ambitious plan to steal coins from half the pay phones in town, Harrogate is chased into hiding by the notoriously implacable "telephone heat"; at last, in desperation, he attempts a robbery and is arrested. In his very crudeness and naivete Harrogate is an ideal expression of the ethic which governs contemporary Knoxville—and more broadly, of the "gnostic" error of attempting to manage the wildness of existence by means of planning and studying. We might think of him as a sort of benign Lester Ballard, considerably less alarming but sharing not only unconventional sexual habits but, what underlies those habits, a pastoral desire to impose order on a chaotic world.

Such efforts, *Suttree* suggests, are deluded and destructive. Suttree does not fully recognize this at first: he seems to be seeking, haphazardly, his own sort of release from flux. He first ventured into McAnally, apparently, in search of a martyr's revenge on a meaningless world:

> I spoke with bitterness about my life and I said that I would take my own part against the slander of oblivion and against the monstrous facelessness of it and that I would stand a stone in the very void where all would read my name. (414)

Suttree is at first determined to extract some sort of stable meaning from life, seeking either religious revelation or death. Later, perhaps despairing of these alternatives, he attempts his own sad versions of ordinary middle-class stability: with the parody of domestic bliss he achieves with the whore Joyce, or with his halfhearted effort to make a fortune in mussel shells with the doomed Reese and his family. But of course all these efforts come to naught, ending in comic disappointment or bloody tragedy: each time he returns to his houseboat on the river.

The river is, to put it mildly, a symbol: of life, since it gives Suttree the fish which sustain him, and of death—in the opening scene the bloated body of a suicide is grappled from its depths—and ultimately (as for Heraclitus) of the mysterious flux at the heart of existence, of everything that Knoxville attempts to deny. Suttree gets his share of clues about its significance: one of the preachers he meets, at a baptism in the river, warns him that the sprinkling he received as an infant in church is insufficient: "It wont take if you dont get total nursin. That old sprinklin business wont get it, buddy boy" (122). Indeed it won't; a line from Conrad comes to mind: "The way is to the destructive element submit yourself, and with the exertions of your hands and feet in the water make the deep, deep sea keep you up" (214).[2] Sut Lovingood would agree, and his namesake learns to at last: Suttree's salvation, such as it is, comes when at last he recognizes this truth. Following a nearly fatal bout with typhoid fever, accompanied by a series of visionary hallucinations, Suttree is able to tell what he has learned: God, he explains to the priest who has come to administer last rites, "is not a thing. Nothing ever stops moving" (461).

And so Suttree mustn't stop moving either; for movement, action, participation in the flux at the heart of experience, is the only alternative to destruction. Disabuse yourself of your gnostic delusions, promised Sut Lovingood, forego plannin' and studyin' and the effort to impose order on experience, and "I'm durn'd ef yu don't git out somehow." And his namesake does get out somehow, leaving Knoxville just one step ahead of the "huntsman," death, which has pursued him throughout the novel. Death is of course a major presence in *Suttree*, essentially bracketing its main action: "Who's dead?" Suttree asks his friend J-Bone early in the novel—an appropriate question in his violent world, and one which needs to be asked repeatedly (148). By the end, as the hero takes his leave from Knoxville, we have at least a negative answer: "Shit," says one of his McAnally friends, "Old Suttree aint dead" (470). This is the nearest thing to affirmation we will find in McCarthy's grim works. He's not dead yet; like the denizens of Red Branch in *The Orchard Keeper*, and unlike most of the author's other protagonists, Suttree manages, for a while longer at least, to keep up his end of the dialogue with death. This is all the deliverance that is available in McCarthy's world: deliverance from the pastoral delusions which have plagued his region—those represented by the ruined mansion, and also those represented by the expressway being built over the ruins of McAnally Flats as he takes his leave, the work of "[g]nostic workmen who would have down this shabby shapeshow that masks the higher world of form" (464). To be saved is to continue swimming in the currents of time; the only cessation, as Lester Ballard knew, is death.

NOTES

[1]McCarthy's work is dense with these buried allusions, some obvious (as when Cornelius Suttree "come[s] to himself in this obscure wood" [287]) and some less so (as when the boys from McAnally, reflecting on the demise last winter of their comrade Cecil, unconsciously echo Auden's elegy for Yeats: "All agreed that the day of his death was a cold one" [175]). Some of these, like Ather's paraphrase of Yeats, have a clear significance; others, it strikes me, do not and thus contribute to our general sense of McCarthy's novels as hieroglyphic—apparently meaningful but often inscrutable.

[2]Stein is speaking to Marlow in *Lord Jim*.

WORKS CITED

Bell, Vereen M. *The Achievement of Cormac McCarthy.* Baton Rouge: Louisiana State UP, 1988.

Conrad, Joseph. *Lord Jim.* 1899. New York: Modern Library, 1931.

Ditsky, John. "Further Into Darkness: The Novels of Cormac McCarthy." *Hollins Critic* 18.2 (1981): 1–11.

Harris, George Washington. *Sut Lovingood: Yarns Spun by a "Nat'ral Born Durn'd Fool."* New York: Dick & Fitzgerald, 1867.

McCarthy, Cormac. *Child of God.* 1973. New York: Ecco, 1984.

_____. *The Orchard Keeper.* 1965. New York: Ecco, 1982.

_____. *Outer Dark.* 1968. New York: Ecco, 1984.

_____. *Suttree.* 1979. New York: Vintage-Random, 1986.

Pocock, J.G.A. *The Machiavellian Moment.* Princeton: Princeton UP, 1975.

Simpson, Lewis P. *The Dispossessed Garden.* Athens: U of Georgia P, 1975.

Williams, Raymond. *The Country and the City.* London: Oxford UP, 1973.

Naming, Knowing and Nothingness

McCarthy's Moral Parables

Edwin T. Arnold

Despite the relatively small amount of criticism presently available on the six novels of Cormac McCarthy, certain critical "truths" have become established about his work, in large part because they have been so effectively set forth by the author of the single book thus far published on McCarthy. Foremost among the readings found in Vereen M. Bell's *The Achievement of Cormac McCarthy*[1] is the idea that McCarthy's books are essentially nihilistic, devoid of conventional plot, theme or moral reference. As a corollary of the first proposition, Bell further states, "Ordinarily the omniscient narrator in McCarthy's novels is recessive—merely narrating— and the characters are almost without thoughts, certainly without thought processes, so neither narrator nor characters offer us any help with the business of generalizing. . . . The motivation of characters is usually tantalizingly obscure. . . . All of the characters threaten to become almost eerily unselfconscious" (4).

While not wishing to dispute Bell on his very able appreciation of McCarthy's work in general, I would like to attempt an argument against this particular thread of anti-interpretation, for it seems to me a reduction of McCarthy's exceedingly rich fiction.[2] McCarthy's characters are clearly motivated by those emotions we all share—love, loneliness, guilt, shame, hope, despair; the narratives are driven by distinct thematic concerns and move at least *in the direction of* some form of resolution; and there is in each novel a moral gauge by which we, the readers, are able to judge the failure or limited success of McCarthy's characters. While I recognize and appreciate the postmodern celebration of McCarthy's exuberant violence, his astonishing approximation of chaos, his grand evocation of the mystery of the world, there is also evident in his work a profound belief in the need for moral order, a conviction that is essentially religious. There is, in addition, always the possibility of grace and redemption even in the darkest of his tales, although that redemption may require more of his characters than they are ultimately willing to give.[3]

According to Bell, *Outer Dark* (1968), McCarthy's second novel,[4] is "as brutally nihilistic as any serious novel written in this century in this unnihilistic country" (34). The world it represents is "an incoherent and unrationalized gestalt of mass and process, without design or purpose, unless it is that some demented and unapproachable God invisibly presides" (38). Yet, as William J. Schafer first noted (112), the book's title comes from the eighth chapter of Matthew, in which Jesus comments on the faith shown by the centurion at Capernaum, who has said, "Lord, I am not worthy to have you come under my roof, but only say the word, and my servant will be healed" (8:8). "Truly, I say to you, not even in Israel have I found such faith," Jesus responds. "I tell you many will come from east and west and sit at table with Abraham, Isaac, and Jacob in the kingdom of heaven, while the sons of the kingdom will be thrown into the outer darkness; there men will weep and gnash their teeth" (8:10–12). Thus, there are two possibilities: the kingdom of heaven as well as the "outer darkness" of hell.

It is this second image that is conjured up in Culla Holme's guilt-ridden and desperate nightmare. Standing in the midst of a "delegation of human ruin," the blind and crippled and leprous, Culla listens with them to a prophet who declares that in the darkness of the nearing eclipse of the sun they will all be healed, made whole. It is the promise of a Second Coming. Culla, who has no obvious physical impairment, struggles forward, crying, "Me . . . Can I be cured?" "Yes," the prophet answers, "I think perhaps you will be cured" (5). But when the dying sun changes day to night and then does not return, and when the crowd find their afflictions and deformities still with them, they turn against "the dreamer," Culla himself. "They grew seething and more mutinous and he tried to hide among them but they knew him even in that pit of hopeless dark and fell upon him with howls of outrage" (6).

Bell and others argue that, like most McCarthy characters, Culla has "virtually no thoughts" (36). Yet Culla is a tormented man, haunted by his sin, embodied by the "nameless weight" (5) in his sister Rinthy's womb. He is a man who wishes to be cured, forgiven, but who can cry out only in his sleep. Awake, he tries to conceal his guilt. "Sickness here. . . . Got sickness" (6), he warns away the tinker who appears in the yard. He refuses, moreover, to get a midwife to tend the difficult birth. "She'd tell," he says. "Who is they to tell?" Rinthy asks. "Anybody," Culla answers (10).

The extent of Culla's guilt, and the impossibility of evading that guilt, is made clear after the child is born. Culla takes it into the "swampy forest" (16) near their cabin and leaves it to die in a glade of cottonwood trees. Taking direction by the sun, he becomes lost as soon as night falls, as in his dream: running in "full flight" (17), he circles through the woods (when he spits in the stream, he thinks, in his confusion, that the saliva floats upstream) and stumbles back into the very glade where he first left the baby. "He would have taken it for some boneless cognate of his heart's dread had the child not cried," howling "execration upon the dim camarine world of its nativity wail on wail . . ." (17–18). The next day, when the misshapen tinker tracks Culla into the woods and discovers the abandoned infant, he notes how Culla's circular path begins and ends: "As if the tracks' maker had met in this forest some dark other self in chemistry with whom he had been fused traceless from the earth" (20). The idea of the "dark other self" is more fully explored in McCarthy's fourth novel, *Suttree*,[5] but here the sense of some dreaded doppelgänger, the embodiment of secret horror, is carefully planted in our minds.

Culla's act is reprehensible, but his need to deny the child is understandable. It is not simply a cruel, mindless deed, and he is haunted by it. Thus, he creates a lie, telling Rinthy the child died after birth, that he has given it proper burial. "It ain't even got a name," Rinthy protests. "We could give it one. . . ." "It's dead," Culla replies. "You don't name things dead" (31). He shows her a false grave to allay her suspicions, but later she digs into it to see the actual body and discovers his lie. When she looks to him, he turns *his* guilt onto *her*: "Now you really went and done it," he cries. "And her own face still bland and impervious in such wonder he mistook for accusation, silent and inarguable female invective, until he rose and fled, bearing his clenched hands above him threatful, supplicant, to the mute and windy heavens" (33).

Surely the passages collected here reveal a tormented and divided soul, so weighed by his own sin and his need to conceal that sin that he interprets his sister's "wonder" for "accusation" and malicious "invective." The siblings' contrasting responses in this scene are significant. Once Rinthy finds her child is not dead, she goes off in search of it. Shortly thereafter Culla himself sets out, telling those who directly ask him that he is looking for his sister. But there is no reason to believe this is the truth. Culla's actions thus far have been attempts to deny, to hide, to flee. One of the first men he meets, the squire who hires him to chop a tree, asks, suspiciously, "Come on man. What is it you've done. Where are you runnin from?" (46). Another stranger, a beehiver, subsequently questions, "How far is it to where you're goin? . . . Or do ye not know where it is you're a-goin?" (81). Even Rinthy, who is the least likely to cast unfair blame, answers when asked about her family, "I ain't got nary'n. Ceptin just a brother and he run off" (102). Rinthy later adds, "He lied all the time" (156).[6]

As most readers of the novel have noted, the story alternates between Culla's and Rinthy's travels and encounters. Rinthy, whose sole purpose is to find her child (for whom she continues to lactate even months after its disappearance) is constantly described in terms of innocence and even a kind of virginal purity. She sets out on her journey "humming softly to herself and so into the sunshine that washed fitfully with the spring wind over the glade, turning her face up to the sky and bestowing upon it a smile all bland and burdenless as a child's" (53). She is at peace with nature, and it with her: "Butterflies attended her and birds dusting in the road did not fly up when she passed" (98).

Rinthy's name is possibly a shortened version of "Corinthians."[7] If so, it would indicate that her and Culla's parents had some knowledge or awareness of the Bible which the children seem to have lost. There are, moreover, numerous images in Paul's first letter to the Corinthians which are appropriate to McCarthy's dolorous mater. "But I, breathern, could not address you as spiritual men," Paul writes, "but as men of the flesh, as babes in Christ. I fed you with milk, not solid food; for you were not ready for it; and even yet you are not ready, for you are still of the flesh" (I Cor. 3:1–3). Rinthy is often described (unfairly, I think) as simple-minded, but, according to Paul, "If any one among you thinks that he is wise in this age, let him become a fool that he may become wise. For the wisdom of this world is folly with God" (3:18–19). Finally, in this book is Paul's magnificent personification of love: "Love bears all things, believes all things, hopes all things, endures all things. . . . So faith, hope, love abide, these three; but the greatest of these is love" (13:8, 13). Such is Rinthy, whose gentleness is generally met with equal kindness. She feels no guilt at having had the child—"I wasn't ashamed," she says quietly (156). Nor does she seem to blame Culla for fathering the baby; rather it is his denial of it that she holds against him.

Culla, on the other hand, is always met with suspicion. Even when he is offered hospitality, as by the snakeman who gives him water—"Wouldn't turn Satan away for a drink," the snakeman says to Culla (117)—Culla becomes fearful, and perhaps with good reason, for everywhere he goes he finds proof of evil in the world. The figures that most constantly dog Culla's flight are, of course, the mysterious dark trio whose violent and horrifying exploits are recounted in the italicized inter-passages of the book. Just as Culla (inadvertently) crosses Rinthy's path, so these figures intersect with Culla, leaving behind them atrocious deeds for which Culla is inevitably blamed. It is as if his own guilt—or his denial of his own guilt—has called these figures forth. The leader of the group is sometimes taken for a minister (by the snakeman, for instance, just before he is killed), and the three of them together are described as having an air of *"spurious sanctity"* ([3]) when they are first introduced.

As is so often the case in McCarthy, even the portrayal of certain evil is given a theological twist: these creatures are malevolent destroyers, but they are also agents of retribution and thus figures of judgment,[8] another of the major themes found in I Corinthians. Paul states, "I am not aware of anything against myself, but I am not thereby acquitted. It is the Lord who judges me. Therefore do not pronounce judgment before the time, before the Lord comes, who will bring to light those things now hidden in darkness and will disclose the purposes of the heart. Then every man will receive his commendation from God" (4:4–5). Culla is drawn to these mysterious dark men on two different nights, and each time he is interrogated, held to trial by the leader of the group. On the first night, Culla is adrift on a ferry whose line has given way (or been cut) and is pulled ashore by the men. Drying at their fire, he is coerced into eating a "black and mummified" meat (171) in awful communion with the strangers. The leader first implies that Culla himself is responsible for the ferry accident and the death (or murder) of the ferryman. He asks Culla's name. "A feller didn't know he'd think you wanted it kept for a secret," he says (174), but then acknowledges that another of the three has no name at all—"He wanted me to give him one but I wouldn't do it" (174)—and boasts that his own name is also hidden—"I expect they's lots would like to know that" (175), he smiles. After questioning Culla further about his past (Culla lies when he answers), the leader returns abruptly to the idea of names and the unnameable: "I wouldn't name him because if you cain't name somethin you cain't claim it," he says, alluding to the third figure. "You cain't talk about it even. You cain't say what it is" (177).

The leader's comments and questions make clear his awareness of Culla's guilt—"How come ye to run your sister off?" he asks (178)—and also recall Culla's determined refusal to give the "nameless weight" in Rinthy's belly an identity, that is (in the leader's philosophy), to claim it as his own. Thus, there is an interesting kinship established here between Culla and the leader. Each hides his own name, and each refuses to give a name (again, perhaps his own) to the son/relation/dependent/companion. The leader also suggests that this denial is the cause of the general disaster which follows Culla and has brought him to this place. Speaking of the unnamed man (the last is identified as Harmon), the leader says, "He's the one set the skiff adrift this mornin. . . . Even if it just drifted off he still done it. I knowed they's a reason. We waited all day and half the night. I kept up a good fire. You seen it didn't ye?" (178). In other words, the unnamed companion has, just by *being*, directed Culla to them to confront his guilt. Finally, forcing Culla to give him his boots (which Culla stole from the first squire who gave him work, the same squire who has subsequently been murdered by these men), the leader initiates a round-robin of boot-swapping which leaves Culla with the "mismatched, cracked, shapeless, burntlooking and crudely mended" boots of the nameless member (180), the grown double of his own unclaimed child.[9] Why do they not kill Culla, as they do every other person they meet? The answer seems to be that there is a purpose yet to be served. Culla's destiny has not yet worked itself out.

"Where was you headin sure enough?" the leader asks Culla as they prepare to leave. "Nowheres," Culla answers. "Nowheres," the leader repeats. "You may get there yet" (181). The second time Culla meets them—having again had a narrow brush with death, a near hanging and a desperate leap from a cliff—the leader greets him: "You got here all right for somebody bound elsewhere. . . . We ain't hard to find. Oncet you've found us" (232–33). This time they have the child with them, taken from the now murdered tinker, and this time the glade is clearly established as a place of judgment, the child stark witness against his father. Half its body is scarred, burned and blind; the other well and whole. "Whose youngern?" Culla asks, apparently in ignorance, unable or unwilling to recognize the result of his deeds. "What happent to his eye?" "Some folks has two and cain't see," the leader replies. What follows is a detailed series of denials, played out on the repetition of nothingness. "It ain't nothin to me," Culla says of the child, beginning a string of excuses which the leader then summarizes: "Never figured nothin, never had nothin, never was nothin, the man said. He was looking at nothing at all" (233). The word play continues: "You ain't nothin to me," Culla tells the man and later adds, "It ain't nothin to you." "I'll be the judge of that," the man says (234–34) in comic portentousness.

Taking the child, he gives Culla one last opportunity to acknowledge his responsibility. "What's his name?" the man asks.

> I don't know.
> He ain't got nary'n.
> No. I don't reckon. I don't know.
> They say people in hell ain't got names. But they had to be called somethin to get sent there. Didn't they.
> That tinker might of named him.
> It wasn't his to name. Besides names dies with the namers. A dead man's dog ain't got a name. (235–36)

"You don't name things dead," Culla had told Rinthy. Now, as the man takes out his knife, Culla is still unable to name, to own his child, "My sister would take him . . . . That chap. We could find her and she'd take him." "Yes," the man agrees, acknowledging Rinthy's willingness to accept the child,[10] but then cuts the boy's throat with Culla as silent observer and gives the dying body to the other nameless man, who (forcing us to remember Culla's earlier meal of "mummified meat") drinks its blood, apparently consumes its sacrificed body (236).

In Revelations, John writes to the church in Laodicea these words of Jesus, "I know your works: you are neither cold nor hot. Would that you were cold or hot! So, because you are lukewarm, and neither cold nor hot, I will spew you out of my mouth" (3:15–16). These are the same cast of sinners, the "neutrals" Dante encounters in the vestibule of Hell. "The heavens drove them forth, not to be less fair, and the depth of Hell does not receive them lest the wicked have some glory over them," Virgil explains. "They have no hope of death, and so abject is their blind life that they are envious of every other lot. The world suffers no report of them to live. Pity and justice despise them. Let us not talk of them; but look thou and pass" (Canto III, 40–42, 46–51). These are the same souls Eliot alludes to in *The Waste Land*.[11] According to Dante, having committed themselves neither to God nor the Devil, these nameless sinners now exist in "nowhere," in a state of nothingness. Dante recognizes one "who from cowardice made the great refusal" (III, 60), a description thoroughly applicable to Culla himself.

The ending of the book is often cited as proof of its nihilistic intent, and admittedly it is a bleak conclusion. Rinthy has found a man who loves her, but she leaves him to continue her search. Wandering at last into the glade where the child has been killed, she pokes among the ashes and finds there "the charred billets and chalk bones, the little calcined ribcage," but she "did not know what to make of it" (237). Then "little sister" goes to sleep, apparently unaware that she has finally found her child. Is this ending cruelly ironic, or is there a sense of resolution? The "glade" recalls the glade in which Culla originally abandoned the child, may in fact (given the circular journeys in the novel) *be* the same glade. And we should remember that Rinthy's original impulse, when first told that the child was dead, was an acceptance and a desire to honor it with a name and flowers. At that time she discovered the grave was a false one and began her search. This time, without actually knowing, she stops her search and sleeps, and in that rest is implied, I think, a final peace, the "frail agony of grace" (237) McCarthy describes. Or, back to I Corinthians, "Lo! I tell you a mystery. We shall not all sleep, but we shall all be changed, in a moment, in the twinkling of an eye, at the last trumpet. For the trumpet will sound, and the dead will be raised imperishable, and we shall be changed" (15: 51–52).

Culla is allowed no such peace, although there is still the possibility of redemption. "In later years he used to meet a blind man, ragged and serene, who spoke him a good day out of his constant dark" (239), we are told. This blind man has been anticipated. When Culla is threatened with hanging, blamed for the death of a swineherder who is carried over a cliff by the rioting hogs,[12] a "parson or what looked like one" (221) appears. This "Reverend," who loudly proclaims Culla's guilt, tells the story of a blind man he once led to Christ. He recalls his words to the man:

> They's been more than one feller brought to the love of Jesus over the paths of affliction. And what better way than blind? In a world darksome as this'n I believe a blind man ort to be better sighted than most. I believe it's got a good deal to recommend it. The grace of God don't rest easy on a man. It can blind him easy as not. It can bend him and make him

crooked. And who did Jesus love, friends? The lame the halt and the blind, that's who. Them is the ones scarred with God's mercy. Stricken with his love. Ever legless fool and old blind mess like you is a flower in the garden of God (226).

The preacher's words echo those of Jesus in Revelations: "For you say, I am rich, I have prospered, and I need nothing; not knowing that you are wretched, pitiable, poor, blind, and naked. Therefore, I counsel you to buy from me gold refined by fire, that you may be rich, and white garments to clothe you and to keep the shame of your nakedness from being seen, and salve to anoint your eyes, that you may see. Those whom I love, I reprove and chasten; so be zealous and repent. Behold, I stand at the door and knock; if any one hears my voice and opens the door, I will come in to him and eat with him, and he with me"(3:17–20). Ironically, they also recall the words of the dark leader, the spurious "minister" who feeds Culla and tells him, "Some folks has two [eyes] and cain't see." And it may well be that these two ministers are one and the same. As in Melville's *The Confidence Man*, a work worth further comparison to this one, the possibility of multiple identities abound in *Outer Dark*.[13] Moreover, the preacher's "sermon" also recalls Culla's dream: perhaps he is also the "prophet" Culla cried to for mercy.

This idea is now reinforced by the blind man, who constantly speaks in terms of sight: "Well . . . it's good to see the sun again ain't it" (239); "But I knowed I'd seen ye afore" (240). The blind man recounts the moment of his salvation, which is an obvious version of Culla's dream (and the passages from Revelations).

They was a bunch of us there all cripple folks. . . . And they was a feller leapt up and hollered out that nobody knowed what was wrong with. And they said it caused that preacher to go away. But they's darksome ways afoot in this world and it may be he weren't no true preacher. . . . I always did want to find that feller. . . . And tell him. If somebody don't tell him he never will have no rest. (241)

Culla continues his habitual denial—"I don't need nothin" (240)—and walks away, only to find the road ends in a swamp, "A faintly smoking garden of the dead that tended away to the earth's curve. . . . He wondered why a road should come to such a place" (242). Retracing his steps, Culla sees the blind man coming and attempts to hide, but the blind man "sees" him, turns his head and smiles at him as he passes. Culla watches: "He wondered where the blind man was going and did he know how the road ended. Someone should tell a blind man before setting him out that way" (242). But Culla, "gracelorn" (241) as he is, is not the one to stop him. And who is to say, finally, that the swamp even awaits the blind man? Just as Rinthy circles back to the secluded glade, so might Culla be returning to the "swampy forest," the "dark wood" on the edge of hell, in which he first became lost after abandoning his child. His sin still unspoken, his guilt yet unnamed, the blind man's message of salvation turned aside, Culla, wandering in his state of nothingness, seems fated to return again and again to the site of his sin. He will likely meet the blind man again; but he is just as likely to meet the three dark figures, or another preacher or prophet, or perhaps he will meet them all with each encounter.

While it is not my intention to examine all of McCarthy's novels in such detail, nor to belabor the points I have tried to make, I again note here that in McCarthy's highly moralistic world, sins must be named and owned before they can be forgiven; and those characters who most insist on the "nothingness" of existence, who attempt to remain "neutral," are those most in need of grace. In none of McCarthy's novels is the division between good and evil easily distinguished nor are the agents easily identified and cast. It is, however, the state of the soul that is being examined and narrated. Culla Holme is a thinking, tortured, conflicted character just as is Arthur Dimmesdale or Hazel Motes, men striving against the frightening prospect of God's grace and mercy, which can blind and scar even as it heals.

The protagonist of McCarthy's next published novel, *Child of God* (1973), is initially more difficult to assimilate than Culla Holme. Lester Ballard is a sneak, a thief, a liar, a poacher, a voyeur, a murderer and, finally, a necrophile. He is an isolate who becomes a hermit and then devolves into a gnome-like creature scampering beneath the surface of the ground. The title, at first, appears to be a wicked joke, except that, when the narrator introduces Lester as a "child of God much like yourself perhaps" (4), there is no sense of irony whatsoever.

Lester is another abandoned child, deserted by his mother, then left fully parentless by the suicide of his father, whose body he finds hanging grotesquely in the barn. When we first see Lester, the rope still hangs behind him from the loft, a constant reminder. "They say he never was right after his daddy killed hisself" (21), a townsperson recounts. By the time Lester is a grown man, he has lost his home and land and been knocked permanently crooked when he attempts to drive the auctioneer and potential buyers away.

The first section of the novel details precisely Lester's gradual withdrawal from human society. He moves into an abandoned house when his own home is sold. He is sexually teased and embarrassed by the daughters of his neighbor, a dumpkeeper who offers him a modest friendship. He goes to church but is stared at as he sits in the back pew, sniffling. When he finds a nearly naked woman, passed out on a deserted mountain turnabout, his first impulse is to inquire, "Ain't you cold?" (42). It is only after she hits him with a rock that he tears away her clothes and walks off with them, making her later charge of rape a lie, as Lester himself insists. "All the trouble I ever was in . . . was caused by whiskey or women or both" (53), he brags in jail, not because it is true but because he has heard other men say it and would like to pretend a kinship with them. Upon his release, the sheriff, appropriately named Fate, finds him examining wanted posters, as if to find a clue to his own identity. "I guess murder is next on the list ain't it?" the sheriff suggests (56). At a fair, Lester wins the most expensive prizes—large stuffed animals—at a shooting booth, and for the moment enjoys some form of admiration; the animals become his solitary companions. In early spring, he chases a robin. "He caught and held one warm and feathered in his palm with the heart of it beating there just so" (76). It is the only scene in which Lester laughs or shows joy. Attempting to ingratiate himself with one of the neighbor girls, he gives the bird to her idiot brother, who chews off its legs. "He wanted it to where it couldn't run off," Lester explains, fully understanding the idiot's motives (79).

McCarthy spends over a third of the book thus setting up the *reasons* for Lester's otherwise unimaginable actions, creating a world in which such actions have a cause. The story is certainly not horror for horror's sake. Lester is both pushed and pulled into this monstrous life (the apparently extraneous story of the carnival ape is worth noting in this regard [58–60]). The first body is practically given to him, by accident, by fate. To say that he "rapes" her, as has one critic (Bartlett 5), misinterprets Lester's own needs, for he is not about violence but about companionship: "He poured into that waxen ear everything he'd ever thought of saying to a woman. Who could say she did not hear him?" (88–89). He woos, romances the dead woman. When he loses her in the fire which consumes his house, he moves into a cave. Shortly thereafter, met on the road by the man who bought his old home, he denies he is Lester Ballard. Soon he begins killing people and taking the corpses underground, creating his own community.

In his growing madness, Lester has no hold on his own identity. He begins to wear the clothing of his victims, and later he will wear their hair as a wig, anticipating the scalp hunting of *Blood Meridian*. After losing everything else, he begins to lose himself. Yet he is not without moments of self-awareness, of recognition, even of introspection. Spotting his own reflection in a pool of water, he reaches out hesitantly to touch it before drawing back, afraid. At night from his cave he "watched the hordes of cold stars sprawled across the smokehole and wondered what stuff they were made of, or himself" (141). During a flood, when he is forced to move his family of bodies, he shouts aloud in weariness and despair: "Whatever voice spoke him was no demon but some old shed self that came yet from time to time in the name of sanity, a hand to gentle him back from the rim of his disastrous wrath" (158). The most touching scene in the book occurs as he lies awake in the cave and imagines "a whistling as he used to when he was a boy in his bed in the dark and he'd hear his father on the road coming home whistling, a lonely piper . . ." (170). That night he dreams (in a delicate echo of Dylan Thomas's "Fern Hill"[14]) of riding a mule through a beautiful woods, and "the world that day was as lovely as any day that ever was and he was riding to his death" (171).

What Lester wants is permanence, even (or especially) the permanence of death, but what he experiences in his life is change in the form of desertion and denial and loss. He expects to be abandoned. When he can't find his prized rifle, he panics, and upon retrieving it says to the inanimate object, "You'd try it, wouldn't ye?" (132). Thus, the dead he collects underground around him. But Lester is also caught between the two worlds, above and below. As his lunacy grows, he tries (outfitted in the dress and hair of one of his female corpses) to reclaim his old home, and perhaps his lost child's life, by killing the owner; he is himself shot, his arm blown away. Now crippled, maimed, he is taken from the hospital by a band of men who threaten to hang him unless he confesses the enormity of his crime. "I never done it," Lester at first says (178). "I don't know nothin about no bodies" (182). Then admitting under duress,[15] he leads them into the cave and, as a creature of the dark, quickly eludes them. He spends three days underground before he finds a narrow passage to the upper world. Digging with his one hand, "He'd cause to wish and he did wish for some brute midwife to spald him from his rocky keep" (189). The image of birth is not inappropriate, for the Lester who emerges above ground is different, "changed." A church bus passes in the night, and Lester shares a stare with a young boy looking out the window: "There was nothing out there to see but [the boy] was looking anyway. As he went by he looked at Ballard and Ballard looked back." The "nothing" the boy sees is Ballard; but what Ballard sees in the boy is "himself" (191). That dawn he returns to the hospital: "I'm supposed to be here, he said" (192), and soon after he dies, apparently a natural death.

In *Child of God*, Lester Ballard arguably faces his guilt with a courage not shown by Culla Holme. He identifies himself as Culla can never do. Thus, in a sense, he escapes from Dante's "nowhere" zone of the uncommitted. Moreover, McCarthy also suggests that Lester serves a larger purpose, is himself a necessary agent. When he almost drowns in the flooded creek, the narrator breaks the action to address directly the reader:

> He could not swim, but how would you drown him? His wrath seemed to buoy him up. Some halt in the way of things seems to work here. See him. You could say that he's sustained by his fellow men, like you. Has peopled the shore with them calling to him. A race that gives suck to the maimed and the crazed, that wants their wrong blood in its history and will have it. But they want this man's life. (156)

In the next section, an old man talks to Sheriff Fate about earlier days. "You think people was meaner then than they are now?" a deputy asks. "No . . . I don't," the old man answers. "I think people are the same from the day God first made one." He then tells another story about "how an old hermit used to live out on House Mountain, a ragged gnome with kneelength hair who dressed in leaves and how people were used to going by his hole in the rocks and throwing in stones on a dare and calling him to come out" (168). The story describes Lester himself. He is created by those around him, a necessary figure of the community, the scapegoat that embodies their weird alienation and stoked violence but also their terrible sadness, their potential nothingness. Thus, Lester Ballard is raised to the level of mystery. He is not one man in one age. "As in olden times so now," the narrator states. "As in other countries here" (191).

Suttree (1979) is such a large book, so full of variety and richness and amazements, that to focus on any one element or theme is to distort the overall achievement. It is useless to attempt to summarize its plot, as I have tried to do with *Outer Dark* and *Child of God*, which is not to say that the book has no plot or thread of development. The chronology distinctly covers six years, from 1950 to 1955, and the narrative is replete with specific dates and holidays and days of the week as well as the passing seasons. The streets, buildings, markets of Knoxville are carefully mapped. There are over one hundred fifty named characters in the book, some of whom appear for one time only and others who weave in and out of the story.[16] Some of them go by different names at different times: J-Bone is Jim is James is James Long, for example. The protagonist, Cornelius Suttree, himself goes by a variety of names: he is Bud or Buddy to his family, Sut or Suttree or Youngblood to his companions, but never his given name of Cornelius. The question of identity and responsibility weighs heavily on his soul. McAnally Flats, "*a world within the world*" (4) with yet another world beneath it, is his own vestibule of hell.

As everyone notes, Suttree is McCarthy's most intellectual protagonist. He is, in fact, almost *too* aware, his sense of self-horror often lapsing into self-pity. He is a fine example of what William James termed the "divided self," the person who strives with the "sick soul" within: "Back of everything is the great spectre of universal death, the all-encompassing blackness," James writes of the sick soul ("Sick Soul" 118),[17] and certainly this description captures the essence of Suttree, who throughout the novel fears the passing of time, the certainty of death. One need only note the prevalence of watches and clocks, from the running wristwatch on the suicide fished out of the river to the sound of ticking at Mother She's to the nightmare of clocks that figure in Suttree's final delirium as he faces the "galactic drainsuck" of death (453). The division within Suttree is further underscored by the many doubles who people the book, from the numerous sets of brothers (Suttree and his dead twin chief among them) to the contrasting yet allied characters (such as the religious goat man and the cynical ragman) who present different sides of dialectical arguments in their relationships with Suttree.

In its broadest, most metaphysical sense, Suttree's divided self is expressed by what Suttree calls the "antisuttree" (28), the term calling forth the idea of the Jungian double but also indicating the threat of negation and nothingness. For example, when Suttree retreats from Knoxville to the mountains of Tennessee and North Carolina, he senses "that another went before him and each glade he entered seemed just quit by a figure who'd been sitting there and risen and gone on. Some doublegoer, some othersuttree eluded him in these woods and he feared that should that figure fail to rise and steal away and were he therefore to come to himself in this obscure wood he'd be neither mended nor made whole but rather set mindless to dodder drooling with his ghosty clone from sun to sun across a hostile hemisphere forever" (287). Suttree, here in the Dantesque "obscure wood," is very much like Culla Holme in his wish to avoid facing the dark figure of his guilt, and with it the possibility of his salvation—to be "mended" or "made whole," the conditions promised by the prophet in *Outer Dark*.

Suttree is another of McCarthy's "neutrals." Like Lester, he has removed himself from the upper world, retreated to the lower slums of Knoxville's McAnally Flats. Like Culla, he has abandoned his own child and the mother of his child. As in *Outer Dark*, the child dies. Suttree's withdrawal is a form of spiritual despair and abasement.[18] Sober, Suttree maintains an order and economy to his life, marked by cleanliness and concern and moderate responsibility. But drunk, he is filthy beyond words (almost): one of the grand artistries of this novel is McCarthy's brilliance in describing various states of befoulment. As Suttree says after one prolonged binge, "My life is ghastly" (348).

Nevertheless, there is a type of brotherhood in Suttree's world—he is much less isolated than either Culla or Lester—and he feels real affection and loyalty for many of the people around him. Indeed, Suttree serves as a kind of guardian for some of them—Ab Jones, the ragpicker, Daddy Watson, Harvey the junkman, Gene Harrogate—as he in turn is cared for by J-Bone and others. He can be inconsistent—like Culla, he leaves a blind man to find his own way home on one dark night—but still he shows a care to this adopted family he has denied to his own relatives. Perhaps one is an effort to make amends for the other, but the impulse is worth noting. "You got a good heart, Youngblood," Ab Jones tells him. "Look out for your own" (203).

Of the many scenes one could mention to illustrate Suttree's "good heart," the most extraordinary is his journey underground to rescue Gene Harrogate, a great comic character, as all have noted, but also a figure of some real pathos. Suttree's feelings for the boy are, I think, deepened by his own son's death. (Excluded from the funeral, Suttree later fills in the grave, but this is a fairly useless gesture. He seems sorrier for himself at this point than for the lost child.) When Harrogate disappears into the caves underrunning Knoxville—off on his fantastic scheme to rob a bank by blasting into its vault—Suttree must go in after him. McCarthy presents it as a trip into the spiritual underworld. Harrogate is described as a "cherrycolored troll or demon cartographer in the hellish light [of his stolen red road lantern] charting the progress of souls in the darkness below" (260). His name (there is a Harrogate, Tennessee) takes on a deeper meaning, for in one sense Suttree "harrows" the "gates" of hell to attempt the rescue, to retrieve Gene from the depths. We should remember that Suttree is a fisherman, although the river he fishes runs out of Eliot's *Waste Land* and he more often resembles the wounded Fisher King than, as here, the Christian fisher of men. He finds Harrogate in shock, covered with dried excrement (for he has burst a sewer main and been engulfed by the filth, another view of hell found in Dante).[19] "True news of man here below," Suttree observes. "I thought I was dead. I thought I'd die in this place," Harrogate says. Then (echoing Lester Ballard), he adds: "There was people down here. . . . I talked to em." "Let's go," Suttree says. "I'd give ten dollars for a glass of icewater," Harrogate concludes. "Cash money" (276–77). Earlier, when Suttree is told to call his father (who would tell him of Suttree's son's death), he refuses, joking, "People in hell want ice water" (148). Suttree could only fill the grave for his own son, but on this occasion, at least, he can return the surrogate boy above ground.[20]

Indeed, it is difficult *not* to follow Suttree's movement as a religious or spiritual quest, even as he tries to deny exactly that aspect of it. In *Blood Meridian*, a preacher says, "Don't you know that he said I will foller ye always even unto the end of the road? . . . He's a goin to be there with ye ever step of the way whether ye ask it or ye dont. . . . Neighbor, you caint get shed of him. Now. Are you going to drag him, *him*, into that hellhole yonder?" (6). The preacher's words are appropriate to Suttree, as well as to McCarthy's other characters. Religion, Faith, God, Death, Grace are constant topics of conversation between Suttree and such figures as the ragpicker, the goatman, Daddy Watson, the street evangelists and numerous strangers he encounters. Although Suttree denies he is "saved" (122), declares himself a "defrocked" Catholic (191), his struggle indicates otherwise. Early in the book he feels that "even a false adumbration of the world of the spirit is better than none at all" (21). By the end he has entered that world of the spirit and has acknowledged its power.

As do the previous characters, Suttree attempts to excuse his failures by insisting on the insignificance and "nothingness" of life. Picked up by the sheriff after his son's funeral, Suttree says, "No one cares. It's not important." The sheriff answers, "That's where you're wrong my friend. Everything's important. A man lives his life, he has to make that important. Whether he's a small town county sheriff or the president. Or a busted out bum. You might even understand that some day. I dont say you will. You might" (157). Visiting the dwarf witch Mother She, he sees a photograph of her family: "I was there when it was took but I never come out," she tells him. Instead, there is a "dead place . . . a greyed-out patch, a ghost in the photo" (279) where she stood, and we are reminded that when Suttree looks through his own family pictures, he likewise never appears in any of the shots. However, after roaming the mountains trailing his "other self," he runs across a startled bow-hunter. "What are you? . . . Are ye lost?" the hunter asks. "I'll tell you what I'm not," the half-crazed Suttree replies. "A figment. I'm not a figment" (288–89). Later, near death with typhoid fever, Suttree envisions a trial in which he is accused of "squandering" his life. "I was drunk," is his first excuse (457), but when he regains consciousness and the attending priest asks, "Would you like to confess?", his simple but all-inclusive answer is "I did it" (461).

Thus, I find it difficult to read the end of *Suttree* as anything but affirming, although some critics find it much less convincing than I do. He leaves McAnally Flats, which is itself being torn down to make way for the new highway system, with a new sense of wholeness. "I learned that there is one Suttree and one Suttree only," he says to the priest, which is not a statement of resignation or nullity. Similarly, his avowal of God—"He is not a thing. Nothing ever stops moving" (461)—seems equally strong. Here the concept of "nothing" or "No thing" is turned into "All things." All things exist and have meaning. The Suttree who at first has "a subtle obsession with uniqueness" (113) learns that "all souls are one and all souls lonely" (459). Thus, "one Suttree" is "all Suttrees," all people. "He had divested himself of the little cloaked godlet and his other amulets in a place where they would not be found in his lifetime and he'd taken for talisman the simple human heart within him. Walking down the little street for the last time he felt everything fall away from him. Until there was nothing left of him to shed" (468). It is a state of rebirth, very much like that experienced by Lester Ballard when he reenters the world. Significantly, the crazed, crippled preacher who has cursed him throughout the book, warning him of his imminent damnation, fails to do so as Suttree leaves town (469). The angelic child, who is "ladling out water" to workmen whose "hands come up from below the rim of the pit in parched supplication" (recalling the earlier mentions of ice water and hell) offers a drink to Suttree (470). Then Suttree is given a ride without even lifting a hand.

Where he goes is unimportant. The fact that the hound of the hunter Death comes to sniff his tracks is simply another indication that he is still alive.[21] We all flee death. What Suttree has lost is the terrible, incapacitating fear of death. Culla Holme wanders still lost; Lester Ballard realizes where he "belongs"; but Cornelius Suttree is not yet done with the business of living.

And then there is the appalling, haunting, brilliant *Blood Meridian* (1985). With its stark recitations of incredible violence, of "death hilarious" (53) in the most brutal landscape imaginable, and with an ending which seems as contrary to the merciful conclusion of *Suttree* as possible, *Blood Meridian* challenges its readers' sensibilities even more than does *Child of God*. The gruesome acts of one mad solitary can be absorbed, even rationalized. Extreme variations of such acts by men united—men who are mostly sane, capable of moral distinctions, bound by certain shared values; men who are our historical forefathers, separated from us by only three or four generations (or by none at all, for we,

McCarthy suggests, are they)—must confound us from every perspective.

I nevertheless maintain that the moral center of this book holds as firmly as in the earlier novels. The unnamed "kid," the apparent protagonist of the narrative, is another of McCarthy's unparented children. "The mother dead these fourteen years did incubate in her own bosom the creature who would carry her off. The father never speaks her name, the child does not know it. . . . He can neither read nor write and in him broods already a taste for mindless violence. All history present in that visage, the child the father of the man" (3). McCarthy's ironic play on Wordsworth is noteworthy, certainly, for it underscores not the child's "natural piety" but the "mindless violence" which overcomes it, as later events will certainly prove.

It is surprising to realize that the kid is only sixteen years old for most of the narrative; he seems so much older. Yet, as the narrator tells us, the "child's face is curiously untouched behind the scars, the eyes oddly innocent" (4). Having run away from home in Tennessee, he ends up in Texas, Mexico and the Far West: "His origins are become remote as is his destiny and not again in all the world's turning will there be terrains so wild and barbarous to try whether the stuff of creation may be shaped to man's will or whether his own heart is not another kind of clay" (4–5). This question is the thematic center of the novel. Although the kid will ride with many men, on this staging ground it is Judge Holden, the mysterious, monstrous Judge Holden, who places the questions before the kid, who contests most strongly for the child's soul.

Blood Meridian comes out of historical record, and there was an actual Judge Holden (see the essay by John Sepich in this volume); but McCarthy, in a sense, had already created him in *Outer Dark*, for the judge and the sinister, supernatural leader of the murderous band are the same manifestation, extended over time and space. Both are creatures of fire, and both exemplify a kind of terrible justice and retribution. And what of the kid? Like Culla Holme, he wanders through a dark land, and, again like Culla, his destiny carries him over and over to the company of the frightening judge.

Judge Holden is clearly satanic, a "great ponderous djinn" from the flames (96), a "sootysouled rascal" (124) known to all men, a magician, a liar, a trickster. Also a child molester and murderer, drawn to the very innocence he needs to destroy. And yet, again, evil is not that simple in McCarthy. As William James put it, "the world is all the richer for having a devil in it, *so long as we keep our foot upon his neck*" ("Circumscription" 48), and the judge is an endlessly fascinating and seductive and even comic character for all his abhorrent vileness. He "smiles" upon the kid the first time he sees him, follows him with his eye and later claims he has loved him "like a son" (306). Most opposed to the judge is Tobin, known as the expriest but actually a lapsed novitiate. He urges the kid to resist the judge at all turns and offers a kind of faith in opposition to the judge's words. "For let it go how it will," he tells the kid, "God speaks in the least of creatures. . . . No man is give leave of that voice." "I aint heard no voice," the kid replies. "When it stops," Tobin says, "you'll know you've heard it all your life" (124).

The heart of the judge's arguments (which stand in direct opposition to those of the sheriff in *Suttree*) is that life is infinitely fascinating but ultimately has no meaning other than that man imposes on it. "The truth about the world," he says, "is that anything is possible. Had you not seen it all from birth and thereby bled it of its strangeness it would appear to you for what it is, a hat trick in a medicine show, a fevered dream, a trance bepopulate with chimeras having neither analogue nor precedent, an itinerant carnival, a migratory tentshow whose ultimate destination after many a pitch in many a mudded field is unspeakable and calamitous beyond reckoning" (245). War, then, "is the ultimate game because war is at last a forcing of the unity of existence. War is god. . . . Moral law is an invention of mankind for the disenfranchisement of the powerful in favor of the weak. . . . Decisions of life and death, of what shall be and what shall not, beggar all question of right. In elections of these magnitudes are all lesser ones subsumed, moral, spiritual, natural" (249–50). Finally, he argues, "Your heart's desire is to be told some mystery. The mystery is that there is no mystery" (252).[22]

"As if he were no mystery himself, the bloody old hoodwinker," responds Tobin, and his point is well taken. Some readers assume the judge speaks for McCarthy himself, but Tobin, I think, comes much closer (or, at least, presents the other side of the dialectic). And it is Tobin who tells the kid to kill the judge when they meet him in the desert after the massacre at Yuma ferry. "Do it for the love of God. Do it or I swear your life is forfeit" (285), Tobin says. The kid resists. "He aint nothin. You told me so yourself. Men are made of the dust of the earth. You said it was no pair . . . pair . . . . No parable. That it was a naked fact and the judge was a man like all men." "Face him down then," Tobin implores (297). But the kid will not take a stand.

This talk of parables comes from Mark 4: 10–13, following Christ's story of the sower and the seeds:

And when he was alone, those who were about him with the twelve asked him concerning the parables. And he said to them, "To you has been given the secret of the kingdom of God, but for those outside everything is in parables; so that they may indeed see but not perceive, and may indeed hear but not understand; lest they should turn again, and be forgiven." And he said to them, "Do you not understand this parable? How then will you understand all the parables?"

The kid "sees" but he does not "perceive" the truth of the judge: "He aint nothin," he insists, blind to the "secret." Tobin says the kid is a "free agent" (284) and thus has the ability to choose. But the judge indicates that it is the lack of choice which damns the kid: "No assassin. . . . And no partisan either. There's a flawed place in the fabric of your heart," he charges (299). (It's worth noting that Dante's uncommitted are condemned to "chase a whirling banner which ran so fast that it seemed as if it could never make a stand" [Canto III, 52–54].) Although it is certain that the kid actively participates in the scalp-hunting atrocities, McCarthy rarely shows us the kid in action: we never actually see him scalping and hacking and raping. As the judge says, "You alone reserved in your soul some corner of clemency for the heathen" (299). (The kid also shows misplaced mercy to other members of the gang, leaving Shelby, for example, alive even though he knows Elias's men will torture him when he is captured.) After the kid is rescued from the desert (by Indians, ironically) and is subsequently jailed in San Diego, the judge accuses him to the authorities of being the cause of the massacre, the "person responsible" (306). In a broad sense he is, for he has failed to confront the heart within, to "face down" the judge.

In jail, the kid "began to speak with a strange urgency of things few men have seen in a lifetime and his jailers said that his mind had come uncottered by the acts of blood in which he had participated" (305). Finally released, the kid roams for almost thirty years before he again meets the judge, this time in Fort Griffin, the "biggest town for sin in all Texas" (319), also a veritable boneyard of slaughtered buffalo. The kid is now a man, forty-five years old. During the interval, he is sometimes taken for a male whore, sometimes for a preacher since he carries a bible with him, one which he cannot read: "but he was no witness to them, neither of things at hand nor things to come, he least of any man" (312). The one time he again attempts to tell his story, it is to a mummified Indian, long dead. Like Lester Ballard, he pours his words into the ear of a corpse. He has, however, lost his taste for "mindless violence." The one time we see him kill after leaving the band, it is out of self-defense. The boy he kills, Elrod, is fifteen, approximately the same age as the kid when he began his exploits.[23]

"Was it always your idea . . . that if you did not speak you would not be recognized?" the judge asks (328) at their later meeting. "You aint nothin," the kid still tells him. "You speak truer than you know," the judge replies (331), underscoring the hidden reality in the kid's double negative. Although he comes "out of nothing," the judge is an active, existing power: "Whatever his antecedents he was something wholly other than their sum," McCarthy writes, "nor was there system by which to divide him back into his origins for he would not go. Whoever would seek out his history . . . must stand at last darkened and dumb at the shore of a void without terminus or origin and whatever science he might bring to bear upon the dusty primal matter blowing down out of the millennia will discover no trace of any ultimate atavistic egg by which to reckon his commencing" (309–10).

By failing to examine his heart, to name and face the judge, to acknowledge responsibility, the kid is another Culla Holme. Yet unlike Culla, he finally runs out of time, embraced (possibly, like the judge's other child victims, raped) by the judge in the outhouse. [24] The judge lives on: "He dances in light and in shadow and he is a great favorite. He never sleeps, the judge. He is dancing, dancing. He says that he will never die" (335).[25] Nor will he, as the epilogue illustrates. Fences will neither hold the judge nor constrain the force he calls to in each of us. But moral choice remains; the judge can still be faced.

McCarthy's newest novel, *All the Pretty Horses* (1992), will, I think, cause further reassessment of the writer's reputation as a nihilist. The first of the proposed "Border Trilogy," it is set, like *Blood Meridian*, in Texas and Mexico, approximately a century later, in the late 1940s. The protagonist is again a sixteen-year-old boy, this time given a name—John Grady Cole. Unlike *Blood Meridian*, this book is quietly restrained, often beautiful, sad, elegiac. Instead of hundreds of deaths, there are exactly two, and the consequences of those deaths haunt the boy. It is a book about the importance of choices and responsibility. It is a book about honor and courage and love. It is a book in which moral decisions count. As one of the characters, Lacey Rawlins, puts it, "Ever dumb thing I ever done in my life there was a decision I made before that got me into it. It was never the dumb thing. It was always some choice I'd made before it" (79). Judge Holden argues, "If God meant to interfere in the degeneracy of mankind would he not have done so by now?" (146). When John Grady Cole asks, "You think God looks out for people?", Rawlins answers, "Way the world is. Somebody can wake up and sneeze somewhere in Arkansas or some damn place and before you're done there's wars and ruination and all hell. You dont know what's goin to happen. I'd say He's just about got to. I dont believe we'd make it a day otherwise" (89). And when John Grady stands before *his* judge at the end of the book to tell his story (and it is a story he *needs* and *wants* to tell), the judge declares, "I've sat on the bench in this county since it was a county and in that time I've heard a lot of things that give me grave doubts about the human race but this aint one of em" (289).

Some of McCarthy's readers may be disappointed in this book, may feel that it is a more traditional, perhaps safer work than he has done in the past, certainly a more reassuring tale than its dark double *Blood Meridian*. It is, of course, impossible to know where the next two volumes will take us, but *All the Pretty Horses* is an affirmation of life and of humanity, however severe the experience. And this is the theme to be found in all of the books of Cormac McCarthy. For it is not that he says there is no mystery. Quite the opposite. The mystery McCarthy propounds is that we are blind to the mystery that is the very stuff of our existence.

NOTES

[1]See also Bell's earlier article, "The Ambiguous Nihilism of Cormac McCarthy," *Southern Literary Journal*, 15 (Spring 1983) 31–41. Bell is also the author of *Robert Lowell: Nihilist as Hero*.

[2]For other critics who have emphasized the nihilistic aspect of McCarthy's work, see John Ditsky, "Further Into Darkness: The Novels of Cormac McCarthy," *Hollins Critic*, 18 (1981) 1–11; John Lewis Longley, Jr., "The Nuclear Winter of Cormac McCarthy," *Virginia Quarterly Review*, 62 (1986) 746–50; Jerry Leath Mills, "Cormac McCarthy: A Great Tragic Writer," *Independent Weekly* 1–7 June 1989: 9–10; and Mark Royden Winchell, "Inner Dark: or, The Place of Cormac McCarthy," *Southern Review*, 26 (1990) 293–309.

[3]For examinations of the question of morality in McCarthy's work, see William J. Schafer; Robert Coles, "The Stranger," *New Yorker*, 26 Aug. 1974: 87–90; and Dianne [Luce] Cox, "Cormac McCarthy," *Dictionary of Literary Biography: American Novelists Since World War II*, ed. James E. Kibler, Jr. (Detroit: Gale Research, 1980) 224–32. More recently, see John Lewis Longley, Jr., "Suttree and the Metaphysics of Death," *Southern Literary Journal*, 17 (1985) 79–90; Frank W. Shelton, "Suttree and Suicide," *Southern Quarterly*, 29.1 (1990) 71–83; and Andrew Bartlett.

[4]For a similar discussion of McCarthy's first novel, *The Orchard Keeper* (Random, 1965), see David Paul Ragan, "Values and Structure in *The Orchard Keeper*" in this volume.

[5]For further analysis of the *double*, see Louis H. Palmer III, "The Use of the Double or Doppelgänger in the Novels of Cormac McCarthy," Thesis, Appalachian State U, 1991.

[6]The fact is that Rinthy is the first to leave home. She hides when she sees Culla coming toward the cabin. Culla, however, has taken the money, sold his gun and apparently made his own preparations to leave.

[7]I am indebted to Dianne Luce for making this suggestion as well as pointing out the later allusion to "Fern Hill."

[8]It is apparently the leader of the three, for example, who at one point leads the band of righteous citizens in the lynching of two men he falsely accuses of the murder of Squire Salter ([95]).

[9]Footwear is important in McCarthy's work. The type and state of a character's shoes or boots often signify the character's moral condition. This is especially true in *Suttree*: "Jesus never had no shoes," one recently saved man points out (123).

[10]In a contrasting scene, Rinthy implores the tinker to give her the child, repeating Culla's statement, "It ain't nothin to you" (193). Rinthy, however, *wants* the child, even though, as she admits, "It's no right child" (194).

[11]"I had not thought death had undone so many.
Sighs, short and infrequent, were exhaled,
And each man fixed his eyes before his feet."
T.S. Eliot, *The Complete Poems and Plays: 1909—1950* (New York: Harcourt, 1971), 39.

[12]The scene recalls Jesus's casting out of the demons into the swine at Gadarene. See Mark 5:1–20.

[13]The minister Culla meets on the cliff wears "a pair of octagonal glasses on the one pane of which the late sun shone while a watery eye peered from the naked wire aperture of the other" (221). Compare to Culla's child: "when it turned to look up at him he saw one eyeless and angry red socket like a stokehole to a brain in flames" (231–32).

[14]"All the sun long it was running, it was lovely, the hay
Fields high as the house, the tunes from the chimneys, it was air
And playing, lovely and watery
And fire green as grass.
And nightly under the simple stars
As I rode to sleep the owls were bearing the farm away. . . ." (11. 29–34)

[15]Compare Culla Holme who, when asked to plead to the charges of trespassing, at first says, "I ain't guilty. . . . I don't figure I done nothin wrong" (201); but, when threatened with jail, says, "I'll take the guilty" (202).

[16]As in *Blood Meridian*, *Suttree* also mixes real and fictional characters. An example is John Randolph Neal, Jr., who was indeed chief counsel for John T. Scopes. Suttree meets him on the streets of Knoxville in 1952, seven years before Neal's death.

[17]I am indebted to Garry Wallace for recording McCarthy's knowledge of James.

[18]Suttree's mother, from whom he is also estranged, is, significantly, named Grace. Near the end of the book, he is specifically identified as "son of Grace" (432).

[19]See, for example, Canto XVIII: "We went there, and thence in the moat below I saw people plunged in a filth which seemed to have come from human privies, and searching down there with my eyes I saw one with his head so befouled with ordure that it did not appear whether he was layman or cleric" (112–17). We should also note that in Canto IX, Virgil recounts how he himself, shortly after his death, was forced to take mortal form and go into hell to retrieve the soul of a traitor: "the circle of Judas, the deepest and darkest place, farthest from the heaven that encircles all. Well do I know the way . . . . This marsh exhaling the great stench goes all round the woeful city, which we cannot now enter without contention" (27–33). McCarthy's description of Harrogate underground—"The wick toppled and dropped with a thin hiss and dark closed over him so absolute that he became without boundary to himself, as large as all the universe and small as anything that was" (274–75)—also recalls Melville's description of the cabin-boy Pip in *Moby-Dick*, who jumps overboard and finds himself swallowed up by the immensity of the sea and goes mad: "the sea had jeeringly kept his finite body up, but drowned the infinite of his soul. Not drowned entirely, though. Rather carried down alive to wondrous depths, where strange shapes of the unwarped primal world glided to and fro before his passive eyes . . . " ([New York: Library of America, 1983] 1236).

[20]But Suttree cannot ultimately save Gene from his rashness. Harrogate is finally sent to prison for attempted robbery.

[21]In Canto XIII, in "The Wood of the Suicides," Virgil and Dante witness two figures who are chased by "hunting dogs," "black bitches, ravenous and swift like hounds loosed from the chain" (11. 125–26), who seize and tear them apart. Suttree has explicitly rejected the possibility of suicide (see Shelton, "Suttree and Suicide," for further discussion of this aspect of the book). Dante also employs a series of negatives to describe the Wood: it is a place of ultimate negation.

[22]Compare the judge's words with those of the strange hermit the kid meets at the beginning of the book. The hermit tells him, "It's a mystery. A man's at odds to know his mind cause his mind is aught he has to know it with. He can know his heart, but he dont want to. Rightly so. Best not to look in there. It aint the heart of a creature that is bound in the way that God has set for it" (19). Perhaps the judge and the hermit are the same: the kid awakes in the night to find the hermit climbing into bed with him, an act which anticipates the kid's final encounter with the judge.

[23]The boy, Elrod, seems, somehow, to come from the judge's own parable of the harnessmaker (142–46), who kills a traveler with a rock and buries him in the woods. Years later, on his death bed, the harnessmaker confesses to his son, who digs up the body and scatters the bones in the woods and then "went away

to the west and he himself became a killer of men" (145). Elrod's "grandaddy was killed by a lunatic and buried in the woods like a dog" (323).

[24]After Suttree's near-death experience, he "lay aneled. Like a rape victim" and he refers to God as a "pederastic deity" (460).

[25]The image of the dance, so important to *Blood Meridian*, is likely derived also from Eliot:

> At the still point of the turning world. Neither flesh nor fleshless;
> Neither from nor towards; at the still point, there the dance is,
> But neither arrest nor movement. And do not call it fixity,
> Where past and future are gathered. Neither movement from nor towards,
> Neither ascent nor decline. Except for the point, the still point,
> There would be no dance, and there is only the dance. ("Burnt Norton,"
> ll. 64–72)

WORKS CITED

Bartlett, Andrew. "From Voyeurism to Archaeology: Cormac McCarthy's *Child of God*." *Southern Literary Journal* 24 (1991): 3–15.

Bell, Vereen M. *The Achievement of Cormac McCarthy*. Baton Rouge: Louisiana State UP, 1988.

Dante Alighieri. *The Divine Comedy*. Trans. John D. Sinclair. New York: Oxford UP, 1939.

James, William. "Circumscription of the Topic." *The Varieties of Religious Experience*. Cambridge and London: Harvard UP, 1985.

———. "The Sick Soul." *The Varieties of Religious Experience*. Cambridge and London: Harvard UP, 1985.

McCarthy, Cormac. *All the Pretty Horses*. New York: Knopf, 1992.

———. *Blood Meridian or the Evening Redness in the West*. New York: Random, 1985.

———. *Child of God*. New York: Random, 1973.

———. *Outer Dark*. 1968. New York: Ecco, 1984.

———. *Suttree*. New York: Random, 1979.

Schafer, William J. "Cormac McCarthy: The Hard Wages of Original Sin." *Appalachian Journal* 4 (1977): 105–19.

Cormac McCarthy's First Screenplay

"The Gardener's Son"

Dianne C. Luce

Nay—the shuttle flies—the figures float from forth the loom;
the freshet-rushing carpet for ever slides away. The weaver-god,
he weaves; and by that weaving is he deafened, that he hears
no mortal voice; and by that humming, we, too, who look on the
loom are deafened; and only when we escape it shall we hear
the thousand voices that speak through it. For even so it is in all
material factories.
                              —Herman Melville, *Moby-Dick*

. . . And wake to the farm forever fled from the childless land.
                              —Dylan Thomas, "Fern Hill"

When *Blood Meridian* was published in 1985, it appeared, to many who had been following Cormac McCarthy's writing career, to represent a significant departure from patterns established in his earlier novels. Here was a novel set in the American Southwest and Mexico of the nineteenth century rather than the mid-twentieth century eastern Tennessee where McCarthy grew up and which is so familiarly detailed in *The Orchard Keeper*, *Child of God* and *Suttree*. Here too was a fully realized historical novel—McCarthy's first in that form, but a magnificent achievement—one in which his characteristic themes of the mysteries of the human soul are played out on the stage of American territorial expansion in the West in such a way as to become emblematic of the history of western man. I do not know whether McCarthy moved to El Paso because he wanted to write a novel such as *Blood Meridian* or whether his shift in novelistic form was a natural, almost necessary, outcome of his desire to move to a new location. But it seems plausible that the researching and writing of a historical novel was a means for McCarthy to make his new locale his own: to steep himself so deeply in the life of the Southwest that he could write of it as concretely as he had of Tennessee. *All the Pretty Horses*, published in May of 1992, is the first of a series of three novels set in the Southwest and Mexico, which McCarthy's publisher is calling "The Border Trilogy." It is not a historical novel, but like *Blood Meridian* it is everywhere informed by McCarthy's mastery of the history, geology, botany, cultural anthropology, language—all the physical and human textures of the region.

McCarthy's apparently unprecedented venture into the historical mode was in fact anticipated by his screenplay, "The Gardener's Son," written after the publication of *Child of God* in January 1974 ("PW Forecasts"). The screenplay is an historical drama based on the 1876 killing of James Gregg, mill superintendent of the Graniteville Manufacturing Company, by Robert McEvoy, of a family of textile workers. The screenplay was directed and co-produced by Richard Pearce, the independent filmmaker whose later feature films "Heartland" (1980) and "Country" (1984) are more widely known. "The Gardener's Son" was filmed on site at the Graniteville textile mill in western South Carolina, the only surviving antebellum textile mill building in the state; and it was aired in January 1977 in the "Visions" series of original works by new American playwrights on PBS (O'Connor; Brown).[1]

Richard Pearce visited South Carolina in the summer of 1974 to explore the possibility of making a film about the Graniteville murder case. He contacted Professor Tom Terrill, the economic historian at the University of South Carolina who was to become the consulting historian for the film, to discuss the project. At that time, according to Terrill,[2] Pearce had read Broadus Mitchell's highly laudatory 1928 biography of William Gregg, James Gregg's father and first president of the Graniteville company and the foremost leader in textile manufacturing in the South. Here Pearce found the story of Robert McEvoy's crime:

> The bad boy of the village was Bob McAvoy [sic]. One who knew him described him: "He would mold nickels, and it was said he would take Confederate money and raise its denomination by pasting a 2 on top of the 1 of a 10-dollar note." Playing about a freight car at the Kalmia station, Bob got a severe injury to his left leg. When Mrs. Gregg knew of it

and learned that the wound was infected, she went to the McAvoy home and bathed and dressed the hurt. The leg had to be amputated, and Mrs. Gregg nursed the boy and took him to Kalmia [her home] to convalesce. When he was well he had a crutch, in the use of which he was remarkably dexterous. He would go hunting all day through the swamps, and could climb a tree like a cat.

One April day in 1876, nobody knows why, he appeared at the door of the mill office in the main factory building, where James Gregg, then superintendent, was working at a desk. He shot Gregg, fled through the passage-way, and swung round the jamb of the door toward the canal, across which he disappeared with uncanny swiftness. One may still see the hole in the door frame torn by the bullet which Gregg sent after him. Gregg died a few days later in Augusta. Mrs. Gregg recorded it in the family Bible that her son was murdered in cold blood.

Bob McAvoy hid in the attic of his father's house in the village. Planning his escape, he employed his handiness with tools to make a wooden leg to replace his tell-tale crutch; he devised a wig, donned woman's clothing, and was accompanied by his sister to the train at Aiken. In indiscreet solicitude for his safety, his sister cautioned him as he stepped on the platform, "Now be careful and don't let them catch you"; the conductor overheard this remark, telegraphed ahead, and McAvoy was captured by officers at Columbia. He was brought back to Aiken, tried, and hung. Many Graniteville people witnessed the execution. One villager, now an old man, told me of seeing Bob's father drive back to the town sitting on his son's coffin. He buried the body in the corner of his yard where he could watch over the grave—this out of fear, so the story goes, that doctors would disinter it to dissect the brain, which was admitted to be "a powerful one." "After times and times," my informant concluded, "the mound disappeared—old man McAvoy had moved the body himself, nobody knew where to." (327–28)

Terrill also recalls that when he first worked with the director in 1974, Pearce was then reading the works of a novelist he had never met: Cormac McCarthy. Pearce may well have been struck by the similarity of some of the details of Mitchell's account to elements in *Child of God*, such as McEvoy's amputated limb, his dressing as a woman and the suggestion that his brain might be dissected, as well as McCarthy's treatment of the outlaw or outcast in his novels. Soon after this, Pearce asked McCarthy to work with him on the project, and they did most—if not all—of the further historical research together.[3] Some of this was done in Graniteville and was recorded in seven "research newsletters" that Pearce sent to the Alicia Patterson Foundation in New York. These are dated from early

April 1975 to 19 November 1975. Pearce states in the first of them that his intention is to explore "both sides of Graniteville's industrial revolution, that is, both her public mythology of monuments and ceremonial heroes, and at the same time her private underworld of ghost villains and legendary characters, family histories and photographs, each preserved and passed down through the generations family by family in solemn testimony to this extraordinary period in our economic history" ([c. 7 Apr. 1975] 8). The newsletters include interviews with older members of the Graniteville community, photographs, quotations from some of the published and documentary sources and, in the last one, the text of several related scenes from not quite the middle of "The Gardener's Son." (McCarthy, of course, is credited.) The earlier newsletters also bear indirect evidence suggesting McCarthy's input. The first one ends with the weaver-god passage from *Moby-Dick* that appears as an epigraph to this article, and which, in light of McCarthy's use of Melville's novel in his own work, seems likely to have been his contribution.[4] And in the sixth newsletter, Pearce follows some comments on Americans' fear of the corrupting influence of industrialization with a quotation from Bernal Diaz's *The Discovery and Conquest of Mexico*: "The Indians thought that the horse and its rider was all one animal, for they had never seen horses up to this time" (8 Oct. 1975: 3)—a passage which looks forward to McCarthy's later work, especially *All the Pretty Horses* (1992).

Pearce's copies of these newsletters, together with his marked copy of the complete shooting script of the screenplay, are now owned by the South Caroliniana Library of the University of South Carolina. They are helpful not only in dating McCarthy's involvement in the project, but also in identifying some of his sources—and in illustrating the nature of his collaboration with Richard Pearce. Pearce was not a co-writer; McCarthy receives sole credit as the screenwriter of "The Gardener's Son," and the screenplay is in every way consistent with McCarthy's treatments of characters, theme and the spoken language in his novels. Yet Pearce and McCarthy were clearly powerful reciprocal influences on one another in their conception of this story; and the screenplay's interpretation of the historical events, I conclude, must represent some kind of concensus reached by the two. (The film itself cuts a few whole scenes and some lines from the script, and these excisions may reflect Pearce's decisions alone. The shooting script shows his penciled marking of some of these deletions—but not all.)

Another profound influence on McCarthy—although filtered through

Richard Pearce—was Tom Terrill. Terrill had little direct contact with McCarthy, but a great deal with Pearce, who stayed at his house for substantial periods of time during the research stages of the film. Terrill pointed Pearce to relevant historical sources and shared his own interpretation of the situation in Graniteville that led to the killing of James Gregg and the eventual execution of Robert McEvoy, an interpretation that differs markedly from Broadus Mitchell's. A full study of the historical backgrounds of "The Gardener's Son" would start not only with Mitchell, but also with Terrill's account, "Murder in Graniteville," by far the most historically detailed telling of the story. Published several years after "The Gardener's Son" was filmed, it presents, for the most part, information Terrill possessed and shared with Pearce in 1974 and 1975. Terrill thinks that Pearce knew "seventy percent" of what is in his article (Interview).

"The Gardener's Son" departs from Mitchell's account in making McEvoy the protagonist of the screenplay and in omitting references to his ineffectual attempts to escape the law and other denigrating details. It traces McEvoy's story from the amputation of his leg, presided over by Mrs. Gregg, through the soul-sickness of his struggle to come to terms with his life, his unpremeditated killing of James Gregg, his trial and execution. McCarthy's screenplay draws on but implicitly challenges the version of McEvoy's history recorded by the "insiders" of the community, much as the structure and authorial perspective of *Child of God* challenges the local versions of Lester Ballard's history that would explain away his actions. Although McCarthy himself echoed the language of Mitchell's footnote when he told a reporter for the Knoxville *News-Sentinel*, "Robert McEvoy grows up being a black sheep, the bad boy of the town," he made it clear that his treatment of the character is very different: "The kid was a natural rebel, probably just a troublemaker in real life. But in our film he has a certain nobility. He stands up and says, 'No, this is intolerable and I want to do something about it' " ("Gardner's Son"). McCarthy's screenplay does not pretend to explain exactly why McEvoy killed Gregg, but it neither dismisses the question nor circumvents it by labeling him "bad." Rather, it subtly depicts the forces that coalesce to create the act, including the provocation by the "victim."

Like all of McCarthy's work, the screenplay functions through the interplay of finely realized concrete textures and mythic or literary allusiveness to achieve its thematic richness. The title of the screenplay alludes both to Adam's sons and to "Hamlet" and links its themes of physical and social corruption, fall from grace and fratricide. Both Robert McEvoy

(Brad Dourif[5]) and James Gregg (Kevin Conway) can be seen as the gardener's son. Robert's father Patrick (Jerry Hardin) is employed as a gardener at the mill, at least until James decides that landscaping the grounds is a waste of money. The film often shows Patrick planting, either in the garden plot of the family's cottage (our first image of him) or in the mill's greenhouse (which later in the film is shown abandoned and falling into ruin). But James's father, William, is also described as a gardener. Mrs. Gregg (Nan Martin) tells James that his father had hoped to establish a "garden of industry" in Graniteville, and at his funeral the preacher describes William Gregg's life's work in similarly post-Edenic terms: "the neat homes, the churches and schools, the gardens and the lovely grounds and last but not least the massive factory structure with its beautiful and perfect machinery" (Script 50, 24).[6]

The historical William Gregg had a troubling mixture of agrarian and urban impulses. In his writing and his experiment at Graniteville, he was a champion of industry in an agricultural state. In his *Essáys on Domestic Industry*, he quoted an opinion that, Mitchell says, he might have written himself: "An exclusively agricultural people, in the present age of the world, will always be poor. . . . They want cities and towns, they want diversity of employment." Though he would also concede, in addressing the planter class, "that agriculture is the natural and 'blessed employment of man'" (Mitchell 15, 171, n. 16), Gregg believed that the economic health of the South demanded abandoning its traditional devotion to a plantation economy. At the same time, he distrusted city workers, and he advised locating factories in rural areas. He devoted his career to manufacturing, yet he surrounded his home, Kalmia (named after the mountain laurel that flourished there), with gardens and extensive peach orchards. Although he encouraged gardening and even farming by the fathers of the girls his mill employed, Terrill points out that his offer of cash for labor meant that for many poor whites "their departure from the farm might become permanent, perhaps meaning never having land of their own, an elemental part of the world of nineteenth-century Americans" ("Murder" 199). It is hard to avoid the conclusion that while Gregg wanted to enlist the good will of the planter class and to preserve the benefits of a pastoral setting in his own life, he was willing to do so at the expense of the under-class of "lint-heads" he was creating. Terrill writes that "the rustic hue of the enterprise in the Horse Creek Valley did not mislead careful observers, Gregg, his successors or the stockholders. This was a different South" ("Murder" 200).[7] Among other things, according to Pearce, "the Valley had become a symbol of the stigma attached to textile millwork throughout the South "([c. 7 Apr. 1975]: 5).

As an experiment in industrialization and modest urbanization, McCarthy's screenplay suggests, the mill village as established by William Gregg already bore the seeds of corruption and the stamp of original sin, if not yet the mark of Cain. The older Gregg and McEvoy are Adam figures in their roles as fathers and gardeners, but in both generations the men of the Gregg and McEvoy families are also paired as Cain/Abel figures. The older men are very different kinds of gardeners: Gregg is associated with the urban, industrial "garden" tending toward Cain's city, while Patrick McEvoy is a tiller of the soil who has left farming in Pickens, South Carolina, to maintain the gardens in Graniteville.[8]

Their sons carry forward these agricultural/urban associations, but both reject their fathers' values of husbandry and rebel against the obligations laid upon them. Robert's rebellion, at least before he loses his leg, can be largely excused because of his youth; when the family farmed in Pickens, probably as tenant farmers or sharecroppers, Patrick remembers, "[I]t was like pullin teeth to get him [Robert] to milk [their cow]" (McCarthy, Script 42).[9] James's rebellion is a more thorough-going rejection of his father's pretense of creating a benevolent if paternalistic social and economic system that would benefit the laboring class of Graniteville. His rebellion is a manifestation of his cynicism, a failure of faith in his fellow man, a rejection of their brotherhood. The abandonment of the father's professed (however hypocritically) ideals by the son is illustrated in a conversation between James and his mother during a visit to the cemetery. She reminds him, "[Y]our father put a great deal of store in the common people. They made this company" (50). Near her husband's grave is that of a nameless child, a stranger who had died in Graniteville twenty years before and whose headstone was erected by the Greggs. In contrast to his parents, James has complained to his mother: "These people think we're running a dosshouse down here. You don't have to put up with it. . . . The world is made up of indigents and diligents. You can't help the indigent. Anything you do for him just makes him weaker. And the diligent doesn't need your help" (49). Earlier we have seen this attitude in action when James rudely turns away a group of hill people who have come seeking work in response to a "dodger" or handbill issued by the company four years earlier. He comments that "God's seed has fallen on barren ground" (34). As an employee hired to sweep Gregg's offices, Robert McEvoy witnesses James's obvious distaste for "these people," his grudging provision of train fare to send them back home and his assistant Captain Giles's outrage that Gregg does that much for them.

The linking of James and Robert, then, as gardener's sons, sons of Adam, the presentation of Robert's killing of James as a figurative fratricide, the prefiguring of that killing by James's refusal to be his brother's keeper (and by Robert's alienation from all of the human family) suggest that the title "The Gardener's Son" functions much as the title *Child of God*, linking all of flawed mankind, who share Adam and Cain's self-will, disobedience and failure in appropriate responsibility to our fellow man. In this sense, the first gardener is God, and as a child of God each of us is the gardener's son. McCarthy points to this in the earliest scenes of the screenplay, when Mrs. Gregg leaves her husband's sickbed to take the doctor to Robert McEvoy, whose leg has been injured and is now corrupted with gangrene. Robert resists the idea of amputation, saying, "I'd rather to be dead. . . . If God put the rot in it then let it rot off." Mrs. Gregg argues that "God doesn't ask that all the flowers in his garden be perfect" (17–18).[10]

Corruption or decay of the flesh, the grossest sign of man's mortality and the wages of his own disobedience, functions throughout the screenplay as a metaphor for man's imperfection and for the corruption of the social bond that results largely from man's inability to accept the imperfection in himself, in others or in his Father's garden. God may not require perfection of man, but man, McCarthy implies, often demands it, thereby setting his will against reality and creating his own hell. After a 1950 framing scene that does not appear in "The Gardener's Son" as filmed, the historical center of the screenplay begins with that common human theme, the death of fathers, as William Gregg lies on his deathbed; and his mortality is juxtaposed in the scenes immediately following with the mortification of Robert's leg. Later, the unburied corpse of Robert's mother is juxtaposed with the killing of James and the hanging of Robert as a symbol of corruption brooding over the entire sequence of events.[11] In his reluctant confrontations with the realities of the corruption of his flesh, the amputation of his leg and later the death of his mother, and in his disillusionment with the Gregg family, Robert reenacts Prince Hamlet's self-destructive struggle to come to terms with life in what he has concluded is an "unweeded garden." The displacement of Hamlet's father by Claudius leads him to conclude that "Things rank and gross in nature possess it merely." Robert's similar disgust with the unmasking of the Greggs' apparent benevolence in James's open cynicism is conveyed nonverbally, but is reinforced by James's decision to abandon the literal gardens established by his father, and by the garden metaphors themselves. In an ironic commentary on Mrs. Gregg's assertion that not all flowers in God's garden need be perfect, McCarthy shows her, in the scene at the cemetery, carrying flowers in one hand while she stoops to pull weeds from a grave with the other, "doing this with a certain practice and ruthlessness" (46). It is, despite her words to Robert and to James, a precise corollary to James's division of people into the diligent and indigent: flowers and weeds. And it prefigures her ruthless (though perhaps not fully conscious) participation in the misrepresentation of her family's character and Robert's that leads to his being hanged.

The parallels between Robert and Hamlet are also drawn very directly in McCarthy's gravedigger scene. Robert has left Graniteville but returns when his sister writes that his mother is very ill. As he passes the cemetery, he confronts two black men, who are taking a break from digging a fresh grave. Robert's gradual recognition that the grave is his mother's, while lacking some of the bitter irony of Hamlet's graveside discovery of Ophelia's death, provokes similar grief and outrage. The gravediggers don't know whose grave they are digging; they tell Robert that they were to have been paid by a Mr. Evans, but that the woman's husband has paid them instead and then lingered in the cemetery picking up the dead flowers: "Said folks ought not to bring flowers if they wasn't fixin to come back" (53). At this, Robert runs them off and declares, "That woman's not to be buried up here. She don't belong to the mill" (54). They see when he leans forward that there is a pistol stuck in his belt, but there is no indication that he consciously means to threaten them with it. He does threaten verbally, however, to "blow a hole in your black ass" (55).[12]

Proud refusal to belong to the mill and especially to James Gregg is portrayed as an important factor in Robert's alienation. Like those other spiritually blind and "legless fools," Melville's Ahab and Flannery O'Connor's Hulga in "Good Country People," Robert seems to be at war with life itself once he has lost his leg. He carves a wooden leg to replace his own, and for a time he does menial labor in the offices of the mill. But soon, like Lester Ballard, he takes to staying in caves—that physical symbol of spiritual dislocation for several of McCarthy's characters. His distressed father complains that he has "kindly infidel ways" and then in a more honest tone admits that Bobby "ain't no heathen. He's just got a troubled heart and they don't nobody know why" (McCarthy, Script 43). But like Hamlet, Robert has a specific focus for his anger and alienation: James Gregg and the hypocrisy of the paternalistic system of which he is the figurehead.

Even in William Gregg's day there were poor whites who resisted placing themselves entirely under his power. Mitchell notes that "Not a few families placing young people in the mill preferred to build their own homes adjacent to the town rather than becoming the company's tenants" (57). Regardless, Mitchell recognizes no disparity between the reality of Graniteville and the image of it William Gregg promulgates in his essays: "A later generation of managers has maintained welfare programs first for profit, and second for the happiness and progress of the workpeople. With William Gregg the human motive ran *pari passu* with the commercial. He acted, in all his plans for the life of the people of Graniteville, from a profound sense of social obligation. . . . The subjects over whom he ruled in his little kingdom were economically as weak as he was strong, and yet no hint of exploitation ever entered his consciousness" (76).

Perhaps it did not enter William Gregg's consciousness that his plan was exploitative (as it does not enter his wife's in "The Gardener's Son"), but even Mitchell makes clear the economic motives that led to the particular social organization established at Graniteville. Early on in his attempts to persuade South Carolina's planters and lawmakers to open up the state to corporate industrial enterprise, Gregg had argued for the use of slave labor because it would result in less turnover than white labor and because "you are not under the necessity of educating" slaves (Mitchell 23–24). But at the Graniteville mill, he employed only white laborers, and in the same essay he had counterbalanced his argument for the economy of slave labor with one for the advantages to the social fabric that would result from providing employment for poor whites, citing their poverty, ignorance and the cheapness of their labor: "It is only necessary to build a manufacturing village of shanties, in a healthy location in any part of the State, to have crowds of these poor people around you, seeking employment at half the compensation given to operatives at the North. It is indeed painful to be brought in contact with such ignorance and degradation; but on the other hand, it is pleasant to witness the change, which soon takes place in the condition of those who obtain employment" (24–25).

Terrill's study amply shows that while the mill allowed poor farmers to participate in a cash economy in a way for which they had few alternatives, the wages were modest, the hours were long, the benefits were certainly not free, nor were they primarily for the workers' benefit. Both Terrill and Pearce quote William Gregg's argument that the compulsory schooling for children of six to twelve was, "[a]side from a charitable point of view . . . most assuredly a source of profit to our Company." Gregg saw the company school as a "nursery for the best class of factory operatives" (Terrill, "Murder" 201; Pearce, 24 May 1975: 1). Moreover, Gregg and the company rigidly enforced rules meant to suppress undesirable behavior or weed out undesirable people. Richard Pearce's comments in his newsletter of 9 September 1975 reveal the degree to which he then rejected Mitchell's interpretation of Gregg's motives: "For William Gregg and his contemporary industrial pioneers in the antebellum South, the question was not whether owned (i.e. slave) labor could be freed, but on the contrary it was whether free labor could be owned or 'controlled' through new manufacturing communities which like their plantation counterparts would create a 'rich harvest' for their philanthropic benefactors" (9).

In "The Gardener's Son," with the passing of William Gregg, the inherent perversion of social responsibility in the mill community becomes more obvious, and Robert's disillusionment with life finds a focus in his growing hatred for James Gregg. There is only one scene before Robert's shooting of James that shows the two of them together: when Robert witnesses James's disrespectful turning away of the poor family who have come seeking work. But James is portrayed as outspokenly contemptuous of the poor whites, and his attitudes strip away any illusions created by the hypocrisy of his parents. We may infer that Robert's closer contact with James and his assistant after he has become crippled makes him understand that to them he is and will always remain an outsider.

Another aspect of James Gregg's ruthlessness is that he makes a game of preying on the girls who work for him. Fairly early in the screenplay, Robert's sister Martha (Anne O'Sullivan) goes to the mill office on a Sunday "huntin my brother." James teases her suggestively about whether she has a boyfriend. When he offers her a cigar in jest, she refuses but says, "I'll take one to my daddy if you're passin em out." He apparently interprets this as evidence that she can be bought, and he places a ten-dollar gold piece on the desk: "She looks at the coin and the full implication of the money strikes her and she looks at James Gregg with an expression partly of disdain but mostly she is just afraid." Then she runs from the office (McCarthy, Script 35–39).[13]

This event, however, is not presented as a motive for Robert's killing James in "The Gardener's Son," and in this McCarthy departs from the historical. After Robert McEvoy was tried and convicted of murder, he wrote his own account of the events, claiming that he killed Gregg in defense of his sister's honor and that a pretrial bargain prevented the testimony of women witnesses about James Gregg's improper advances towards the girls who worked in the mill.[14] But in the screenplay, though the whole village knows of James's habitual abuse of his position, Martha declares convincingly, in her hopeless attempt to persuade Mrs. Gregg to save Robert from the gallows, that "Bobby couldn't have knowed nothin about it. He couldn't of. You know I wouldn't of told him hotheaded as he was" (113). For Robert, James's lechery seems to be just one more aspect of his abuse and cynicism, not a personal assault. Ironically, though, both his sister and Mrs. Gregg fear that James's attempt to seduce Martha is the motivation for Robert's act. Mrs. Gregg uses her influence specifically to protect her family from implications of this kind, and Robert's lawyer refuses to let him testify in his defense, telling Patrick McEvoy, "We won't get anywhere in an attempt to blacken the Gregg name. People don't want that. We've agreed with Mrs. Gregg to call no female witnesses" (94).

In the screenplay, Robert's central problem always comes back to his alienation from life, from himself and from all human ties. The death of his mother brings him part way back to his family, and his insistence that she be buried "back home" in Pickens implies that he may be beginning to define for himself a sense of belonging to his immediate family, separate from the wider Graniteville community. But he has made only a beginning, and in the scenes between his return to Graniteville and his shooting of James, he and his father are shown hunting one another without success.[15] The screenplay tantalizes us with the hope that Patrick, Robert and Martha might come together in their grief, relieving some of their pain. Each has had jarring revelations of the corruption in their "garden." When Robert seeks his father in the mill greenhouse, an old man tells him, "[H]e ain't the gardener. Not no more he ain't. You see any gardens? . . . Not big on gardens here no more" (63). And it seems that Patrick has as a result felt some of the same alienation as his son, because he has rejected the mill community's financial assistance in burying his wife.[16]

Robert's struggle with his feelings of loss and isolation is suggested in his angry outbursts in three scenes after he returns to Graniteville. When he arrives at his father's house, he finds a wake in progress. He drives out the grim mourners who are there to do their duty, saying, "I don't know you" (57). Moments later, when Martha tries to comfort him, he lashes out at her, "You don't know how I am. You don't know me." Her response is as it will be to the end: "You're still my brother" (61).[17] Finally, when Robert goes to the mill office the next day, still looking for his father, James Gregg comes in to find Robert sitting at his desk. James asks what he is doing there:

MCEVOY
I was huntin my father.

GREGG
Your father.

MCEVOY
He was the gardener.

GREGG
I know who he was.

MCEVOY
No you don't.

GREGG
What do you mean I don't?

MCEVOY
You might know his name is all. (82)

The circumstances immediately preceding the shooting combine with Robert's long-standing disaffection to create the tragic disintegration of his family. Robert's anger that his father intends to bury his mother in the Graniteville cemetery feeds into his fixed brooding over the Greggs' assumption of authority over the lives and deaths of the people of the village—a brooding that has had its beginning when Mrs. Gregg asserts her will over his in ordering the amputation of his leg. During his fruitless search for his father, sympathetic villagers offer consolation and advice that only deepen Robert's despair. At the ruined greenhouse, the old man unwittingly describes his father's pain at the time of his mother's illness. Then he tells Robert, "You wasn't wrong to of come here. Trouble will make folks hunt out the places where they've knowed better times" (64). In the next scene, which Pearce cut before the filming, Robert continues his search in the Greggs' neglected peach orchards. There Mrs. Gregg's black carriage driver suggests that Robert's father might be drinking to assuage his grief: "Night my Ella died I went to a cardhouse and got drunk. Laid in my own vomit. That's what I thought of the hand of the Lord. Lay dead drunk in ye own vomit like a dog. I ain't proud of it. But I give up lyin same as I done the drinkin." Cynically, Robert asks, "What did it get ye?" and the black answers, "Ain't what it got me. It's what it got me from. . . . Death. I seen his face. Know where he uses. I know how he loves the unready." Unready to listen to such advice, Robert replies, "He loves us all" (66–67).

The next scene shows Robert entering a doggery, where he is affection-
ately welcomed by the proprietor, Pinky (Ned Beatty), who commiserates
the loss of his mother and encourages him to drink and talk. While the
compassion of Pinky and some of the other men is genuine, suggesting
that in this stratum of society Robert, rather like Suttree, finds a tentative
sense of belonging, their conversation reminds him of their grievances
against the mill—and his own. When asked if he plans to "get on at the
mill," Robert responds, "I ain't lost nothin down there." Pinky says, "I
hear ye. Only way to get ahead down there is to get your woman knocked
up by the boss. Give ye a little leverage." Later they refer to the hypocrisy
of the mill's prohibition of alcohol: "They hate for *you* to drink it. That
ain't sayin they won't take a drink their own selves." Pinky recalls, "The
old man would by god not take one," but about James, he says, "That son
of a bitch will take a drink." And another man remarks, "Thing about
James. He never did want to put the jam on the lower shelf where the little
man could get some" (73–76). Trying to be helpful, one of the men suggests that Patrick might be at church, until Pinky reminds him, and Robert,
that Graniteville has no Catholic church. Pinky's well-meaning comment
and the man's remark, "Well now that is right. I forgot about him bein
catholic" (73), can only reinforce Robert's sense of difference.[18]

Woven into these comments are faint allusions to the depression that had
beset the region in the 1870s, when the mill reduced wages and the workers
staged strikes. Also, a "second man" talks compulsively about murders of
whites by blacks in the region. While these references evoke the violence
of Reconstruction and the frustration felt by the white mill workers, their
full significance is clear only if the history of the Graniteville community
is known. Terrill relates that in 1875 during a strike over a cut in wages,
a mill superintendent was shot and wounded by a worker. In response, the
company threatened to close the mill, and the wage cut was not rescinded
("Murder" 209).

The reference to blacks' murdering whites has less relevance to Robert's
mind-set, but together with the reference to violence against the mill
supervisors it helps to elucidate the coming trial scenes, in which Robert
is found guilty of murder by a predominantly black jury and is sentenced
to hang. In November of 1877 (the year after Robert's crime but before
his hanging), there was in Graniteville a public execution of five blacks
who had been convicted of murdering two whites, an execution that appeared "a bizarre combination of carnival and revival meeting." Terrill
shows that Robert McEvoy's punishment was determined more by reac-

tions to these events than by impartial justice. He states that after this shameful public execution, "Blacks demanded that white murderers receive the same fate black murderers did" ("Murder" 214). In addition, the elite of the state saw the shooting of James Gregg as a threatening escalation of violence in that section. "As the election of 1876 approached," Terrill writes, "the elite became desperate to reassert their dominance clearly and finally over blacks, in particular, but also over the lower orders of whites. Strikes and violent assaults on the elite could not, must not, be tolerated" ("Murder" 211). In spite of the extenuating circumstances of the case, a petition signed by 340 citizens of Graniteville to commute McEvoy's sentence to life in prison was denied by Governor Hampton, and McEvoy was hanged on 19 April 1878 ("Murder" 212–14).[19]

The references by the men in the doggery to the violence in Graniteville thus set the stage for the scenes to come. In their depiction of a society divided by class and racial conflict, they also advance the themes of social corruption and the failure of fraternal bonds evoked by the screenplay's title. The men's casual talk of these things finally may serve to intensify Robert's feeling that this community is utterly divided against itself and against him. Drink, frustration, anger, despair sap his resolve, and though he repeatedly says he needs to continue his search for his father, he makes no move. Later, in a brief scene reminiscent of *Outer Dark*, but not included in the filmed version, Robert staggers through the dark toward Graniteville: "[S]everal dogs have come into the road behind him and circle to pick up his scent and howl. . . . [T]heir hackles are up and they howl after McEvoy who wobbles on into the darkness" (77).[20]

These events bring Robert to James Gregg's office the next morning, still presumably in search of his father. The confrontation between him and James proceeds as we would expect between two such disaffected souls. Gregg, however, is the more suspicious and fearful of the two, and the more aggressive. He accuses Robert of being a thief, and when Robert calls him a liar, he recreates the gesture that had sent Martha running from his office. "What do you want," he asks. "Money?" Then he flips a ten–dollar gold piece onto his desk, saying, "Take it and get out." As Robert's eyes reveal his hatred, James panics. As he reaches for his desk drawer, Robert draws his gun and warns James, "Don't." Then "Gregg scrabbles in the desk drawer for his pistol and McEvoy fires," wounding him. James again reaches, and Robert fires again. James is still alive when Robert walks out of the office, but James pursues him, firing at his back. Now there are witnesses. Robert turns: "Gregg is standing in the doorway, swaying, holding his pistol at his waist in both hands and looking down at McEvoy. There is a frozen moment and then McEvoy's face turns anguished and he raises the pistol and cocks it and levels it at Gregg. It hesitates for just a moment. Then it fires" (83–88).

In the middle of the argument between Robert and James, the scene has cut away to Patrick, who is told by a fellow worker that Robert has headed toward the mill office. With a sense of "impending doom" Patrick has started after him. Now he and his son find each other. Crying, but with dignity, Patrick reaches for the gun. "McEvoy turns the pistol on his father for a moment. The older man takes yet another step toward his son. He is almost close enough now to put his arm around his son. He is crying quietly. McEvoy lowers his head. He hands the pistol to his father" (89).

The remainder of the screenplay establishes the violation of justice in the trial and execution of Robert, compressing the two years that these events actually covered, but reflecting the historical vulnerability of the McEvoys in the face of the social class power represented by the Greggs. However, in these scenes, Robert becomes, to a degree, more accepting of his fate. He is willing to accept the consequences of his actions. He is shown to have the understanding and good will of the sheriff and some of the members of the community. He makes what efforts he can to help his father and sisters, and he prepares for death quietly and with self-possession, "like a priest being dressed for a sacrament" (126).

Patrick and Martha, on the other hand, are plunged deeper into despair at the turn their lives have taken. Out of his utter helplessness in the situation, Patrick goes to see the black attorney who is helping to defend Robert. Whipper (Paul Benjamin) receives Patrick "without compassion" (100) and offers him the false comfort of cynicism. When Patrick tries to hold firm to his belief that God, at least, is just, Whipper mocks him: "If God's justice was all we had there'd be no peace in this world. Everywhere I look I see men trying to set right the injustices God's left them with." As Patrick persists in arguing for a principle of justice at work in human events, Whipper tells him, "I tried a law case in Beaufort a few months back. In the course of the proceedings I turned to the court and I said: Is there anybody here who believes in justice? . . . There were in the courtroom at that time seven or eight of the most notorious scoundrels in the state and every man jack of them raised his hand. Nobody else. Even the judge busted out laughing."[21] The destructiveness of this counsel is clear when Patrick echoes Robert's despairing attitude before the amputation of his leg: "We come here seven year ago. Tried to stay on at home after the

war but they wasn't no way. If I could of foresaw what has happened
I'd rather to of been dead" (103–04).

This scene is paired with a conversation between Martha and Mrs.
Gregg—one of the most affecting scenes in "The Gardener's Son" because
in it a small hope for the redemption of the human family seems to be raised
and then squelched. Martha goes to Mrs. Gregg to apologize for her loss
of her son, but at first Mrs. Gregg receives her with cold suspicion, much
as her son had received Robert. Martha's very innocence leaves her open
to Mrs. Gregg's misunderstanding her, and when Martha begins, "I know
what people said about James," Mrs. Gregg repeatedly interrupts her in
such a way that makes it clear that her denial of James's nature is a self-
delusion: "My people learned to live with slander a long time ago. With
envy and with ingratitude. . . . No, I'm sorry. There was a family here.
A community of people working together, joined in a common enterprise.
But my ʰusband's . . . my family's bond to this community, was of the
spirit, not of the flesh" (109). Crying, Martha finally is able to say, "I just
wanted you to know that your son never done nothin to me. I just come
to say I was sorry." This softens Mrs. Gregg, who now realizes "that
Martha has not come to beg for Bobby but to console her, Mrs. Gregg"
(110). She orders tea, and reassured that Martha has not come to accuse
her son, she expresses her bewilderment about the killing: "These things
must have beginnings somewhere. Be put in motion at some point. . . . But
when I look at you I see nothing. I can see nothing in you to do with death
and murder" (112). Attempting an honest response to this, Martha again
blunders into the issue Mrs. Gregg will not hear, her son's treatment of
his female employees:

> I cain't help but think it was just a mistake   some kind. If they'd of
> got me up there . . . I'd of maybe had to tell em about that gold piece
> and it would of sounded worse than what it was. . . . He done that with
> . . . I mean he would do stuff like that, you know, just in fun?

Mrs. Gregg asks, "Do what?" And still very openly Martha responds,
"Well, you know. Like offer ye money" (113).

Whether Mrs. Gregg perceives this as blackmail—a threat of exposure—
or whether it merely threatens the image of her family she must maintain
in her own mind, Martha's innocent remark drives her into a defensive
posture. She says to Martha, "Oh you are a little darling, aren't you?" and
she ends the conversation affirming her son's cynicism while Martha
launches into the plea she has meant not to make, that Mrs. Gregg do

something to save Robert's life (114). As Martha is shown out of the house, she says, "I don't blame you Mam. . . . God bless you Mam," but Mrs. Gregg "turns from her and puts her hands over her ears" (115).

Though Martha understands little of the dynamics of this conversation, her failure to reach Mrs. Gregg's humanity initially seems to have a devastating effect on her, undermining her trust in herself and others. Robert's lawyers' agreement with Mrs. Gregg to prevent testimony about James's behavior with women employees and with Martha in particular has ironically implicated her in her brother's crime. Her dismal failure to save her brother, and Mrs. Gregg's bad opinion of her, now seem to intensify her sense of guilt. She meets Robert on the street soon after her visit to Mrs. Gregg (he has been taken to sit for a photograph and is being returned to the jail), and though she has been all honesty in word and deed up to that visit, now she tells her brother that even though James did nothing to her, "I'd of told em anything, Bobby. I swear it. They wouldn't let me. I'd of told em any kind of lie. I wouldn't care. I'd of swore it on ten Bibles if it sent my soul to hell forever and ever I wouldn't care" (120). In a community divided against itself, even the instinct to be one's brother's keeper risks becoming perverted, and responsibility and integrity begin to seem possible only within very narrow limits.

Martha's despair elicits from Robert a similar affirmation of narrow family bonds rather than more inclusive social bonds. He has been expressing his anger at the pervasive dishonesty of his society, its unwillingness to face the reality of James Gregg, the lies that made a murderer and a scapegoat of him, a man to be expunged in spite of his willingness to atone for his crime in the penitentiary. Now he expresses a hope for his sister's future that disturbingly echoes the judgmental attitudes of the Greggs themselves: "You forget you ever had a brother. Find the best man . . . you find the best man in the world. *Don't take no culls.* And you make him be good to you. . . . And you have a good life. Little sister. The best that anybody ever had in this damned world" (121; italics added).[22]

The opening and closing scenes of the screenplay, not included in the filmed version, further comment on the fates of the two families, especially Martha's, and on the impact of the past on the present. Set in 1950, the opening scene shows an unidentified young man being guided through the old mill office by a "timekeeper," an old man who was a boy in Graniteville when McEvoy was hanged. There are hints that the young man is connected with the Greggs. When the timekeeper contrasts James with his father, saying "[James] was all right, but the blood runs thin"

(2), he catches himself and adds, "No offense" (3). Soon after this, the young man says, "I guess if you hire these people you have to take the consequences"—a remark that structurally foreshadows and chronologically repeats James's comment about the poor whites. The timekeeper smiles and repeats, "No offense" (3).

As the young man begins to look through boxes of old papers, the timekeeper tells him, "You won't find it here. . . . They ain't the thing. Old papers or pitchers. Once you copy a thing down you don't have it no more. You just have the record. Times past are fugitive and cain't be kept in no box" (3–4). This serves as entree to the living recreation of history represented by the screenplay itself. It would seem to affirm the value of memory and imagination over documentation as an avenue to reality, truth. It may also reflect the idea that documents are created by the literate and powerful and thus do not speak the whole truth.[23] In his research newsletter of 8 October 1975—which cites the record of the court proceedings against Robert McEvoy to the effect that after being found guilty, "HE SAITH NOTHING"—Pearce quotes historian Jesse Lemisch, "No contention about the people on the bottom of society— neither that they are rebellious nor docile, neither that they are noble nor that they are base—no such contention even approaches being proved until we have in fact attempted a history of the inarticulate" (10).

"The Gardener's Son" attempts a history of the inarticulate (as do, in another sense, *Outer Dark*, *Child of God* and *Blood Meridian*), and the final scene suggests that a true vision of the past or of our own inarticulate brothers is a potential avenue of redemption for the human family. Here the young man of the first scene is identified as William Chaffee, grandson of Mrs. Gregg. After hearing the story of Robert McEvoy from the timekeeper, he has traveled to the State Hospital in Columbia, the insane asylum, to see Martha McEvoy. His gentle and respectful treatment of her indicates that his humanity has been touched if his forebears' was not. He brings Martha flowers. He and Martha confess to each other that they have only a partial understanding of their families' experiences.

Martha still has the gentle and charitable soul we have seen in her as a young girl; she has not done her brother's bidding. The younger sister Maryellen has forgotten her mother and presumably her brother, repressing their memories, and she is the one who has married and had a family. But Martha, who has never married, has become an advocate of memory (though, like that other repository of eternal values, Arthur Ownby in *The Orchard Keeper*, she is exiled in her old age in the asylum).[24] She shows Chaffee a photograph of Robert and says, "Sometimes I wisht I'd not even of kept it. That lawyer said that the image of God was blotted out of his face. That's what he said about Bobby. I ort not even to of kept it. I think a person's memory serves better. Sometimes I can almost talk to him. I cain't see him no more. In my mind. I just see this old pitcher" (140). The screenplay ends with an image of these two survivors of the Gregg and McEvoy lines together in Martha's room, their eyes focused elsewhere, presumably on the living memory of their families.

"The Gardener's Son" is as impressive an achievement as a first screenplay as *The Orchard Keeper* is as a first novel. McCarthy has more recently written other dramatic works. A screenplay set in the West was completed ten years ago, and McCarthy's first stage play, entitled "The Stonemason," was to have been performed at the Arena Stage in Washington, DC in the fall of 1992 (Woodward 28). The author has been involved with this now postponed production, as he was with the filming of "The Gardener's Son"; he was in Washington and New York in the spring of 1992 to participate in the auditioning of actors and in readings of the play. McCarthy continues to write novels as well; *All the Pretty Horses*, the first of three projected novels, has recently been released. The second is finished, and the third well underway.[25] McCarthy's dramatic works, then, do not represent an abandonment of his work in the fictional mode, but another and important dimension of his still evolving writing career—one which invites reassessment of the whole.

NOTES

[1]The series was funded with grants from the Corporation for Public Broadcasting, the Ford Foundation and the National Endowment for the Arts.

[2]I am grateful for Professor Terrill's gracious and helpful sharing of information concerning "The Gardener's Son."

[3]O'Connor's *New York Times* article offers a misleading description of how the film came to be: "Barbara Schultz, executive director of public television's 'Visions' series, heard about Mr. Pearce's research, and Cormac McCarthy . . . was recruited to write his first screenplay, working closely with Mr. Pearce." When McCarthy read my paraphrase of this in a draft of my sketch on his life and work for the *Dictionary of Literary Biography*, he made it clear that Pearce had asked him to work with him nearly at the beginning of the project. Terrill's comments to me confirm this, as does Pearce's statement in his "research newsletter" of 19 November 1975 that "During the past months, novelist Cormac McCarthy . . . and I have been working together on a screenplay" (3).

Richard Pearce said on a different occasion that McCarthy "was as intimately involved in the project as a writer can be. When I was casting bits and extras he came along. We saw over 1000 people in the State of South Carolina and he came to every session." McCarthy's comments to the same reporter indicate that he was on-site for the filming as well: "It's back-breaking work. On location for 30 days, and the last week we were working 16 to 18 hours a day. You've got to be some kind of weirdo to think that it's fun. But it sure kept my interest up—and writers are basically pretty lazy people" ("Gardner's").

[4]This passage would seem to be a literary source for Tobin's sermon to the kid in *Blood Meridian*. Tobin says the Lord has:

> an uncommon love for the common man and godly wisdom resides in the least of things so that it may well be that the voice of the Almighty speaks most profoundly in such beings as lives in silence themselves. . . .
> For let it go how it will, . . . God speaks in the least of creatures. . . .
> The kid spat into the fire and bent to his work.
> I aint heard no voice, he said.
> When it stops, said Tobin, you'll know you've heard it all your life. (123–24)

For a historical source for the metaphor of all men's waking when horses cease grazing, which Tobin adds to his argument, see John Sepich's "'What kind of indians was them?'" elsewhere in this volume.

[5]Dourif had received an Academy Award nomination for Best Supporting Actor for his portrayal of Billy Bibbitt in "One Flew Over the Cuckoo's Nest." In 1979, he played the role of Hazel Motes in "Wise Blood" directed by John Huston.

[6]McCarthy draws here on a eulogy delivered at a meeting of Gregg's friends shortly after his death, quoted in the Edgefield *Advertiser*, and repeated by Mitchell: "When we consider all the circumstances of the case, the almost entire ignorance of our people on this subject [of establishing manufacture], their prejudice against it and the consequent difficulty of enlisting capital in its favor, the conversion of a barren wilderness into a beautiful village with its neat cottages, its flower gardens, and beautiful grounds, its churches, its factory structure built of solid Granite obtained on the spot, the beautiful and perfect machinery; all these things, never before seen, or dreamed of, by the natives, seemed as if created by magic" (280–81, n.30).

[7]Mitchell seems to have been misled, however. He takes at face value Gregg's promotional claims for having created a nearly utopian mill community in Graniteville, and while he acknowledges that the laborers found themselves in a paternalistic system comparable to a feudal barony, he minimizes the importance of their loss: "if they gave up something of an unmeaning freedom, they gained in the substantial asset of security" (60). Mitchell's interpretation reflects the interests of the Gregg descendants and members of the community who were ready to reinforce the most positive view of William Gregg, especially when dealing with outsiders. In "The Gardener's Son" we see indications that lionizing of

William Gregg by his widow has begun and is being reinforced by the community's resentment of his son James. Pearce's newsletter of 9 September 1975 quotes Raymond Williams's *The Country and the City* on this phenomenon: "The real ruling class could not be put in question, so they were seen as temporarily absent, or as the good old people suceeded [sic] by the bad new people—themselves suceeding [sic] themselves. We have heard this sad song for many centuries now: a seductive song, turning protest into retrospect, until we die of time" (1).

[8]Terrill's work with the censuses of the nineteenth century shows that the historical Patrick McEvoy was in Graniteville at least by 1856, twenty years before his son killed James Gregg ("Murder" 212). There is no evidence that he had worked a farm in South Carolina. On the contrary, Pearce's research newsletter of 8 October 1975 says without documentation that in 1825 Patrick emigrated from Ireland across the Atlantic and up the Savannah River. He married a South Carolina woman, and Robert J. McEvoy was born in 1854. Pearce identifies Patrick McEvoy as one of the many cottier tenants evicted by Irish landlords (4). Thus the screenplay's presentation of Patrick as emblematic of the tenant farmer dispossessed by the gentry may have some historical basis though the details of his history are changed.

[9]Ben Robertson, in *Red Hills and Cotton: An Upcountry Memory*, discusses the transition of Pickens County poor folk from tenant farmers to textile laborers and notes that "A man is never free from a cow" (160). This memoir about upcountry values, traditions and everyday life may have been one of McCarthy's sources for the socio-historical contexts of "The Gardener's Son," although its chapters on the industrialization of South Carolina refer mostly to the 1920s.

[10]In *Outer Dark* the preacher who provokes the hog drovers to threaten hanging Culla Holme claims to have saved a blind man by preaching a similar sermon, and one that is especially apt in Robert's case: "The grace of God don't rest easy on a man. It can blind him easy as not. It can bend him and make him crooked. And who did Jesus love, friends? The lame the halt and the blind, that's who. Them is the ones scarred with God's mercy. Stricken with his love. Ever legless fool and old blind mess like you is a flower in the garden of God" (226).

[11]The unburied corpse which outrages the McEvoys' neighbors and further alienates them from the community, and which Patrick McEvoy finally burns, seems borrowed from William Faulkner's *As I Lay Dying*. I am aware of no historical basis for it.

[12]McCarthy's gravedigger scene in "The Gardener's Son" is adumbrated in a more comic version in *Outer Dark*. Hired to dig the graves for the victims of a lynching, Culla finds two black men already digging a grave in the ceme-

tery. After some cross-talk, he realizes that they are digging a grave for some-one else, and he begins to dig his graves in the "place for buryin anybody that ain't spoke for"—a faint allusion to the controversy over burying Ophelia in hallowed ground (143–45).

[13]In *Outer Dark* the son of the family that befriends Rinthy tries to seduce her by showing her money:

It's a bunch of it ain't it? he said. Bet you ain't never

. . .

I got to go, she said. (74)

She walks decisively away from him.

[14]The historical James Gregg seems to have been more of a ruffian and even more widely disliked than he is portrayed to be in "The Gardener's Son." "In 1860," Terrill writes, "James and his brother had been charged with assault and battery with intent to kill." The legal case raveled out, the brother died during the war years and eventually James was "allowed to pay seventy–five dollars on a riot and assault charge." Terrill believes that the directors of the Graniteville company went out of their way to keep James in a relatively subordinate role after the death of his father. And he writes that "James Gregg's behavior toward female employees was the subject of local gossip. Some of the Gregg family may have thought or even known that James Gregg was an adulterer" ("Murder" 212–13, 221, n.65).

[15]The image of family members wandering at cross purposes is of central significance in *Outer Dark*.

[16]The historical Patrick is known to have owned $2,300 worth of stock in the Graniteville company (Terrill, "Murder" 212). Later in the screenplay Robert comments that his father has the money to bury his wife in Pickens.

[17]Martha's unwavering affirmation of kinship links her with Rinthy in *Outer Dark*, though near the end of "The Gardener's Son" Martha is wracked with guilty self-doubt in ways that Rinthy never is.

[18]McCarthy commented in his remarks to the Knoxville *News-Sentinel*: "The McEvoys . . . were Irish Catholics living in a Southern town, like my family was. . . . Everyone else was Methodist or Baptist" ("Gardner's"). Near the beginning, the screenplay hints that as Roman Catholics the McEvoys are seen as outsiders. There is something of cold reserve in the manner in which Mrs. Gregg questions Robert's sisters about their given names when she takes the doctor to their house. The youngest answers that her name is Maryellen; Mrs. Gregg responds, as if this confirms something to her, "Yes. And Martha" (13). According to Mitchell, William Gregg was originally a Quaker and Marina Gregg was Episcopalian.

[19]Terrill quotes the description of McEvoy's end given by the Augusta *Chronicle and Sentinel* the day after the hanging: "Cool and unterrified, yet softened

by religion . . . his will which sustained him so long in life, left him not in the hour of facing his fate" ("Murder" 214).

[20]See also the ending of McCarthy's *Suttree*:

An enormous lank hound had come out of the meadow by the river like a hound from the depths and was sniffing at the spot where Suttree had stood.

Somewhere in the gray wood by the river is the huntsman and in the brooming corn and in the castellated press of cities. His work lies all wheres and his hounds tire not. I have seen them in a dream, slaverous and wild and their eyes crazed with ravening for souls in this world. Fly them. (471)

[21]In *Blood Meridian* the judge tells Glanton's men, "Moral law is an invention of mankind for the disenfranchisement of the powerful in favor of the weak. Historical law subverts it at every turn" (250).

[22]Robert's advice prefigures Judge Holden's argument that children should be raised by subjecting them to historical law: "If God meant to interfere in the degeneracy of mankind would he not have done so by now? Wolves cull themselves, man. What other creature could? And is the race of man not more predacious yet? The way of the world is to bloom and to flower and die but in the affairs of men there is no waning and the noon of his expression signals the onset of night" (McCarthy, *Blood Meridian* 146).

[23]Compare Judge Holden's assertion of his will over historical reality when he destroys historical artifacts after making a record of them in his book: "A Tennessean named Webster had been watching him and he asked the judge what he aimed to do with those notes and sketches and the judge smiled and said that it was his intention to expunge them from the memory of man." Webster replies that "them pictures is like enough the things themselves. But no man can put all the world in a book. No more than everthing drawed in a book is so." The judge's response, "Well said, Marcus," intimates that this is precisely how he will expunge reality from memory—by making a mere record of it (McCarthy, *Blood Meridian* 140–41).

[24]McCarthy recast parts of this scene for his description of Suttree's visit to his great-aunt Alice in the asylum. For example, compare *Suttree* (433–34) with the following passage from the screenplay:

Me and Mama went back up to Pickens one time. It was right fore she died. I was just a young girl. Went up on the train. We'd had this horse and his name was Captain and I used to ride him just everwheres and he'd foller me around like a dog and I remember whenever we got ready to leave from up there why they sent me over to Maa-maw's cause the feller was fixin to come and get him. They'd done sold him, you see? But when me and Mama went up there. It was right fore she died. We was in Greenville on Saturday afternoon and I looked and there in the street was old Captain. He was harnessed up in a express wagon standin there in front of a store and whenever I seen him I just run across the street and throwed my arms around his neck and kissed him and I reckon everbody thought I was crazy. I mean I was about growed and me standin there in the middle of the street huggin and kissin a old horse and just a bawlin to beat the band. (139)

The detail of Suttree's great-uncle Jeffrey, Alice's brother, who was hanged for murder in 1884 (433), may also owe its existence to McCarthy's work on the Robert McEvoy story. Thomas D. Young, Jr. points out that Jeffrey also figures in Suttree's imagination when he asks, "What family has no mariner in its tree? No fool, no felon. No fisherman" (128; see Young's "The Imprisonment of Sensibility: *Suttree*" in this volume).

[25]Woodward implies that the screenplay set in the West contains the germ of McCarthy's "Border Trilogy," of which *All the Pretty Horses* is the first novel to be published. McCarthy, after attempting unsuccessfully to arrange with Richard Pearce for the filming of this screenplay, apparently has decided to re-write it as the third novel of his trilogy (Woodward 40). I am grateful to Edwin T. Arnold and John Sepich for sharing information about McCarthy's progress on the trilogy and about his activities relating to "The Stonemason." Their source was McCarthy himself.

WORKS CITED

Brown, Les. "'Visions' Gets New Grants." *New York Times* 14 May 1977: 47.

"'Gardner's [sic] Son' on PBS This Week, Written by Louisvillian." *News-Sentinel* [Knoxville, TN] 2 Jan. 1977: G7.

McCarthy, Cormac. *Blood Meridian or the Evening Redness in the West.* New York: Random, 1985.

————. *Outer Dark.* New York: Random, 1968.

————. Shooting script of "The Gardener's Son," ts. Richard Inman Pearce Collection. South Caroliniana Library. U of South Carolina.

————. *Suttree.* New York: Random, 1979.

Mitchell, Broadus. *William Gregg: Factory Master of the Old South.* 1928. New York: Octagon, 1966.

O'Connor, John. "TV: WNET Showing Haunting 'Gardener's Son.'" *New York Times* 6 Jan. 1977: 59.

Pearce, Richard Inman. Research newsletter, [c. 7 Apr. 1975]. Richard Inman Pearce Collection. South Caroliniana Library. U of South Carolina.

————. Research newsletter, 24 May 1975. Richard Inman Pearce Collection. South Caroliniana Library. U of South Carolina.

————. Research newsletter, 9 Sept. 1975. Richard Inman Pearce Collection. South Caroliniana Library. U of South Carolina.

————. Research newsletter, 8 Oct. 1975. Richard Inman Pearce Collection. South Caroliniana Library. U of South Carolina.

_____. Research newsletter, 19 Nov. 1975. Richard Inman Pearce Collection. South Caroliniana Library. U of South Carolina.

"PW Forecasts." *Publishers Weekly* 29 Oct. 1973: 31.

Robertson, Ben. *Red Hills and Cotton: An Upcountry Memory.* 1942. Columbia: U of South Carolina P, 1960.

Terrill, Tom E. "Murder in Graniteville." *Toward a New South?: Studies in Post-Civil War Southern Communities.* Ed. Orville Vernon Burton and Robert C. McMath, Jr. Westport, CT: Greenwood, 1982. 193–222.

_____. Personal Interview, 5 Mar. 1992.

Woodward, Richard B. "Cormac McCarthy's Venomous Fiction." *New York Times Magazine* 19 Apr. 1992: 28–31, 36, 40.

The Imprisonment of Sensibility

Suttree

Thomas D. Young, Jr.

Suttree (1979) is anomalous among Cormac McCarthy's novels in two obvious respects. First, it is an urban novel, set in and around Knoxville, Tennessee, during the years 1950–1955. And second, in taking Cornelius Suttree as its protagonist, the book provides a texture of experience that is considerably more intricate and layered than elsewhere in McCarthy's work, Suttree having been the beneficiary of an affluent upbringing and a college education. Despite his departure from the strict rustication and stolid, inarticulate protagonists of the other books, however, McCarthy's fictional terrain here is not really so different. Knoxville in 1950 is an embryonic city, something like medieval London or Jerusalem at the time of Christ, with the striations of its growth still plainly visible. It has, as McCarthy points out, been "*constructed on no known paradigm, a mongrel architecture reading back through the works of man in a brief delineation of the aberrant disordered and mad*" (3). This primitive structure is a living record of that elemental and highly ambiguous activity of human "settlement" which is essentially the subject of all McCarthy's fiction. Eventually it will lie concealed beneath the involutions of the modern city: by the end of the novel McAnally Flats, the particular Knoxville ghetto Suttree calls home, is being razed to facilitate the construction of an expressway. But for the moment Knoxville is another glimpse into what Conrad called "the true world," before it is "buried under the growth of centuries."

The legacy of the original obsessive, Bible-haunted pioneers—the *"old teutonic forebears with eyes incandesced by the visionary light of a massive rapacity, wave on wave of the violent and the insane"* (4)—is still apparent on every Knoxville streetcorner. The sprawl of peddlers, psalmists, blind singers, beggars and wild street preachers radiates a volatile, pristine energy which Suttree has come to prefer to university life or formal vocation. In Suttree's eyes, this detritus bears the clear mark of its pioneer ancestry, upon whom the entitlements of socialization—commerce, institutionalized government, law and order—still sit somewhat uneasily. In some ways these misfits and human oddities are reminiscent of the fossilized forms Suttree keeps noticing embedded in the city's stonework architecture, the trilobites and "vanished bivalves and delicate seaferns, . . . stone armatures on which once hung the flesh of living fish" (82). They are the residue of archaic forces by which the city, and all civilization, originally were generated but which have been used up, rejected or absorbed in that same process. This same strain Suttree—the self-styled "[r]eprobate scion of doomed Saxon clans" (136)—has located beneath his own cultural enfeeblement, and he endeavors to have it reveal itself further. Thus *Suttree*, like McCarthy's other novels, is an account of the rise of this "western world" of human culture[1] as observed in dramatically ontogenetic terms. Here, as in the other works, the message is: *"Ruder forms survive"* (5).

McAnally Flats, the particular "world within a world" which Suttree calls home, is an especially rich study in this kind of cultural ferment. Suttree has two sets of friends there. One is "a collection of drunks" and borderline criminals—J. Bone and Junior Long, Red Callahan, Hoghead Henry—who carouse together and share their impoverished circumstances. The other, a group largely disdained even by this rabble, is the black population down along the river, among whom Suttree enjoys several warm friendships, most particularly with the tavern-keeper Abednego Jones. Together these friends constitute, in Suttree's view, a kind of "fellowship of the doomed. Where life pulsed obscenely fecund" (23), and Suttree's purposes among them are determinedly lowbrow and atavistic. He is at pains, in word and deed, to deny his intellectual and cultural endowments. He shares with his friends the badge of a rebelliousness that borders on criminality: as the novel opens, Suttree has already had several brushes with the law on charges of vagrancy and public drunkenness; in 1950 he served seven months in the Knoxville workhouse for his role in the robbery of a drug-store. Following his release he has taken up residence on a ramshackle houseboat, where he makes a desultory living running trotlines on the Tennessee River.

The two "anomalous" aspects of *Suttree* ultimately are aligned, then. The city as aberrant accretion of the pioneering impulse—aberrant because it rises from the need to check the very impulses that give it being—is replicated in Suttree's unwelcome intellectuality. Similarly, his attempt to live simply on the river, to penetrate into ever more primitive realms of being, is the same as his other great quest in the novel: the attempt to understand his own past. The lineaments of the family drama, which hold for Suttree such elemental significance, are, for the reader, only imperfectly at hand. They must be pieced together from four elliptical and widely separated episodes in the novel: the appearance of the blacksheep Uncle John at the houseboat early in the book (15–20); a Sunday afternoon visit Suttree makes to his Aunt Martha and Uncle Clayton's home downriver (119–36); and a trip to an insane asylum to interview his great-aunt Alice, which follows hard upon his paranormal experience with the black fortune-teller Mother She (423–34). From these four scenes the following account may be constructed. It is Suttree's father who has been largely responsible for Suttree's self-exile in McAnally. He believes, according to his son, "that the world is run by those willing to take the responsibility for the running of it." In a last letter before the permanent rupture of their relation-ship, he has advised Suttree that "If it is life that you feel you are missing I can tell you where to find it. In the law courts, in business, in government. There is nothing occurring in the streets. Nothing but a dumbshow composed of the helpless and impotent" (13–14). The aristocratic elder Suttree's contempt also apparently extends to the low breeding of his wife and her family, something he has remarked in both the alcoholic Uncle John and the near-alcoholic Suttree as well.

As if to validate this judgment, Suttree chooses to trace his own lineage primarily through his mother's family (both Aunt Martha and Aunt Alice are maternal relations), this "Old distaff kin coughed up out of the vortex, thin and cracked and macled and a bit redundant" (129). His recollections of them, as is not uncommon in southern families, are especially attached to their deaths or funerals. His Uncle Milo was lost off the coast of Chile with a boatload of guano. The death of the beatific Robert at age eighteeen, apparently in the first World War, is crucial to Aunt Alice's family narrative (433) and may be the subject of Suttree's half-meditative, half-memorial reconstruction ("[t]he patriot in his sam browne belt and puttees" being taken in his coffin from the train [129]). But Suttree's most conspicuous interest is trained upon his great-uncle Jeffrey, another of Alice's brothers, whom he knows to have been hanged in Rockcastle County, Kentucky, on 18 July 1884 (433). Jeffrey represents the isomer of violence present in the family bloodlines ("What family has no mariner in its tree? No fool, no felon. No fisherman" [128]), and it is his influence that Suttree is at pains to defend himself against in his delirious dream-trial (454–55).

The two deaths which Suttree can recall from his childhood with particular vividness—those of his grandfather and of his Aunt Elizabeth—have had a formative effect upon his consciousness. He can recall his grandfather saying goodbye to him from his deathbed: "His caved and wasted face. The dead would take the living with them if they could" (13). And looking at the grainy photograph of Elizabeth that he sees at Aunt Martha's house, he remembers the old woman in her casket: "Bloodless skull and dry white hair, matriarchal meat drawn lean and dry on frail bone . . . by candlelight in a cold hall, black lacquered bier on sawhorses wound with crepe. I would not cry. My sisters cried" (130). Such experiences are common enough, perhaps, among young children exposed to death for the first time. Suttree's fixation upon death, as it turns out, however, does not derive primarily from these two memories after all. They are merely masking memories of the true source of his obsession, later unlocked under the influence of Mother She's drugs. This ancient witch reputedly has the power to look into the future. Instead Suttree is whirled through a chaotic revisitation of his past. At the bottom of his remembrance he comes once again to the image of Aunt Elizabeth in her casket—"that old lady who had sat in the stained and cracked photograph like a fierce bird lay cold in state . . . . Black lacquer bier trestled up in a drafty hall"—and his father's arms lifting him up "to see how quietly the dead lay" (428–29). Suddenly, however, a deeper, more concealed memory rises to consciousness, a memory which causes Suttree to sit bolt upright on Mother She's cot:

> He saw in a small alcove among flowers the sleeping doll, the white bonnet, the lace, the candlelight. Come upon in their wanderings through the vast funeral hall. And the little girl took the thing from its cradle and held it and rocked it in her arms and Clayton said you better put that thing up. She took it through the halls crooning it a lullaby, the long lace burial dress trailing behind her to the floor and Suttree following and a woman saw them pass in the hall and called softly upon God before

she ran from the room and someone cried out: You bring that thing here. And they ran down the hall and the little girl fell with it and it rolled on the floor and a man came out and took it away and the little girl was crying and she said that it was just lying in there by itself and the little boy was much afraid. (429)

In this primal memory, which has long lain dormant, the "thing" the little girl takes from among the flowers is not a "sleeping doll" at all but, as Suttree now realizes, a dead baby. It is the same image that he has encountered at Aunt Martha's, one of whose family photographs is of "a fat dead baby" in a casket, "garishly painted, bright fuchsia cheeks. Never ask whose" (130). Whoever the child in the funeral parlor may have been, there is no question with whom Suttree associates it: it calls to consciousness the key event of his mental life, as he believes, the still-birth of his twin brother.

Suttree has first learned of this child's birth only because of a drunken lapse on the part of his Uncle John, and presumably he holds this conceal-ment against his family as well. The child is buried in the Woodlawn cemetery, which Suttree on occasion drunkenly visits, "A maudlin mad-man stumbling among the stones in search of a friend long dead" (302). While he could still maintain the Catholic faith in which he was reared, Suttree prayed for his dead brother's soul, "Believing this ghastly circus reconvened elsewhere for alltime." In this dispensation the nameless brother was a sort of "ordinary," a clergyman attendant upon Suttree's own self-proclaimed criminality—"He in the limbo of the Christless righteous, I in a terrestrial hell" (14). But with the loss of his religious faith Suttree's ruminations come to center around more fundamental questions of being. The existence of this spectral other—"Suttree and Antisuttree," as he sometimes thinks of it (28)—is the constant reminder of his own putative nonexistence.

The ambiguous circumstances of this twin's creation and disappear-ance seem, in fact, to have attenuated Suttree's own existence as well, reducing his status to that of mere imago. Suttree is lefthanded; the "mauve halfmoon" he bears on the left side of his head is identical (he im-agines) to the mark on his brother's right temple; Suttree is his brother's "Mirror image. Gauche carbon" (14). Even his heart seems to have been displaced in this mirror reflection. He has been found to be a dextrocar-diac, and it is the magnitude of feeling himself twinned with a creature consigned to the parallel universe of death that has made his heart "[w]eathershrunk and loveless" (13).

He neither spoke nor saw nor does he now. Perhaps his skull held seawater. Born dead and witless both or a terratoma grisly in form. No, for we were alike to the last hair. I followed him into the world, me. A breech birth. Hind end fore in common with whales and bats, life forms meant for other mediums than the earth and having no affinity for it. (14)

The task which Suttree's consciousness thrusts upon him in this novel is to determine the difference between "dead and witless" inanimate nature and the peculiar phenomenon of human life that has proceeded out of it. If animation alone is the distinction, then death really does have the primacy throughout the entire natural world that Suttree's preoccupation with it suggests. Life becomes an improbable deviation from the eternally uniform, comfortable stasis of inorganicism. Suttree's aim, then, is to draw as close as possible to "that still center where the living and the dead are one" (447). He wants to know the miracle by which the individual consciousness emerges out of the massive, impersonal process of 'the world, how the "[b]lind moil in the earth's nap cast up in an eyeblink between becoming and done" gives rise to the "I am, I am" (129).

His path there is not unlike Thoreau's. The idea is to reduce life "to its lowest terms, and, if it proved to be mean, why then to get the whole and genuine meanness of it; or if it were sublime, to know it by experience." Like Thoreau too, Suttree's first task comes to be to demythologize reality, to free it from cultural deadlock—most men, as Thoreau says, having "*somewhat hastily* concluded that it is the chief end of man here to 'glorify God and enjoy him forever.' " As the novel opens, Suttree is lying face down in his leaky skiff, peering into the polluted depths of the river from the distance of about one foot, "as if something unseen" might be stirring below (7). What lurks there, as he is soon reminded by the appearance of a rescue crew, is no river god but the corpse of yet another suicide who has leapt from the bridge above; "They always seem to jump in hot weather," Suttree observes (12). Among the other river debris, he frequently notes shoals of bobbing condoms and, on more than one occasion, "*the beached and stinking forms of foetal humans*" (4, 306). Such is the elemental but apparently accidental organization of being and not-being at their source, as between Suttree's form and that of his dead twin. And it is the gravity of this impression that keeps placing Suttree himself up on the bridge, wondering what it would be like "To fall through dark to darkness. Struggle in those opaque and fecal deeps, which way is up" (29).

Suttree's choice of life on the river keeps the "twinned" facts of life and death continually before him and ensures that he enact his own mortality in the most personalized terms. Living there he is conspicuously uninsulated by middling concerns with family, employment or career. Instead the core meaning of his existence, with the death of his twin as its dramatic first moment, is continually made explicit in the complex beveling of natural fact and memory. One example of how the full weight of such memory bears upon every moment of Suttree's experience may suffice. When the corpse is hauled from the river at the beginning of the novel, Suttree notices "with a feeling he could not name that the dead man's watch was still running" (10). A little later, lying on his cot, he recalls that the "old tin clock on Grandfather's table hammered like a foundry" when he saw the old man on his deathbed (13). Suttree remembers his grandfather timing a racehorse with a stopwatch and suggesting "that they had witnessed a thing against which time would not prevail"—something even as a boy Suttree knew was not true, for he "had already begun to sicken at the slow seeping of life. . . . Lives running out like something foul, nightsoil from a cesspipe, a measured dripping in the dark" (136). This preoccupation with time and mortality is one of the charges entered against Suttree at his dream-trial, when—in a scene that clearly recalls Quentin Compson in *The Sound and the Fury*—he stops in front of a clockshop, sees his face in the glass and notices that some of the clocks are stopping (453–54). When his grandfather dies, Suttree sees himself reflected in the dead man's spectacles (80, 129).[2] The image of Suttree's face reflected in a shop window or "twinned and blown in the smoked glass of a blind man's spectacles" (80) returns him to the contemplation of his doppelgänger, the Antisuttree of his dead twin, who is a "[m]ore common visitor" to his dreams than even his grandfather (14). All this weight of memory is with Suttree in his skiff as he rocks gently and hears—in what is the working paradox of the novel— "the clocklike blade of the cradle" (80).

Fishing is thus for Suttree an activity which he does not bother to try to strip of metaphor. He accepts without comment its many complexities— the image of the dead man raised from the river with a grappling hook in his mouth (9), an economic system that demands the careful distribution of his goods among both white and black markets (67–69), his distaste for his own product ("I dont much like fish" [205]). The title "fisherman" is an honorific one which helps define the true dimensions of this life, and he claims it without reservation. Lying in his houseboat at night, pondering simultaneously the sounds of fish sloshing in his skiff and the Catholic iconography of his youth, he decides "that he might have been a fisher of men in another time but these fish now seemed task enough for him" (14). The facticity of the river is for him the symbolic equivalent of the world of spirit.

This same transposition occurs regularly throughout the novel. Enroute to his Aunt Martha's house, Suttree comes upon a baptismal scene at the river where a preacher, standing waist-deep in the water, is immersing a series of communicants. In the course of his conversation with some of the other onlookers—one of them a lay preacher—Suttree reveals not only that he is "not saved" but that his own baptism was "[j]ust on the head." "That aint no good," the lay preacher tells him. "That old sprinklin business wont get it, buddy boy" (122). To his entreaties—"Go on, he said. Get down in that water" (123)—Suttree remains outwardly sanguine. For one thing, as another bystander says, "It aint salvation just to get in the water. . . . You got to be saved as well." For another, Suttree's thoughts that morning have, as usual, been running in a far more protomorphic vein: along this same stretch of river he has just seen three gars lying "like dogs, heavy shapes of primitive rapacity" (121) and recalled from his youth an old hunter who murdered turtles with an ancient musket (119–20). Watching one young girl emerge from her baptism with her wet dress plastered to her body, his thoughts are far from religious, and he chuckles with some others at a wiseacre's remark about one flailing celebrant: "Boys, he said, that ought to take if it dont drownd him" (124). Finally, getting up to leave, Suttree does show a trace of annoyance with the lay preacher: "You better get in that river is where you better get to, said the one in overalls. But Suttree knew the river well already and he turned his back to these malingerers and went on" (124–25).

In Suttree's private vulgate, it is he who knows the river, not they. They are "malingerers" caught in the cultural petrifaction of history, who reflexively recreate the river along animistic lines compatible with their own egos and fear of death. Suttree's resolutely unanthropomorphic perspective is the precise opposite of theirs. "The color of this life is water," as he observes later (415), by which he means that both are bred of the same fecund neutrality. The natural world, in Emerson's phrase, is absolutely "inconsiderate of persons": it "tingles your blood, benumbs your feet, freezes a man like an apple." This is the lesson Suttree later has to explain to his friend Gene Harrogate, who thinks it has gotten so cold that the world may be coming to an end. "You're funny, you squirrely son of a bitch," Suttree has to tell him. "Do you think the world will end just because you're cold?" (173).

Suttree's acquaintance with the river follows this strict naturalistic bent, and he is forever seeking out mentors in its lore. One such figure is an Indian named Michael, a prodigy at Suttree's chosen trade, whom Suttree seeks out after seeing the eighty-seven pound catfish he has landed. They become friends, Suttree helping Michael recover his stolen skiff and Michael sharing his secret bait and—in an image that recurs[3]—instructing Suttree in the conversion of seemingly inedible turtle meat into a delicacy for the pot. Michael is a true avatar of the path Suttree is seeking to follow. As an Indian, he is by definition socially disenfranchised, the target of the white man's taunts and a likely candidate for his jails. His home is a cave across the river, before which he sits "crouched like an icon. . . , solemn and unaccountable and bizarre" (240). As his personal totems, he wears a pair of doll's eyes taken from the belly of a fish and lead medallions advertising whiskey, objects he believes may empower him within the difficult cultural niche he occupies. After sharing the turtle stew, Michael provides Suttree with an amulet similarly suitable to the path his friend would travel. It is "a small lozenge of yellowed bone" with a hole bored through it—perhaps a tooth—which Michael has found on the floor of his cave (239). This is the first of several such talismans Suttree receives in the novel that mark the direction of his personal journey.

As it turns out, Suttree—however he may aspire to it—proves incapable of the kind of oneness with the river which Michael has attained. The stench of the "secret bait" is more than Suttree can stand, and he soon goes back to the cutbait and doughballs of the less ardent fisherman. "You wont stay," Michael has predicted (240), even after Suttree has been on the river for two years, and by that fall he has pulled his lines and headed off for what proves a harrowing six-week trek through the Great Smokies near Gatlinburg. In entering the wilderness Suttree becomes more than ever "a hermetic figure, . . . gaunted and sunken at the eyes" (284). He purposely loses himself in the wilderness, straying from all roads and trails, living off roots and nuts, angling for fish with a small hook baited with rice-grains; like his mentor Michael, he sits "crouched like an ape in the dark under the eaves of a slate bluff" (287). He consciously courts the more primitive realms of being he has sought also on the river, and after some weeks of privation he induces in himself that state of visionary power that allows him to see the world as it is. Some of what he sees is essentially what he already knows. He recognizes the fundamental indeterminacy of the universe, "The cold indifferent dark, the blind stars beaded on their tracks and mitered satellites and geared and pinioned planets all reeling through the black of space" (284). Within this same perspective he sees "with a madman's clarity the perishability of his flesh" (287), what he later calls "the mathematical certainty of death" (295). In his delirium he can be sure only that he alone, of all the figures he meets in the woods, is neither "figment" nor phantom. Wrapped in a ragged blanket and with his hair and beard long and matted, the reality of his irreducible self is not to be denied. Most of all, Suttree grasps more powerfully than ever his covenant with the world precisely along these lines of mortality and facticity. Stopping at a stream to drink after days without food, hardly knowing whether he is awake or asleep, Suttree looks around

> at a world of incredible loveliness. Old distaff Celt's blood in some back chamber of his brain moved him to discourse with the birches, with the oaks. A cool green fire kept breaking in the woods and he could hear the footsteps of the dead. Everything had fallen from him. He scarce could tell where his being ended or the world began nor did he care. . . . He could feel the oilless turning of the earth beneath him and the cup of water lay in his stomach as cold as when he drank it. (286)

The radical mediation which society works on this natural experience is apparent as soon as Suttree wanders out of the woods into Bryson City, North Carolina, some days later. He scarcely recognizes the images he sees in a diner there: "the huge and blackened trout" mounted on a board, "the naked leather squirrel with the vitreous eyebulbs," "the dull tocking of applewood clockworks" (292). From this perspective all nature seems misshapen, reduced to incomprehensible relics by the human appropriation of it.

Some of what emerges from Suttree's Gatlinburg experience, however, is less a matter of supposition. For one thing, there is his increasing sense, over the weeks, that he has "begun to become accompanied" (285):

> In these silent sunless galleries he'd come to feel that another went before him and each glade he entered seemed just quit by a figure who'd been sitting there and risen and gone on. Some doublegoer, some othersuttree eluded him in these woods and he feared that should that figure fail to rise and steal away and were he therefore to come to himself in this obscure wood he'd be neither mended nor made whole but rather set mindless to dodder drooling with his ghosty clone from sun to sun across a hostile hemisphere forever. (287)

The immediate assumption is, of course, that the "ghosty clone" involved here is the figure of Suttree's dead twin which McCarthy has carefully foregrounded in the book. In this chapter, however, the device of the dead twin falls away. What is left is a sense of doubleness that is more meta-phorical, a way of explaining what seems to be the primary mechanism of Suttree's consciousness. His mental operations, in this chapter and frequently throughout the novel, typically involve the twinning of a discrete physical fact with an involuntary and often alogical or visionary blossom-ing of that fact. In the mountains, for example, Suttree crosses a stone bridge, above which runs an old logging road leading to an abandoned CCC camp. Just the arrangement of the scene is enough to trigger in Suttree, spontaneously it seems, its own native myth: two boys must once have been fishing from this bridge when a rider on horseback came clattering across the bridge and passed down to go beneath it. The boys switch sides of the bridge to see him ride out, but only the horse emerges, running free, and when they look inside the arch below they see the rider "dangling by his skull from a steel rod that jutted from the new masonry, . . . his eyes slightly crossed as if he would see what was the nature of this thing that had skewered his brains" (285).

Examples of this same sort proliferate throughout the Gatlinburg chap-ter. A drop of rain strikes a stone with a bell-like note, and in the next instant Suttree sees "with no surprise mauve monks in cobwebbed cowls" (286). The clash of rain and lightning over the trees produces a vision of medieval merrymaking, the principals of which are figures out of some fantastic bestiary: a caged wivern "and other alchemical game, chimeras and cacodemons," a mesosaur, trolls and gnomes, a whole carnival of outlandish revelers (287–88). What such scenes demonstrate, it seems, is the impossibility of a human animal such as Suttree remaining among the simple facts of existence, however much he may revere those facts. The irreducible self, which Suttree has so carefully coaxed forth in his flight from respectable society and now stripped in this chapter to its primal form, is still forever altering the fundamental terms of its existence. Suttree's evasion of cultural restraint and social responsibility does nothing to abro-gate the observational and aesthetic privilege incumbent upon human life, which here increases rather than decreases in a state of nature. For a mo-ment his "old distaff Celt's blood," or some other atavistic impulse, may make him feel one with the world, but the fundamental organization of human life precludes it from resuming its original place in the world of fact—as is apparent also in Arthur Ownby's assumption of the responsi-bilities of stewardship in *The Orchard Keeper*, and even in such autoch-thonous forms as Culla and Rinthy Holme in *Outer Dark*, Lester Ballard in *Child of God* and the kid in *Blood Meridian*.

Such subjective conversion of natural fact increases, of course, in proportion to the evolution of self, and with Suttree self-consciousness has reached acute levels. In part this is a function of his much-disdained education; he dislikes his McAnally friends' thinking he is one of those "educated pisswillies" who has gone "to college but . . . cant roll a newspaper" (47). Still, Suttree's education is everywhere apparent—in his status as observer, in the unattributed snippets from Auden (175), Frost (179), cummings (195) and Faulkner (453–54). His assertion that "From all old seamy throats of elders, musty books, I've salvaged not a word" (14) is clearly self-deluding. The privilege of consciousness can emerge especially in his rather mannered responses to the natural experience he seeks. In his first days at Gatlinburg, watching the yellow leaves drop into the river, he thinks first of them as a "perishable currency, forever renewed," then seizes upon the appropriate literary analogue: "In an old grandfather time a ballad transpired here, some love gone wrong and a sabletressed girl drowned in an icegreen pool . . ." (283). Suttree's imagination is always doubling back upon pure perception in this way and obviating his entry into the world. His solipsism is apparent at times even to himself. Near the end of his Gatlinburg experience he recognizes momentarily "what a baleful heart he harbored and how dear to him" (290); he reproaches himself for his "maudlin" disposition (302). At such moments Suttree overtly acknowledges the level of his self-involvement. His problems are almost beyond his capacity for expression, and the curious shorthand references to his dead twin and shadowy family history have for him an emotional valence—as Eliot says of Shakespeare's literarization of experience in *Hamlet*—"in excess of the facts as they appear." The power these departed figures exert over Suttree emanates from their conversion into counters for his private self-questioning, as "explanations" for emotions to which they are not causally connected. The tragedy of his life is the inevitability with which his living relationships are likewise so converted.

Suttree's loss of connection with the possibilities of intersubjectivity is continuously apparent. When his mother comes to visit him at Christmas in the workhouse—her only appearance in the novel—"the son she addressed was hardly there at all," although an abstract, decentralized imagining of the scene ("See the mother sorrowing") brings forth a paroxysm of grief (61). This sort of emotional dysfunction is also manifest in Suttree's actions when, during the fall of his first year on the river, his own son dies. This child, who has been living with Suttree's "abandoned wife" in west Tennessee, has appeared once before in the novel, in a dream Suttree recounts.

A dark figure, which he takes to be his father, emerges from an alley and grasps Suttree's hand. "Yet it was not my father but my son who accosted me with such rancorless intent" (28). The confusion of allegiances between father and son—and the replication of a kind of "rancorless" betrayal from generation to generation—certainly suggests Suttree's feelings of guilt in having abandoned his son, as perhaps he feels himself to have been similarly forsaken. Having learned of the child's death, Suttree makes the overnight trip across the state, where he clashes violently with his ex-wife's hostile parents, attends the funeral services at a distance and—in a rush of insupportable grief—fills in the earth over the child's coffin before the hired gravediggers can finish the task. Later the same day he is peremptorily ushered out of town by the local sheriff.

But it is the thinking that Suttree does during the two days of this ordeal that is most revealing. Throughout the course of his trip across the state, Suttree keeps trying "to see the child's face in his mind but he could not." He can remember only the child's "tiny hand in his as they went to the carnival fair and a fleeting image of elf's eyes wonderstruck at the wide world in its wheeling" (150). And this memory of the ferris wheel and skyrockets is a kind of generic one for Suttree, recurring at two other points in the novel. One such moment takes place while Suttree is in the workhouse and is detailed, with some other prisoners, to pick up trash at the fairgrounds:

> A sad and bitter season. Barrenness of heart and gothic loneliness. Suttree dreamed old dreams of fairgrounds where young girls with flowered hair and wide child's eyes watched by flarelight sequined aerialists aloft. Visions of unspeakable loveliness from a world lost. To make you ache with want. (50)

The other is elicited later in the novel by Suttree's sadness at the demise of his relationship with the prostitute Joyce:

> In the distance the lights of the fairground and the ferriswheel turning like a tiny clockgear. Suttree wondered if she were ever a child at a fair dazed by the constellations of light and the hurdygurdy music of the merrygoround and the raucous calls of the barkers. Who saw in all that shoddy world a vision that child's grace knows and never the sweat and the bad teeth and the nameless stains in the sawdust, the flies and the stale delirium and the vacant look of solitaries who go among these garish holdings seeking a thing they could not name. (408–09)

Neither of these two passages evokes Suttree's son as an object of recollection, both instead being given over to a collective memory of "young girls" with "wide child's eyes" and speculation upon whether Joyce could have ever been such a girl. If, as seems likely, this loss of wonder in the world is really Suttree's own, recollected from the perspective of his present adult "solitariness," then the one memory he can summon of his son is actually a memory of himself as a child. The child Suttree grieves is the emblem of his own irrecoverable innocence, not a flesh and blood son discrete in his own humanness; and in his solipsism the dead son becomes indistinguishable from the dead twin: both are simply facets of Suttree's own present self, lost possibilities buried beneath his current anomie.

Other details of the funeral episode support this impression. Of his wife Suttree can recall only—as some Poe narrators can of their allegorical lost loves—that her hair in the morning was "black, rampant, savage with loveliness" (153), something like that of the sable-tressed ballad-girl in the pool at Gatlinburg. When he calls the funeral home to learn where the burial will be, it is the phrase "*Suttree funeral*" that causes him to drop the telephone receiver from his ear (152). Standing on a hill at some distance from the service, he hears not a word the preacher is saying "until his own name was spoken. Then everything became quite clear. He turned and laid his head against the tree, choked with a sorrow he had never known." The only sound that can penetrate the amnesic weatherlessness of his grief is that of his own name. The whole incident returns Suttree to the emotional ground of his dead twin, his other self. In both cases, he is able to rationalize the self-absorption of his sorrow by supposing that it is really the living who suffer death:

> How surely are the dead beyond death. Death is what the living carry with them. A state of dread, like some uncanny foretaste of a bitter memory. But the dead do not remember and nothingness is not a curse. Far from it. (153)

Such a characterization is useful enough in the case of Suttree's twin, in whose death he is only irrationally implicated, to deflect whatever grief or guilt has accrued. To deploy the same defense in the case of his son, for whose presence in the world he has been directly responsible, is disingenuous at best. It reduces the significance of the boy's death to yet another justification for Suttree's "congenital disaffection." His self-involvement, which insulates him from any full recognition of familial responsibility, thus finds an ironic parallel in Culla Holme's abandonment of his son in *Outer Dark*. Suttree merely stands to Culla as the civilized man to the primitive, with both the development of his consciousness and the terms of his socialization correspondingly more complex.

Suttree's alliances among the social castoffs of McAnally Flats are, on the other hand, concessions to exteriority, and his attention does attach itself there in a naturally generous and unforced manner. Some of his finest moments occur as a result of his friendship with the black tavern-owner, Ab Jones, in his one-man campaign against the persecutions of the Knoxville Police Department. So deeply felt are Suttree's sympathies that they lead to his climactic act of civil disobedience in the novel—stealing a police patrol car and running it off into the river, an action which ultimately forces him to leave the city. Suttree is also especially concerned with two of his nearest neighbors, a misanthropic old rag-picker who lives under a bridge and Daddy Watson, a retired railroader. He makes a practice of checking on the two old men whenever the weather turns inclement, and his solicitude for them seems genuine and deeply felt. It should be remembered, however, that the last time Suttree sees Daddy Watson—who turns up confined in the same mental institution as Suttree's Aunt Alice—he pretends not to know the old man. As with Aunt Alice's unspoken desire for visitors or an occasional ride outside the grounds, there are certain emotional encumbrances which Suttree feels incapable of undertaking, certain "modes for which he had neither aptitude nor will" (434).

Suttree's most significant relationship among the McAnally rabble turns out, somewhat surprisingly, to be with the chronic and disaster-prone miscreant Gene Harrogate. Suttree first meets Harrogate in the work-house, just after the eighteen-year-old youth has been brought up on charges of "bestiality" with a field of watermelons. Harrogate, by any estimate, is "not lovable"; he is "[s]ly, ratfaced. . . . But something in him so transparent, something vulnerable" (54). He is also "[b]right with a kind of animal cognizance, with incipient good will" (42)—traits which he immediately begins to deploy in tireless stratagems against the world, while the incredulous Suttree stands by as witness. Except that Suttree seldom stands completely by. Ensconced beneath the First Creek viaduct, Harrogate extends the tentacles of his ingenuity, Robinson Crusoe-fashion, into the urban wasteland around him. He rigs a lightpole to electrocute pigeons, pilfers porch furniture and road lanterns, makes a boat from two welded car hoods. In all these enterprises gleams a certain primitive ingenuity—equal parts low cunning, unsinkable resilience and predisposition to catastrophe—which Suttree finds irresistible. When

Harrogate is riding high—as he is, briefly, after plugging the coin returns of 286 Knoxville pay telephones—he is the picture of capitalistic success:

> And this was Harrogate. Standing in the door of Suttree's shack with a cigar between his teeth. He had painted the black one and it was chalk white and he had grown a wispy mustache. He wore a corduroy hat a helping larger than his headsize and a black gabardine shirt with slacks to match. His shoes were black and sharply pointed, his socks were yellow. Suttree in his shorts leaned against the door and studied his visitor with what the city rat took for wordless admiration. (418)

Against his better judgment, Suttree keeps finding himself involved in Harrogate's schemes. It is he who obtains the strychnine which Harrogate uses to poison the feeding bats—he shoots it up to them by slingshot—in an effort to collect the one-dollar Board of Health bounty. And Suttree involves himself in an even more addle-brained plot to enter a Knoxville bank vault by way of the extensive cave system underlying the city. In this latter instance, Suttree's interest is perhaps understandable. Early in the novel his cronies defer to his authority on the legendary Knoxville caves (23–24), and, like Harrogate, he is witness to an incident one morning in which a truck on a downtown street falls five feet through the pavement (259). Suttree's fascination is not just with the flimsiness of the urban edifice; it is with the cultural substrata of a modern city, the underlying increments by which "civilized" life has evolved. Harrogate's explorations "in this nether region so gravid with seam and lode," which transforms him into "a bloodcolored troglodyte" (259), correlate with Suttree's own inquiries above ground—along the river and in the mountains at Gatlinburg. Even the literal-minded Harrogate begins "to suspect some dimensional displacement in these descents to the underworld, some disparity unaccountable between the above and the below" (262).[4] In that primordial darkness the demarcations between human and inhuman, between nature and culture, are once again demolished. When Harrogate's light fails, the "dark closed over him so absolute that he became without boundary to himself, as large as all the universe and small as anything that was" (274–75). This experience, it will be recalled, is almost identical to the one Suttree has in the Gatlinburg woods, when he "scarce could tell where his being ended or the world began nor did he care" (286).

It is little wonder that Suttree is soon drawn into the project, helping Harrogate take his crude bearings and poring over obsolete city maps with him, "the small face of the apprentice felon nodding at his elbow" (260).

The characterization of Harrogate as the "apprentice felon" is not gratuitous, for Suttree's disaffection from society runs both more deeply and more dangerously than does Harrogate's. In Harrogate's misdeeds there is always a buoyant innocence, as if he were merely making his way through the world by the same amoral wiles everyone else uses but is at pains to disguise. At one point, listening to Harrogate's unvarnished account of burning down an old woman's house as a boy, Suttree reflects that "other than the melon caper he'd never heard the city rat tell anything but naked truth" (145). In Gene Harrogate Suttree locates the amoral, acquisitive center of the human animal, prior to the development of a socially expedient moral sensibility.

In the end, of course, Harrogate disappears into this underground world and Suttree has to go in after him. Below ground Suttree experiences the same sort of temporal displacement as his young associate. The life of the city seems "gone altogether." Below there is only "a distant timeless dripping"; the cave roof looks like the "ribbed palate of a stone monster comatose, a great uvula dripping rust" (275). Holding in his palm "pale newts with enormous eyes," watching "their tiny hearts hammer under the blue and visible bones of their thimblesized briskets" (276), Suttree finds himself at the incunabular still point at which life and lifelessness first diverged. The only signs of human presence here seem impossibly old and as far removed as myth: "Cimmerians passed on without progeny. Some lack of adventure in the souls of newer folk or want of the love of darkness" (275). When, on the fourth day, Suttree does find the city rat, Harrogate looks "like something that might leap up and scurry off down a hole." He has accidentally dynamited a city sewer main and been wandering through these caverns ever since. When Suttree comes face to face with his own prehistoric simulacrum, Harrogate is practically naked and covered with dried sewage: "True news," Suttree thinks, "of man here below" (276).

Suttree's fascination with Gene Harrogate represents, then, a continuation of the direction he seeks in living on the river and wandering through the mountains. There is an elemental kind of knowledge here, evidence of the primal forces out of which both the human animal and his culture were originally organized. In his big brotherly fosterage of Harrogate, Suttree arrives at a vision of human innocence distinct from any saccharine Golden Age associations. Harrogate represents a part of Suttree now buried beneath the irreversible accession of culture and consciousness— a part of himself also carried in the metaphor of the dead twin. On the day Harrogate arrives in Knoxville, Suttree is in fact dreaming of "his brother in swaddling, hands outheld, a scent of myrrh and lilies. But it was the voice of Gene Harrogate that called to him" (113). When he stands up for Harrogate against the workhouse bully Byrd Slusser, Suttree once again sees himself "twinned" in Slusser's eyes (52). Suttree's defense of Harrogate's innocence, his transparence and vulnerability, is a defense of both his dead brother and of what he thinks of as the "child buried within him" (119). Ultimately, however, Suttree has the same difficulties availing himself fully of such experience in its human manifestations as in its nonhuman ones. In his two most intimate human relationships in the novel—his love affairs with the child-woman Wanda and the prostitute Joyce—Suttree's self-absorption undermines his efforts at outwardness.

In the former case it is apparent that Wanda's presence is in some ways a function of the natural world in which Suttree encounters her. He meets her during his third year on the river, when her family's houseboat ties up for a while near Knoxville. Suttree's awkward suspension between the city and the river has begun to wear on him. He feels like another bit of jetsam disgorged by the city and washed down to the river, "a bit of matter stunned and drying in the curing mud, the terra damnata of the city's dead alchemy" (306). When Wanda's father Reese offers Suttree a chance to join the family in their musselling operation later that summer up the French Broad River, Suttree accepts. Being in the wilderness again initially makes him feel "alien and tainted. . . . As if the city had marked him. So that no eldritch daemon would speak him secrets in this wood" (316). Suttree's first weeks musselling do little to dispel this lassitude. The unexpected impoverishment of the camp itself, the harsh labor and Reese's extraordinary capacity for mismanagement of their scant resources frustrate him to the point of prostration. After one memorable drinking bout with Reese in nearby Newport, Suttree staggers back into camp and collapses. "My life is ghastly, he told the grass" (348).

Little by little, however, Suttree begins to be released from this debilitation. For one thing, there is the rhythm of successive weeks along the pristine river and Suttree's re-immersion in the little intensities of natural experience. Once again, as he did in Gatlinburg and with his fisherman friend Michael, Suttree rededicates himself to life at this level. One day he finds a "gray and alien stone of a kind he'd never seen" (328), on which is faintly carved "two rampant gods addorsed with painted eyes and helmets plumed, their spangled anklets raised in dance." Suttree threads a thong through this "carven gorget," the token of his affiliation with a more primal order of being, and places it around his neck. "For a cold moment the spirit of an older order moved in the rainy air" (327).

In some ways, too, he comes to appreciate the Reese clan, scruffy as they are, as the natural heirs of this "older order." On the same afternoon when, in the throes of his hangover, Suttree has concluded that his life is "ghastly," he awakens to a somewhat incongruous scene. Reese is squatting by the fire smoking a cigarette while his wife prepares their meager meal; Reese's son is coming up the riverbank with a load of driftwood for the fire—"All this with a quality of dark ceremony." When one of the younger daughters puts the coffeepot on the fire, she does so "with a studied domesticity which in this outlandish setting caused Suttree to smile." Suttree ponders the significance of what he is seeing throughout the evening meal. What seems apparent is that he and Reese, in their temporary defection from the family unit, have triggered this reflexive, ceremonial impulse toward reintegration.

> There was about them something subdued beyond their normal reticence.
> As if order had been forced upon them from without. From time to time
> the woman awarded the round dark a look of grim apprehension like
> a fugitive. (348)

Suttree's reconnection with the natural world includes, in this instance, some awareness of how primal human bonds were forged in reaction against that world. His covenant with the "vanished race" whose amulet he wears is not the same thing as the pantheistic immersion in the natural world to which they were so richly attuned. It implies as well a loyalty to the fact of human life, which arose essentially in reaction to natural forces which threatened its discreteness. Thus, when Suttree awakens again later that night to the sound of the family's voices, he associates them with images of alienation and dislocation, like "the thin clamor of some company transgressed from a dream or children who had died going along a road in the dark with lanterns and crying on their way from the world" (348). Readers of *Outer Dark* will recall a similar instance when Rinthy Holme, wandering in the wilderness, is attracted into the "votive" light of a farm family, where she is able to hold off "the untenanted night out of which she had come" (58). This sense of relation, of course, stands in sharp contrast to the destructive fragmentation of family life which has been Suttree's own experience.

Suttree's entry into this expanded family truly begins with his affair with Wanda. She is a vision of nascent sexuality: black hair, "perfect teeth, her skin completely flawless, not so much as a mole" (353). When Suttree kisses her for the first time, he tastes her "child's breath, an odor of raw milk" (352). Their passionate dalliance coincides with Suttree's rediscovery of what John Crowe Ransom calls "the world's body":

> He'd lie awake long after the last dull shapes in the coals of the cookfire died and he'd go naked into the cool and velvet waters and submerge like an otter and come up and blow, the stones smooth as marbles under his cupped toes and the dark water reeling past his eyes. (353)

Lying at night in the shallows, watching the stars, he finds that the "enormity of the universe filled him with a strange sweet woe" (353). A few nights later, watching the same constellations, he is "struck by the fidelity of this earth he inhabited and he bore it sudden love" (354). His love for the girl frees him to love the world by releasing him from the burden of knowledge. For a while the two are one: "With his ear to the womb of this child he could hear the hiss of meteorites through the blind stellar depths" (358). Characteristically, however, once Suttree is invited to commit himself more fully, the impulse flees. Reese drops one nonetoo-subtle comment about how good a cook Wanda is (354), and by the next page Suttree is breaking things off. The lovers have one final, passionate rapprochement before tragedy strikes: the rain-soaked slate cliff above the campsite gives way one night, and Wanda is crushed to death beneath the debris.

In terms of Suttree's prepotent mental life, however, the relationship has already expired the previous evening when two possum hunters show up in camp. They are twins named Vernon and Fernon, identical "to the crooks in their stained brown teeth. The creases about their eyes, the quilting of their dry bird necks" (358–59). Their appearance strikes Suttree dumb, and he can only watch and listen as Reese excitedly extracts their history. So closely do they resemble each other that originally not even their parents could tell them apart. "We dont rightly know which one of us is which noway," Vernon tells them. The identification bracelets they were given as babies they soon tore off; up until they were old enough to identify themselves, there is no way of knowing how many times their names might have interchanged. The twins' subsequent lives, they go on to explain, have been ruled by a pattern of startling doubleness. When, as a boy, Fernon fell out of a black walnut tree and broke his arm, he learned that Vernon had done the same thing—fallen from a black walnut tree "at the identical same minute" on his grandfather's farm eight miles away. Even Reese's credulity is strained by this account, so the brothers arrange a demonstration. "We can tell what one another is thinkin," Vernon says, and he has Reese whisper a word into Fernon's ear. Vernon closes his eyes for a moment, and when he opens them he has it. "*Brother*," he says, spinning around and facing "his unarmed image across the fire, his sinister isomer in bone and flesh." Stunned, Suttree can only take up his bedding and go off into the woods; the next morning he is ready to resume his former life, walking out to the highway and thinking he "could have just walked off down the road" (360–61).

In obvious ways this scene returns Suttree to the constitutive question of his own existence: to what he calls "[h]is subtle obsession with uniqueness" (113). Fernon is Vernon's "sinister isomer" just as Suttree is his dead twin's "gauche carbon." Facing each other across the fire, their hands "palm up on the ground before them in the manner of apes" (359), these twins challenge once again the notion of personal identity—or, more correctly, any definitions of humanness which would distinguish it from the unindividuated and unsignified proliferation of other life forms. Suttree's doubts about his own ontological claims upon the domain of the dead resurface in near allegorical form here and pull him away, as always, from the instinctual freedom he seeks. But it must be added that Wanda herself, in Suttree's mode of perception, seems mostly allegorical as well. With her wild black hair and perfect beauty, she is reminiscent both of Suttree's abandoned wife and the Gatlinburg ballad-girl he imagines in the pool. Like them, she seems more emblem than person, the dream of a perfect—and therefore either lost or unattainable—passion. And like them she falls into the special vacuum of Suttree's habitual conversion of experience into the language of thought. The possibility of true outwardness, of the unfettered life of the instincts, is for him always retained within the all-comprehensive brackets of the self.

The same process may be seen at work in Suttree's other extensive relationship in the novel, his affair with the prostitute Joyce. This episode, which begins late in the fall after Suttree has returned from the French Broad in August, is of longer duration than his liaison with Wanda and involves a more fully functioning partner. Suttree has once again moved off the houseboat to winter in the city, renting a cheap basement room and—with Harrogate as his conscious model—scavenging the neighborhood for furnishings (381). He meets Joyce in a cafe and likes her immediately. She is honest and worldly, with a natural sensuality that sometimes makes Suttree go "awash in the sheer outrageous sentience of her" (393).

Her ribald wit is a match for his own, and her scorn for conventional notions of morality and law and order are, of course, dear to Suttree's own heart. Joyce is, in short, the only other character in the novel who approaches equal footing with Suttree both intellectually and verbally. Together they enjoy caricaturing the pleasant rituals of bourgeois courtship: eating out, going to movies and nightclubs, taking vacations—while always secretly thumbing their noses at the respectable folk around them engaged in identical rites. Their romance is based upon an iconoclastic anti-romanticism. Joyce makes no apologies for her occupation and has no intention of "reforming" for Suttree or anyone else. Suttree, for his part, proudly registers neither moral scruple nor emotional qualm. He accedes unprotesting—not "all that sure what she was talking about" (396)—to serving as something of a pimp for her, handling the proceeds of her business. He allows her to buy him clothes, personal accessories, a radio, "all manner of things that he hardly knew the use of" (395).

For Joyce, it becomes apparent, the anti-romantic trappings of their relationship are more apparent than real; she is not ashamed of what she is and sees no reason to exclude the prospect of love from such a life. Suttree's cynicism is more genuine. In the beginning he can laugh with her at their pantomime of celluloid romantic wholesomeness. Putting her on the bus for one of her periodic out-of-town sorties, Suttree can "[smile] to himself at this emulation of some domestic trial or lovers parted by fate and will they meet again?" But once she is gone the real extent of his dissociation becomes apparent. He wanders up and down the corridors of their hotel, clutching his new pigskin shaving case, "like a ghost through ruins" (397). He becomes "a sitter at windows, a face untrue behind the cataracted glass, . . . eyes vacuous." When he receives the hundred-dollar bills she sends him through the mail, he looks at them "without really understanding them at all" (398). Upon her return they take an apartment together, escalating the level of their involvement, but Suttree can only sit in their rooms "staring into space, detached, a displaced soul musing on the hiatus between himself and the Suttree moving through these strange quarters" (402). When his old friend Michael from the river knocks on his door, this new Suttree is too deep in his hibernational sleep to be awakened (404). He spends most of his days sitting in the apartment and drinking. Once, staring out the window, he catches sight of an old man across the way "washing at a sink, pale arms and small paunch hung in his undershirt," and he self-mockingly toasts this image of himself as domesticated apartment dweller, "a gesture indifferent and almost cynical that as he made it caused him something close to shame" (402).

In the end, despite the anesthesia of one final gift—a Jaguar convertible—and a romantic taxi ride to Gatlinburg, Suttree's catatonia destroys the relationship. He begins to notice Joyce's bovine heaviness, the "[l]ight tracery of old razor scars on her inner wrists," her endless trips through the apartment "always bearing her douchebag about with the hose bobbling obscenely" (404). As with Wanda, the failure of love comes to turn upon the image of his own self in death:

> He surveyed the face in the mirror, letting the jaw go slack, eyes vacant. How would he look in death? For there were days this man so wanted for some end to things that he'd have taken up his membership among the dead, all souls that ever were, eyes bound with night. (405)

By summer things are passing "in monotone," and Suttree falls victim more than ever "to a vast inertia" (407). He makes an oblique effort to share with Joyce the reasons for his disaffection. He takes her to a lake, and they spend a Sunday talking to an old fisherman and scaling rocks out across the water. There Suttree discovers first an arrowhead—something Joyce, a city girl, has never seen before—and then "a huge blue musselshell wasted paper thin" (408). These artifacts he aligns before Joyce as an explanation of himself: his past life as a fisherman, the two aboriginal talismans he has taken up, the idyll-tragedy of the mussel-brailing. But, of course, his presentation of these symbols remains mute and private. He makes no attempt to explain them, or any offer—however inchoate—out of his own emotional life, so their significance is totally lost on her. For Suttree the formal presentation is all, and he is left to ponder his own loneliness and to wonder if Joyce were ever "a child at a fair," seeing in "that shoddy world a vision that child's grace knows" (408–09). At midnight, as they watch a fireworks display in the distance, she begins to cry—perhaps indeed for her lost innocence, perhaps because of Suttree's impenetrable reticence, "he didnt know why" (409). By October their relationship is over, Joyce brutalizing the prized automobile and thrusting great handfuls of money out on the street in her own mute enactment of frustration. As he walks away from her forever, she is hurling some last drunken curses after him, but—as at his son's funeral three years earlier—"all he could make out was his name. He seemed to have heard it all before and he kept on going" (411).

The resolution of the novel, given Suttree's lack of real spiritual progress in it, remains problematical. The book's last two major sections—

Suttree's visit with Mother She and his long, delirious bout with typhoid fever the following spring—make Suttree confront the key facts of his family past. His psychic journey takes him so deeply into his being that he imagines his relation to "the first germ of life adrift on the earth's cooling seas, formless macule of plasm trapped in a vapor drop and all creation yet to come" (430). This sense of his own origins, as opposed to genealogical or theological models, restores the wonder of his life and validates the sacramental communion with pure experience as one's highest priority. No dead brother or hanged relative need be summoned to testify to what it means for Suttree to be. His spiritual hunger, apparent in the novel's rich but adumbrated Christology, can be satisfied by the things of this world. Thus, in the throes of his typhoid delirium, Suttree sees that "there is one Suttree and one Suttree only" (461) and, furthermore, that "all souls are one and all souls lonely" (459). The assertion of the ultimate integrity and sufficiency of the self and of the value of a human community based on an affiliation of such selves is what Suttree—and McCarthy's fiction in general—comes to affirm.

The final pages of the novel, in which Suttree puts behind him the decaying shell of McAnally Flats, conclude things on a decidedly affirmative note. He divests himself "of the little cloaked godlet and his other amulets in a place where they would not be found in his lifetime" and takes up in their stead "for talisman the simple human heart within him" (468). In allegorical terms the novel achieves perfect resolution. The *"hunter with his hounds"* (5)—the familiar death-figure that Suttree frequently imagines on his trail (136, 282)—emerges benignly from the woods as an "enormous lank hound," sniffing the spot where Suttree has been standing (471). The water bearer in his rainy-day Saxon reverie who "does not come, and does not come" (136) is resolved into a new golden-haired waterboy who walks over unbidden from a construction site to offer him a drink. In the eyes of this samaritan Suttree beholds himself "twinned and dark and deep in child's eyes" (471), an image that suggests his new resolution to find his brother among the living rather than the dead. This moment certainly supports the notion, as Vereen Bell expresses it, that "[for] McCarthy a belief in the reality of other people is the first principle of responsible existence" (114). Clearly it is Suttree's sincere wish to live within and be satisfied with the facticity of the world.

But perhaps a cautionary note is in order, too. The two cathartic episodes that conclude the novel are preceded by a curious scene back on Suttree's houseboat. Sitting in his chair one night, he has a conversation with the "quaking ovoid of lamplight on the ceiling." This circle of light, which Suttree has associated earlier with "the zygote dividing" (113) and hence with his dead brother, questions him about the value of his life. While professing to being "not unhappy," Suttree does repent one thing:

> One thing. I spoke with bitterness about my life and I said that I would take my own part against the slander of oblivion and against the monstrous facelessness of it and that I would stand a stone in the very void where all would read my name. Of that vanity I recant all.
>
> Suttree's cameo visage in the black glass watched him across his lamp-lit shoulder. He leaned and blew away the flame, his double, the image overhead. (414)

There is no explicit indication elsewhere in the novel of what Suttree means by taking his own part "against the slander of oblivion" or standing a stone "in the very void where all would read my name." It appears to be yet another emotion "in excess of the facts as they appear." In the novel Suttree's reading habits extend only to the occasional newspaper and religious tract and, once, to some old pulp magazines he finds (358); he is never seen to write. But given his irrevocable disposition toward formalizing experience and the literariness of his perceptions, it seems reasonable to assume that the "vanity" he is recanting is that of the artistic sensibility. It is this doubleness—the coextensiveness of the world of fact and the observational status of the human mind among such facts—that plagues him most, and which will be most difficult to shed. Suttree clearly has learned the precept that the outer world is beautiful and real. Whether this can truly be more than precept for him, however, must remain in doubt.

Notes

[1]McCarthy's first five novels, taken together, are a sort of interior account of the pioneering of America. The first sentence of *The Orchard Keeper* (1965) announces that "the sun was already reddening the western sky." *Blood Meridian or the Evening Redness in the West* (1985), as both its title and subtitle suggest, carries this subject to its eschatological conclusions, marked by the farthermost excursion of these "settlers" to the western edge of the North American continent, circa 1850.

[2]There are, of course, two different grandfathers involved here. Suttree's maternal grandfather, as Uncle John happens to mention, died when Suttree was a baby and "was a fine man"; Suttree claims to remember him (17). This is probably

the grandfather whom Suttree has to be lifted up to see, in whose spectacles he is "twinned" (80, 129), and whose photograph is in Aunt Martha's album. It is the paternal grandfather, on the other hand, whose "favorite saying" was "Blood will tell" (19) and who is associated with the ancestral mansion which lies "stripped and rotting in its copse of trees above the river" (121). He is the one whom Suttree remembers timing the racehorse, and "in the oratory to which he was prone," suggesting that "they had witnessed a thing against which time would not prevail" (136). In a dream he has of this grandfather, the oratory is stripped away: "the old man's talk was filled with incertitude. I saw how all things false fall from the dead. We spoke easily and I was humbly honored to walk with him deep in that world where he was a man like all men" (14). The grandfather that Dr. Neal knew (366) and whom Suttree remembers at the train station with his hat and stogie (367) is also the paternal grandfather.

The conflation of the two grandfather figures in this paragraph does not affect the point being made.

[3]Vereen Bell suggests that the "turkles," through all their manifestations in the novel, function as kind of primal fact, something "loathsome and beyond knowing, akin to what we are but certainly apart from what we wish to be" (72).

[4]In the depths of the cave system, Harrogate even finds indication of a primal murder, along the lines of the one in *The Orchard Keeper*. He holds up some bones he has found: "Bet me, he said softly. They's somebody down here murdered" (262).

WORKS CITED

Bell, Vereen M. *The Achievement of Cormac McCarthy*. Baton Rouge: Louisiana State UP, 1988.

McCarthy, Cormac. *Suttree*. New York: Random, 1979.

_____. *Outer Dark*. New York: Random, 1968.

"What kind of indians was them?"

Some Historical Sources in Cormac McCarthy's *Blood Meridian*

JOHN EMIL SEPICH

A number of critics have remarked that Cormac McCarthy's *Blood Meridian* is based on "history."[1] In fact, the dust jacket of the novel's hardcover edition states flatly that Glanton, Holden and "a number of their followers . . . actually existed, and various accounts of their exploits can be found in chronicles of the period." An under-informed reading of *Blood Meridian* is comparable to the kid's question to Sproule, just after their filibustering expedition to Sonora has been devastated by an Indian attack: "What kind of indians was them?" (56). In some ways, the assailant's name hardly matters. But readers of historical novels expect to know such names, to know background information and relationships.[2] Because McCarthy's story unfolds in a relatively forgotten mid-nineteenth century some thirty years in advance of cowboys, trail drives and rail heads in the Southwest, and because his protagonist aligns himself, for better or worse, with professional scalphunters, a glance at the historical record from which McCarthy draws for settings and characters in *Blood Meridian* can provide context needed for a reader's appreciation of the novel, and can provide a glimpse not before possible of McCarthy at work translating "bare historical facts" into "something rich and strange."[3]

Cormac McCarthy's gangleader is, indeed, an historical figure:

> The identity of [the] regions [between El Paso and Chihuahua City]
> with the names of certain stormy characters supports the law of the survival
> of the fittest. Among the hardiest of these persons were certain Apache
> chiefs and scalp hunters like Captain Santiago Kirker, Captain John Joel
> Glanton, Major Michael H. Chevallie, Major J.S. Gillett, Colonel
> JaquinTerrazas, and Captain Juan de Mata Ortiz. (Smith, "Indians" 38)[4]

John Glanton is found as a character in Jeremiah Clemens's 1856 romance
Bernard Lile (226–29). As recently as 1956 he appears in the pages of
Samuel Chamberlain's long-lost personal narrative of the late 1840s, *My
Confession* (39–40, 259–97).[5] His name punctuates any number of histories
of the mid-nineteenth-century Southwest, and even when nameless his
legend is unmistakable:

> [D]isplaced emigrants . . . [were] . . . turning into horse thieves, gamblers,
> and even murderers. One set up a business killing Apache Indians and
> selling scalps to the Mexican government for two hundred dollars each,
> and collecting two hundred and fifty for each prisoner. If Indians were
> scarce, he even killed Mexicans to profit from their scalps. (Horgan 787)

His tale is unsettling, his misfit excess horrifying.

The Comanches had moved eastward into what would be north central
Texas at least a hundred years before the Anglos began their settlements.
They had come for the buffalo, and for the area's convenient access
to trails southward into Mexico (Smith, "Comanche Invasion" 4–8). John
Hughes describes them as "uncompromising enemies" (131). Annual
trips into Chihuahua, as far south as Zacatecas, provided the Comanches with Mexican horses, livestock and slaves, all of which could be
traded to more northern Indian tribes, and with Anglo traders on the
Arkansas river:

> For [the] decade [of the 1840s] columns in gazettes of north Mexican
> states overflowed with pitiful tales about Indians sweeping away unfor-
> tunate persons and confirm what one historian of the Comanches (Rupert
> N. Richardson) has described as "the most horrendous holocaust ever
> enacted against a civilized people in the Western World." In exchange
> for their staples of trade, they received from the civilized people cloth,
> paints, rifles, powder, lead, knives, guns, and iron from which to make
> arrow and lance points. Eastern tribes moved by the United States
> government to the Indian Territory sold many of their government-issued
> rifles to Comanches for five dollars each. Mexican authorities complained

about American traffic with these Indians and also saw the Yankee image behind Apache raids. (Smith, "Indians" 41)

During the time in which *Blood Meridian* is set, the Comanches were following an established economic pattern based in part on the productivity of the Mexicans, but more recently fueled by what Ralph A. Smith calls "a taste for European manufactures" ("Mexican" 102–03). The Indians at this time also found swelling numbers of westward-bound caravans of gold seekers. "As the Forty-niners swarmed across the vast vacancies of west Texas, there were hardly enough warriors to go around, but the Indians did the best they could" (Sonnichsen 130).

The decade of the 1840s had seen the northern Mexican State of Chihuahua, in its attempt to break the cycle of Indian incursions, hire Anglo aliens to kill the raiders. James (don Santiago) Kirker, in particular, brought hundreds of "proofs" of the deaths of Indians and thousands of head of livestock to Chihuahua City during the first half of the decade.[6] "Proofs": that is, the scalps of the Indians, "receipts." James Hobbs, a professional Indian hunter when with Kirker's gang, took scalps throughout his life. Of one later instance he wrote: "We scalped the Indians, though some of the party said it looked barbarous; but I kept on scalping, saying that business men always took receipts, and I wanted something to show our success" (409).[7] Smith quotes Marcus Webster explaining to "those of posterity who considered scalping a 'grewsome business ... that it was a war necessity' " ("'Long' Webster" 106).[8] In the absence of instantaneous electronic communication, in the absence of a photographic craft stream-lined enough to travel with the band of hunters, "evidence" of the death of an Indian rested on a hunter's producing a scalp as an indication that a most-dear aspect of the Indian had been taken from him. And an Indian's scalp was dearer than is immediately obvious. Richard Dodge described "two ways in which the Indian soul can be prevented from reaching [its] paradise":

> The first is by scalping the head of the dead body. Scalping is annihilation; the soul ceases to exist. This accounts for . . . the care they take to avoid being themselves scalped.
>
> Let the scalp be torn off, and the body becomes mere carrion, not even worthy of burial.
>
> The other method by which an Indian can be cut off from the Happy Hunting Grounds is by strangulation.
>
> Should death ensue by strangulation, the soul can never escape, but must always remain with, or hovering near the remains, even after complete decomposition. (101–03)

The scalp is both a neutral "proof" of an Indian's capture, given the stipulation that the scalp must show the crown of the hair (and in some cases, for further specificity, the ears), and an emotional "proof" of the Indian's death, given the lengths to which an Indian would go to protect against this disfigurement (Smith, "Comanche Sun" 39). Traveling with Wild Tom Hitchcock to meet Glanton's gang, Chamberlain witnessed an incident that demonstrates one Indian's desire to keep his scalp:

> The wounded warrior presented a ghastly sight, he tried to call his pony to him, but the affrightened animal stood at a distance, snorting in terror. The savage then gave a wild startling yell, and by his hands alone, dragged himself to the brink of the deep barranca, then singing his death chant and waving his hand in defiance towards us he plunged into the awful abyss.
>
> "Cincuenta pesos gone to h—l, muchacho," cried Tom. "The doggone mean red nigger done that thar, to cheat us out of his har!" (263–64)

Chihuahua not only paid scalp bounties to licensed alien parties, but also to peon guerilla bands who found that the government payment on a single scalp exceeded the amount which a gang member could earn by hard labor in a year (Smith, "Scalp Hunt" 125). Even for the Anglos, the money was attractive. Pay as a private in the United States Army at about that time averaged about fifteen dollars a month, when bonuses were included (Nevin 24). A group of Indian hunters averaging about fifty men and paid two hundred dollars a scalp would have to bring only four scalps into Chihuahua City in order to exceed the army's rate of pay, and for work not much more hazardous than the army's. Kirker's group was known to have killed as many as two hundred Indians on a single trip, bringing in one hundred and eighty-two scalps. Taking the averages, this is sixty times the amount the men would have earned in other employment. At one point, Chihuahua owed James Kirker $30,000 (Smith, "King" 30). Chihuahua was desperate to have the Comanche invasions stopped. Aliens, peons, even some Indians, were paid by the scalp for their contribution to Chihuahua's protection (Richardson 202).[9]

The *New York Daily Tribune* notes on 1 August 1849 that:

> The Government of Chihuahua has made a bloody contract with an individual named Chevallie, stipulating to give him a bounty of so much per head for every Indian, dead or alive, whom he may secure. The terms of this atrocious bargain are published in the Mexican papers, which, to their credit be it said, denounce them as inhuman and revolting. The Chihuahuans themselves are disgusted with the treaty. (1)

Michael Chevaille had been a Texas Ranger and a volunteer in the Mexican War. On his way to California for the gold, and out of money, he took a scalp contract with Chihuahua on 27 May 1849 (Wharton 34–37). The "inhuman" aspects of such a job apparently did not stop him from applying for a license, nor John Glanton either, as he also contracted with Chihuahua on 27 June of the same year (Smith, "Poor Mexico" 90–91). Thus, Captain Glanton filled a void, did the thing the state hired him to do.

The scalphunters' business, though, is thought to have reached a "peak" in late 1849 and early 1850 (Smith, "Scalp Hunter" 20). A "depletion" of the number of Indians venturing into Mexico, due in part to Chihuahua's willingness to pay for the scalps of women and children (though at a rate below that of warriors), seems to have occurred (Smith, "Scalp Hunter" 21; "Comanche Sun" 44).[10] Chihuahua's desire for an end to Indian incursions, signaled to all in the fabulous amounts of money involved, had stretched to the breaking point the state's ability to account for the origins of scalps. Chihuahua had a large Indian population ante-dating settlement, as well as mestizo population, whose hair was within the averages of Comanche color and texture. Fighting and farming Indians looked about the same, if one limited one's attention only to their hair. Scalpers found Chihuahua's "problem" of identifying hair to be to their benefit. A temptation thus arose in Chihuahua for the Anglo alien, a temptation to which John Glanton, historically, succumbed.

Glanton's "second in command," and *Blood Meridian*'s most imposing character, Judge Holden, is also historically verifiable, but only through Samuel Chamberlain's *My Confession*, a personal narrative unknown until its publication in 1956.[11] Chamberlain, later a decorated Union general in the Civil War, had entered the nineteenth-century Southwest as a private during the war with Mexico, and his adventures during the 1846–1848 conflict comprise the bulk of *My Confession*. War Department records list him as an army "Deserter" as of 22 March 1849 (Chamberlain 4). He had met Holden as he joined Glanton's gang of scalphunters in the process of this desertion (Chamberlain 259–97).[12] Little of Chamberlain's introduction of Holden is a surprise to McCarthy's readers:

> The second in command, now left in charge of [Glanton's] camp, was a man of gigantic size called "Judge" Holden of Texas. Who or what he was no one knew but a cooler blooded villain never went unhung; he stood six feet six in his moccasins, had a large fleshy frame, a dull tallow colored face destitute of hair and all expression. His desires was blood and women, and terrible stories were circulated in camp of horrid

crimes committed by him when bearing another name, in the Cherokee
nation and Texas; and before we left Frontereras a little girl of ten years
was found in the chapperal, foully violated and murdered. The mark of
a huge hand on her little throat pointed him out as the ravisher as no
other man had such a hand, but though all suspected, no one charged
him with the crime.

Holden was by far the best educated man in northern Mexico; he conversed with all in their own language, spoke in several Indian lingos,
at a fandango would take the Harp or Guitar from the hands of the
musicians and charm all with his wonderful performance, and out-waltz
any *poblana* of the ball. He was "plum centre" with rifle or revolver,
a daring horseman, acquainted with the nature of all the strange plants
and their botanical names, great in Geology and Mineralogy, in short
another Admirable Crichton, and with all an arrant coward. Not but that
he possessed enough courage to fight Indians and Mexicans or anyone
where he had the advantage in strength, skill and weapons, but where
the combat would be equal, he would avoid it if possible. I hated him
at first sight, and he knew it, yet nothing could be more gentle and kind
than his deportment towards me; he would often seek conversation with
me and speak of Massachusetts and to my astonishment I found he knew
more about Boston than I did. (271–72)

Interestingly, the complete book version of *My Confession* includes
a black and white illustration of Chamberlain and Holden in the desert
after the massacre—Holden with what appear to be eyebrows and a mous-
tache (293), suggesting that it is Chamberlain's description of Holden's
"face destitute of hair" which has been generalized by McCarthy into
Holden's total, infant-like baldness. The cowardice Chamberlain observes
in the man " 'Judge' Holden" is not reflected in McCarthy's character
Judge Holden, though *Blood Meridian*'s sustained interest in "deceptions,"
if they are viewed as non-confrontational winning, may in fact be related
to "cowardice."

Of particular note in Chamberlain's introduction of his Judge are the
words that "terrible stories were circulated in camp of horrid crimes committed by him when bearing another name, in the Cherokee nation and
Texas." "When bearing another name" seems a particularly apt point of
departure for McCarthy's enhancement of the historical Judge Holden.
Holden's ability to appear, disappear, reappear, in McCarthy's novel, an
ability which tends to reinforce the reader's belief in his claims of a life
which will never end, is first suggested in Chamberlain's mention of the
judge's routine change-of-name.[13]

The reader's next view of Holden in *M   Confession* seems to inform at least two incidents in the novel:

Glanton proved that he was well fitted to be the master spirit of the fiendish band. Drinking deeply, he swore with the most fearful oaths that we were all sinners bound to eternal Perdition, that it was his mission to save us. He then knelt down and in well chosen words prayed with all the fervor of a hard shell Baptist for the salvation of all. Suddenly he sprang up and drawing his revolver opened fire on us right and left. One of the Canadians received a shot in the leg, as a gentle reminder to flee from the wrath to come. Judge Holden seized the madman in his powerful arms, laid him down and soothed him as a mother would a fretful child, and Glanton soon sank into a drunken sleep. (274)

In *Blood Meridian*, at Jesus Maria, Glanton

in his drunkenness was taken with a kind of fit and he lurched crazed and disheveled into the little courtyard and began to open fire with his pistols. In the afternoon he lay bound to his bed like a madman while the judge sat with him and cooled his brow with rags of water and spoke to him in a low voice. . . . After a while Glanton slept and the judge rose and went out. (191)

A second scene in the novel probably shaped by this passage from Chamberlain occurs as the idiot James Robert nearly drowns at the Yuma crossing. There, the judge

stepped into the river and seized up the drowning idiot, snatching it aloft by the heels like a great midwife and slapping it on the back to let the water out. A birth scene or a baptism or some ritual not yet inaugurated into any canon. He twisted the water from its hair and he gathered the naked and sobbing fool into his arms and carried it up into the camp and restored it among its fellows. (259)

When the novel's gang rides through "sandstone cities in the dusk" (113) on their way to the mines of Santa Rita del Cobre, another set of Chamberlain influences may be discerned. Riding with the gang in search of Cibola, Chamberlain found the "golden mirage" of El Dorado, which "for three hundred years haunted the misty frontiers of Spanish America" (Lister 133):

We sat in silence gazing on this realization of our hopes, when the mocking laughter of Judge Holden broke the spell. "So, Glanton, this is El Dorado, is it? The city of gold and fair women! I wish you joy of the discovery— a city of sandstone built by dame nature!" (275)

> Looking back, the summit of the hill from which we first espied this
> El Dorado appeared crowned with a frowning fortress with plumed
> warriors on its walls! The illusion was perfect, yet it was only walls of
> marl with yuccas and cactus growing behind them.
>   Judge Holden mounted a rock for a rostrum and gave us a scientific
> lecture on Geology. The Scalp Hunters, grouped in easy attitudes, listened
> to the "Literati" with marked attention. The whole formed an assemblage
> worthy of the pencil of Salvator Rosa. Holden's lecture no doubt was
> very learned, but hardly true, for one statement he made was "that *millions*
> of years had witnessed the operation producing the result around us,"
> which Glanton with recollections of the Bible teaching his young mind
> had undergone said "was a d—d lie." (276)

The sequence of events and the characters' responses are similar in
McCarthy's novel. The "sandstone cities in the dusk" in McCarthy almost
immediately precede the judge's disquisition on "geological evidence"
(108, 113, 116). And in both stories the judge's remarks are rejected on
scriptural grounds, although in his phrase "a few would quote him scripture," McCarthy declines to make the historical Glanton's religious upbringing a part of his fictional character's background.

Another of Chamberlain's Holden stories contributes to *Blood Meridian*'s "geological evidence" section. On the gang's trip to the junction
of the Colorado and Gila rivers, as they follow the Colorado River west,
Holden advises Glanton that a particular route will be best. Once started
on this path Chamberlain writes:

> Judge Holden rode with me and stated that he knew that we would
> be obliged to retrace our steps, but that Glanton's plan gave him an
> opportunity of seeing the greatest natural wonder of the world, the
> unexplored Great Canyon of the Colorado, reported by hunters as a "cut
> through the plain from one to five miles in depth, and extending some
> three hundred miles." As we rode along Holden, in spite of my re-
> pugnance of the man, interested me greatly by his description of the
> great cut and how it might have been formed. He also was fluent regard-
> ing the ancient races of Indians that at a remote period covered the
> desert with fields of corn, wheat, barley and melons, and built large
> cities with canals bringing water from rivers hundreds of miles distant.
> To my question "how he knew all this," this encyclopaedian Scalp
> Hunter replied, "Nature, these rocks, this little broken piece of clay
> (holding up a little fragment of painted pottery such are found all over
> the desert), the ruins scattered all over the land, tell me the story of
> the past." (283–84)

The judge's statement in McCarthy that "Books lie," but that God's "words" are spoken "in stones and trees, the bones of things" (116) echoes Chamberlain's story.

Chamberlain's depiction of Holden as a child molester, quoted in his introduction of the judge, is not his only notice of this depravity:

> While I was sketching an uproar arose in the village caused by Holden's seizing hold of one of the girls and proceeding to take gross liberties with her person. A dozen cocked rifles brought to bear on him drove the brute from his prey, but the whole village was in ferment, and it seemed as if we stood a chance of being wiped out. However, Holden made some explanation to the crowd in Spanish that appeased them. (287)

Chamberlain's closing thought, that Holden appeases his adversary in Spanish, and his remark that Holden "conversed with all in their own language" (271), are reflected throughout the novel, especially in McCarthy's scene of the judge's convincing Sergeant Aguilar, in Spanish, that the sale of guns from Speyer to the gang is not to be disturbed (84–85), and in his scene of Governor Angel Trias's banquet for the Anglos.

Of Angel Trias, governor of the Mexican State of Chihuahua who hired Glanton for scalp hunting, McCarthy writes that he "had been sent abroad as a young man for his education and was widely read in the classics and was a student of languages" (168). A similar description of Trias is given by John Russell Bartlett, who was in charge of a United States Boundary Commission in 1851–53 which surveyed the eventual border between the United States and Mexico in advance of the Gadsden Purchase, and who published a thousand pages on his experiences:

> General Trias, who was for several years Governor of the State of Chihuahua, is a fine gentleman of large wealth and fine accomplishments. After receiving his education he went to Europe, where he spent eight years travelling in various parts, although he remained most of the time in England and France. He is well versed in several of the European languages, and speaks English with great correctness. Of English literature he told me he was very fond; and he considered that no native appreciated the beauties of Shakspeare and Milton better than he. With Addison and the belles-lettres writers of England he was also familiar. (2:426)[14]

It is little wonder that the judge sits at Trias's right hand "and they at once fell into conversation in a tongue none other in the room spoke at all saving for random vile epithets drifted down from the north" (169). Tobin says in the novel that Holden "speaks dutch" and that "Him and the governor they sat up till breakfast and it was Paris this and London that in five languages, you'd have give something to of heard them" (123).

McCarthy stresses the judge's erudition by contrasting with it the ignorance of the rest of the scalphunters, departing from his historical source to do so. At the fictional banquet:

> Patriotic toasts were drunk, the governor's aides raising their glasses to Washington and Franklin and the Americans responding with yet more of their own country's heroes, ignorant alike of diplomacy and any name at all from the pantheon of their sister republic. (169)

This detail springs from Bartlett's mention that at a dinner given in his Boundary Commission's honor, hosted by General Trias:

> Patriotic toasts were drunk, and among those given by the Mexicans were Washington and Franklin. In return we gave the heroes of the Mexican revolution, Iturbide, Hildalgo, Allende, and Jiminez. (2:427)

McCarthy's adaptation of Bartlett's detail underscores the gang's ethnocentrism, and so distances his reader from them.

John Woodhouse Audubon, a son of artist John James Audubon, traveled the Southwest at mid-century, keeping a journal, and is the apparent source for the Tarot reading tent show which travels with McCarthy's gang to Janos (89–99). Audubon's 13 June 1849 entry at Cerro Gordo describes a similar troupe:

> Here we were visited by a member of a Mexican travelling circus, who asked our protection as far as El Valle, which we promised them. The party consisted of five, one woman and four men. The lady rode as we used to say in Louisiana "leg of a side," on a small pacing pony; the two horses of the ring carried only their saddles, two pack mules, four small trunks, and four jaded horses the rest of the plunder. The four men went on foot, driving the packs and continually refitting and repacking, the other three riding. One man had two Chihuahua dogs about six inches long, stuffed in his shirt bosom, another a size larger on the pommel of his saddle. A second man was in grand Spanish costume, on a small but blooded grey horse, with a large dragoon sword on his left, and a Mexican musket made about 1700, which would have added to an antiquary's armory. They told us they had everything they owned with them, so that if alone, and attacked by the Apaches, whom we hear of continually but never see, their loss would be a very serious one to them. (100–01)

The Mexican party traveled with Audubon for several days, and he later writes:

> Our circus party left us [at El Valle on 17 June]: the woman who was really the queen of the show came to thank us for our protection, which she did most gracefully, and gave us a courteous invitation to her show and fandango, the termination to every Mexican entertainment, wedding, christening, and even battle. I could not go, but several of the party did, and pronounced the senoritas quite good looking. (102)

Audubon's account contains none of the ominous quality of Black John Jackson's performance with the Gypsies in *Blood Meridian* (99), but the relentless winds that contribute so dramatically to the atmosphere of McCarthy's scene may derive from Bartlett's note that during his survey expedition "one of the tents was hurled from its fastenings [by a storm] and blown more than a hundred yards before it was arrested" (2:302).

The germ of the idea for McCarthy's scene of the "conducta" óf quicksilver heading east into Jesus Maria, which Glanton's gang decimates (194-95), may also be found in Audubon. His entry for 14 July reads:

> Everything used [in Jesus Maria] is brought from the Pacific side, quicksilver, irons, wines and liquors; even flour is sometimes brought, but most of that comes from Sonora which is ten days' travel to the east. (121)

West of Jesus Maria on 28 July, Audubon writes that his party was delayed by an unusually long quicksilver train:

> We did not leave camp until nearly noon, waiting for a train of one hundred and eighty-two mules packed with nothing but flasks of quicksilver; the usual length of trains is about forty to fifty, with six or eight men. (129)

In the novel, Glanton displays no such patience. Angry at his losses in Jesus Maria, on treacherous mountain trails Glanton simply shoves past the pack-mules and "methodically rode them from the escarpment, the animals dropping silently as martyrs" (195).

Grannyrat's story of the Lipan mummy burials in *Blood Meridian* (77–78) can be found in the memoirs of the German doctor Adolphus Wislizenus, who traveled in the Southwest during the years of the Mexican War. Grannyrat, the veteran, recalls:

> There was a cave down there [towards Saltillo which] had been a Lipan burial. Must of been a thousand indians in there all settin around. Had on their best robes and blankets and all. Had their bows and their knives, whatever. Beads. The Mexicans carried everything off. Stripped em

naked. Took it all. They carried off whole indians to their homes and
set em in the corner all dressed up but they begun to come apart when
they got out of that cave air and they had to be thowed out. Towards
the last of it they was some Americans went in there and scalped what
was left of em and tried to sell the scalps in Durango. I dont know if
they had any luck about it or not. I expect some of them injins had been
dead a hundred year. (77–78)

Wislizenus's description of a find in a cave, in the area between Chihuahua and Saltillo, is similar in detail if not in tone:

On the right hand, or south of us, a chain of limestone mountains was
running parallel with the road. At the foot of a hill belonging to that
chain, Senor de Gaba pointed out a place to me where some years ago
a remarkable discovery had been made. In the year 1838, a Mexican,
Don Juan Flores, perceived there the hidden entrance to a cave. He
entered; but seeing inside a council of Indian warriors sitting together
in the deepest silence, he retreated and told it to his companions, who,
well prepared, entered the cave together, and discovered about 1,000 (?)
well preserved Indian corpses, squatted together on the ground, with their
hands folded below the knees. They were dressed in fine blankets,
made of the fibres of lechuguilla, with sandals, made of a species
of liana, on their feet, polished bones, &c. This is the very insufficient
account of the mysterious burying place. The Mexicans suppose that
it belonged to the Lipans, an old Indian tribe, which from time imme-
morial has roved and is yet roving over the Bolson de Mapimi. I
had already heard in Chihuahua of this discovery, and was fortunate
enough there to secure a skull that a gentleman had taken from
the cave. At present, I was told, the place is pilfered of everything;
nevertheless, had I been at leisure, I would have made an excursion
to it. (69–70)

McCarthy's note that some of the mummies had been scalped foreshadows
the introduction of Glanton's hunters only a few pages later in his book.

John Hughes, a soldier during the Mexican War, kept a journal which
appears in several places to be another of *Blood Meridian*'s sources, most
strikingly in McCarthy's scene of the kid's experience in the mountains
as he and Tate attempt escape from Elias's scouts. McCarthy's Anglos
have "rolled in their blankets" to sleep in the foot-deep and still falling
snow that night. The Mexican scouts are "five men and they came up
through the evergreens in the dark and all but stumbled upon the sleepers, two mounds in the snow one of which broke open and up out of
which a figure sat suddenly like some terrible hatching" (211). In Hughes,

McCarthy could have found a mountain setting with men sleeping in falling snow, a consequent invisibility of the sleepers and a hint toward his scene's birth imagery:

> Having no tents, the soldiers quartered on the naked earth, in the open air; but so much snow fell that night, that at dawn it was not possible to distinguish where they lay, until they broke the snow which covered them, and came out as though they were rising from their graves; for in less than twelve hours the snow had fallen thirteen inches deep in the valleys, and thirty-six in the mountains. (70)

The Englishman George Frederick Ruxton, again a mid-nineteenth-century witness in the Southwest, writes, "The stranger in Mexico is perpetually annoyed by the religious processions which perambulate the streets at all hours" (*Adventures* 35). He continues:

> A coach, with an eye painted on the panels, and drawn by six mules, conveys the host to the houses of dying Catholics who are rich enough to pay for the privilege: before this equipage a bell tinkles, which warns the orthodox to fall on their knees; and woe to the unfortunate who neglects this ceremony, either from ignorance or design. On one occasion, being suddenly surprised by the approach of one of these processions, I had but just time to doff my hat and run behind a corner of a building, when I was spied by a fat priest, who, shouldering an image, brought up the rear of the procession.

This passage presumably informs McCarthy's paragraph of the kid and other Chihuahua prisoners who observed, as they moved about their work in the streets of the city:

> A small bell was ringing and a coach was coming up the street. They stood along the curb and took off their hats. The guidon passed ringing the bell and then the coach. It had an eye painted on the side and four mules to draw it, taking the host to some soul. A fat priest tottered after carrying an image. The guards were going among the prisoners snatching the hats from the heads of the newcomers and pressing them into their infidel hands. (75)

The "annoyance" Ruxton describes may also contribute to the tension resulting in McCarthy's scene of the bar fight at Nacori (178–80), as this event is prefaced by a Mexican religious procession (177–78).

McCarthy's use of the unusual dialect word "thrapple" in the scene of Glanton's death (275) links him to Mayne Reid's 1850s romance *The Scalp-Hunters*. In a scene late in Reid's book, a Coco Indian, El Sol, a member of scalp-hunter Seguin's band, has killed an attacking Indian. A witness, one of the white scalpers, answers the main character's question about the outcome of the fight:

> "How was it?"
> " 'Ee know, the Injun—that are, the Coco—fit wi' a hatchet."
> "Yes."
> "Wal, then; that ur's a desprit weepun, for them as knows how to use it; an' *he* diz; that Injun diz. T'other had a hatchet, too, but he didn't keep it long. 'Twur clinked out of his hands in a minnit, an' then the Coco got a down blow at him. Wagh! it *wur* a down blow, an' it wan't nuthin' else. It split the niggur's head clur down to the thrapple. 'Twus sep'rated into two halves as ef't had been clove wi' a broad-axe! Ef'ee had 'a seed the varmint when he kim to the ground, 'ee'd 'a thort he wur double-headed." (212–13)

"Hack away you mean red nigger," Glanton says in McCarthy, "and the old man raised the axe and split the head of John Joel Glanton to the thrapple" (275).[15] In addition to the obvious correspondences between passages, it is of note that Reid's "Coco" Indians are the Coco-Maricopas who inhabit the Gila River area only a short distance from McCarthy's Yumas (Eccleston 211; Chamberlain 287).

Although McCarthy worked extensively with nineteenth-century eyewitness sources, the twentieth-century historian J. Frank Dobie seems to have recorded the information on which one of McCarthy's characters' conversations is based. Relating the words of a western treasure hunter, Dobie writes:

> I had my hat over my face so as to shut out the fierce light and was dozing off when all at once something aroused me. I think it was the sudden ceasing of the horses to graze. A grazing horse makes a kind of musical noise cropping grass and grinding it, and men out, with their lives depending on horses, often notice that music or the absence of it. Anyhow, when I raised up, I saw every animal with head up and ears pointed to the range of mountains we had last crossed. I looked too and saw a thin, stringy cloud of dust. (282–83)

McCarthy makes from Dobie's observation on men and horses an analogy expressing the ex-priest Tobin's continuing sense of God's presence, no matter that his vocation in America is scalp-hunting. The kid asserts that he has never heard God's voice, and Tobin contradicts him:

> At night, said Tobin, when the horses are grazing and the company is asleep, who hears them grazing?

Dont nobody hear them if they're asleep.
Aye. And if they cease their grazing who is it that wakes?
Every man.
Aye, said the ex-priest. Every man. (124)

A bare fraction of the correspondences found between McCarthy's
Blood Meridian and the literature, historical and contemporary, on the
American Southwest, these few items nevertheless allow the "history"
mentioned on his book's dust wrapper to be more knowledgeably
approached. The sense of McCarthy's novel is fully available, for me, only
with the recognition that the book is founded to a remarkable degree on
the reports of first-hand observers traveling in the mid-nineteenth-
century Southwest.

Many of the novel's scenes (the lottery of arrows, the bull's goring of
James Miller's horse, Jackson's death in the river) are essentially found
objects: available for explication (Shelby as articulate and romantic,
the bull as a mythic creature, death by water), and yet an explication
of any particular matter in the novel vies with the sense that McCarthy
may have included many of the book's details out of a concern for
(and, in fact, some need of) historical confirmation. If its historical
base is overlooked, McCarthy's novel might appear as nothing more
than three hundred pages of circumstantial evidence (all gory) to
assert Judge Holden's claim of war's dominance as a metaphor in the
lives of men.

Nothing can "be said to occur unobserved" (153) the lawyer in Judge
Holden, or, more relevantly here, a historian, might say. The wounded
Shelby wants to hide from his fate at the hands of Elias's troops (208).
When Tobin and the kid cross the desert west of the massacre, late in
the book, and the "path" of their footprints, by which Holden trails
them, is taken by the wind (296–97), yet their "fates" unshakably find
all three.[16] Fundamentally—and even to account for Holden's view that
the kid's negligence contributes to his fellow gang members' deaths at
the ferry (306–07)—observers, arriving by separate routes, are essential
to the novel. Chamberlain, Bartlett, Audubon, Wislizenus, Reid, Ober,
Smith, Dobie and what appear to be a host of sources, are such observers.
McCarthy has gone out of his way to lock a great deal of *Blood Meridian*
to them. Of the items here, source to novel, McCarthy's character
Holden has undergone a minimal departure from the "history" which
Chamberlain's narrative provides. Yet it is also in this diabolical charac-

ter, ubiquitous, immortal, laced with arcane allusion, that McCarthy's genius at ordering his universal romance *Blood Meridian* is most apparent.

NOTES

[1]Arnold notes that both Glanton and Holden are "apparently historical figures" (Review 103). Mills writes that in the novel "all but a handful of the named characters are historical figures" (10), and Winchell proposes that "*Blood Meridian* is loosely based on history" (308; see also Witek 60). Bell, with a textual approach, does not touch on this point. Some of this "history" is presented in my masters thesis "Notes Toward an Explication of Cormac McCarthy's *Blood Meridian*." A revised and much expanded version of that work exists as "Notes on *Blood Meridian*." Good historical information on Glanton is contained in the thirty-page "Appendix C" of Thomas D. Young, Jr.'s dissertation "Cormac McCarthy and the Geology of Being."

[2]A grasp of what is historically verifiable in *Blood Meridian* brings to light, for instance, the fact that eight of its characters are named after Tennesseeans: The Reverend Robert Green (Carroll 113); Governor Peter Burnett (Melendy 25; Burnett 1); Captain John Glanton (Woodward, "Side Lights" 7; Martin 142) though Glanton's birth is more properly placed in South Carolina (Chamberlain 268; Smith, "John Joel Glanton" 14); Doctor Able Lincoln (Woodward, *Feud* 26) though his birth is better placed in New York (Martin 138–39); Ben McCulloch (Samuel Reid 23); Lt. Cave Couts (Martin 128); General Patterson [also known as Anderson] (Foreman 336; Woodward, *Feud* 24); and Sarah Bourdette (Woodward, "Great Western" 4). Both filibustering William Walker and freebooting Henry Alexander Crabb, sources and analogs for the novel's Captain White, are also natives of Tennessee (Rosengarten ix; Forbes 7). Information of this sort necessarily quali-fies the assertions that *Blood Meridian* is McCarthy's first novel set outside the South (Arnold, "Cormac McCarthy" 1036; Winchell 307), in that McCarthy's story surrounds his Tennessee "kid" with a good many others claimed to have his same Old South birthplace. No other state, in fact, is as well represented in this novel of the opening years of the American Southwest.

[3]Dust jacket, *Blood Meridian*.

[4]Much of the supporting documentation for this section is based on the works of historian Ralph A. Smith. His works are, of those I have seen, the only articles routinely based on both Mexican and United States documents of the period. This attention to the Mexican perspective, when taken with some evidence that McCarthy had seen at least one of Smith's bibliographies (that of "John Joel Glanton"), makes him the authority of choice here.

[5]Besides Chamberlain, the best sources of information on Glanton, as McCarthy

has written him, are Douglas Martin's *Yuma Crossing* (138–50) and Arthur Woodward's *Feud on the Colorado* (20–30). McCarthy read scores of books in order to write *Blood Meridian*; as an abbreviation of several hundred pages of the "Notes on *Blood Meridian*" manuscript: Chamberlain, himself youthful and compassionate (280, 288–89, 293), appears to be a historical analog, in many instances, of McCarthy's "kid," as is Ruxton's character La Bonte (*Life* 73, 111). The historical massacre survivor William Carr's deposition supplies McCarthy with some details: for instance, the historical Carr, *Blood Meridian's* "Billy Carr" (263), takes an arrow in his leg escaping the ferry massacre, a wound analogous to the kid's (277, 308). Theodoro Goodman's letter (also quoted in Woodward, *Feud*) supplies information on David Brown's escape from the San Diego jail. George Evans notes Glanton's murder of a lone and "very aged squaw" (133; *Blood Meridian* 97–98). Jay Wagoner (306) provides McCarthy with historical verification for his unusual choice of an axe as the weapon with which to kill Glanton. And, among other parallels, Chamberlain's narrative (280–81) is McCarthy's source for his lottery of arrows scene (205–09). Glanton's use of a Bowie knife in Chamberlain (39–40) may inform *Blood Meridian's* scene of White John Jackson's death, and the knifing of Grimley at Nacori. Frederick Ober (287, ills. 286) supplies color-detail for McCarthy's "Serenos" (100, 103). John Russell Bartlett's sentences on floating mountains and "*playas*" (1:218, 2:371) are likely the origin of McCarthy's similar sentence (108, see also 46). Bartlett's Tucson meteorite (2:297–98, illus. facing 298) partly informs McCarthy's scene at Pacheco's blacksmith shop (240). David Lavender's book on western traders (98–99) probably assists McCarthy's description of Mexican "ciboleros" (120).

[6]McGaw's is the only book-length biography of Kirker; Smith ("King") and Brandes provide article-length information.

[7]General Elias's troops had nine pairs of ears tacked to their cannon trucks when they met John Coffee Hays in 1849 (Greer 243). The tradition of "trophies and verifications" continues into the present day. Drinnon writes that "Once bagged, [the Viet Cong] were statistics fed into Westmoreland's computer, with their severed ears on occasion tied to the antenna of a troop carrier as trophies and verifications of the body count" (451). Also see McWhiney on southern troops beheading enemy dead during the Civil War (182).

[8]Also worth considering is a twentieth-century interest in translating dead enemies into numbers (nineteenth-century "scalps") in war. Lifton writes: "When at some future moment, ethically sensitive historians get around to telling the story of the Vietnam war . . . I have no doubt that they will select the phenomenon of the 'body count' as the perfect symbol of America's descent into evil. What better represents the numbing, brutalization, illusion (most of the bodies, after all, turn out to be those of civilians), grotesque competition (companies and individuals vie for the highest body counts), and equally grotesque technicizing (progress lies in the *count*) characteristic of the overall American crime of war

in Vietnam" (Falk 25). The literature of "atrocities" in Vietnam seems consistent, in its language, with that of Glanton's "atrocities."

⁹"Many of the most intelligent backed [the payment-for-scalps] scheme for dealing with the Indians, but others looked upon it with horror. The national government never sanctioned it. In this it followed a course similar to that of the government of the United States, which never bought Indian scalps; although many American states, counties, and cities did" (Smith, "Mexican" 102). Bourke notes an 1870s instance in which Indians found it necessary to carry the heads of slain criminals to General Cook for identification (220).

¹⁰In *Blood Meridian* Glanton must deal with an absence of raiding Indians (148).

¹¹*Life* published an abridged version of Chamberlain in three installments in the summer of 1956, of interest to the reader for a color plate published of Chamberlain's watercolor of Sarah Borginnis (6 August: 72). The complete narrative, published in book form in the same year, includes the illustration in black and white (242).

¹²*My Confession* concludes as Chamberlain exits the desert west of the Yuma Crossing within days after the massacre.

¹³McCarthy's weaving of Tarot and Masonic symbolism into his story, and particularly into his Holden character, is explored in my essay, "The Dance of History in Cormac McCarthy's *Blood Meridian*."

¹⁴Bartlett's *Narrative* was published as two volumes in one binding. Page citations here refer first to volume (1 or 2) and then page.

¹⁵The "mean red nigger" phrase McCarthy includes in this sentence is present in Chamberlain (264).

¹⁶The fight in the novel's first chapter between the kid and Toadvine in Nacogdoches, on batboard walkways laid on mud, is, for me, a graphic representation of Holden's claim of intersecting, conflict-ridden destinies (330). Not all dancers take or long hold the center stage. The novel's dust jacket speaks of paths crossing and of fates: the setting for their fistfight is a very simple representation of that concept. Holden's murder of the kid at the jakes in the book's last chapter also occurs at the end of just such a path.

Works Cited

Arnold, Edwin T. "Cormac McCarthy." *Popular World Fiction 1900–Present*. Washington: Beacham, 1987. 1036–43.

_____. Rev. of *Blood Meridian*, by Cormac McCarthy. *Appalachian Journal* 13 (Fall 1985): 103–04.

Audubon, John Woodhouse. *Audubon's Western Journal: 1849–1850*. 1906. Glorietta, NM: Rio Grande P, 1969.

Bartlett, John Russell. *Personal Narrative of Explorations and Incidents In Texas,*

New Mexico, California, Sonora, and Chihuahua. New York: Appleton, 1856.

Bell, Vereen M. *The Achievement of Cormac McCarthy*. Baton Rouge: Louisiana State UP, 1988.

Bourke, John G. *On the Border with Crook*. 2nd ed. New York: Scribner's, 1896.

Brandes, Ray. "Don Santiago Kirker, King of the Scalp Hunters." *The Smoke Signal*. Tucson, Westerners. No. 6 (Fall 1962): 2–8.

Burnett, Peter H. *An Old California Pioneer*. Oakland: Biobooks, 1946.

Carr, William. "Depredations by the Yumas: Declarations Taken in Relation to the Massacre of Dr. Lincoln and His Party on the Colorado River.—Deposition of William Carr." *Annual Publication of the Historical Society of Southern California and the Pioneers of Los Angeles County, 1903*. 52–56.

Carroll, J.M. *A History of Texas Baptists, Comprising a Detailed Account of Their Activities, Their Progress and Their Achievements*. Ed. J.B. Cranfill. Dallas: Baptist Standard, 1923.

Chamberlain, Samuel E. "My Confession." *Life* 23 July 1956: 68–91; 30 July 1956: 52–71; 6 Aug. 1956: 64–86.

———. *My Confession*. 1956. Lincoln: U of Nebraska P, 1987.

Clemens, Jeremiah. *Bernard Lile: An Historical Romance, Embracing the Periods of the Texas Revolution and the Mexican War*. Philadelphia: Lippincott, 1856.

Dobie, J. Frank. *Apache Gold and Yaqui Silver*. New York: Bramhall, 1939.

Dodge, Richard Irving. *Our Wild Indians: Thirty-Three Years' Personal Experience*. Hartford, CT: Worthington, 1883.

Drinnon, Richard. *Facing West: The Metaphysics of Indian-Hating and Empire-Building*. Minneapolis: U of Minnesota P, 1980.

Eccleston, Robert. *Overland to California on the Southwestern Trail: The Diary of Robert Eccleston*. Ed. George P. Hammond and Edward H. Howes. Berkeley: U of California P, 1950.

Evans, George W.B. *Mexico Gold Trail: The Journal of a Forty-Niner*. Ed. Glenn S. Dumke. San Marino, CA: Huntington, 1945.

Falk, Richard A., Gabriel Kolko, and Robert Jay Lifton. *Crimes of War*. New York: Random, 1971.

Forbes, Robert H. *Crabb's Filibustering Expedition into Sonora, 1857: An Historical Account*. [Tucson]: Arizona Silhouettes, 1952.

Foreman, Grant. *Marcy & the Gold Seekers: The Journal of Captain R.B. Marcy, With an Account of the Gold Rush Over the Southern Route*. Norman: U of Oklahoma P, 1939.

Goodman, Theodoro. "Los Angeles Correspondence." *Daily Alta California* 8 Jan. 1851.

Greer, James Kimmins. *Colonel Jack Hays*. New York: Dutton, 1952.

Hobbs, James. *Wild Life in the Far West: Personal Adventures of a Border Mountain Man*. Hartford: Wiley, Waterman & Eaton, 1872.

Horgan, Paul. *The Great River: The Rio Grande in North American History:*

Mexico and the United States. Vol. 2. New York: Rinehart, 1954.

Hughes, John T. *Doniphan's Expedition: Containing an Account of the Conquest of New Mexico.* Rpt. New York: Arno, 1973.

Lavender, David. *Bent's Fort.* New York: Doubleday, 1954.

Lister, Florence C., and Robert H. Lister. *Chihuahua: Storehouse of Storms.* Albuquerque: U of New Mexico P, 1966.

Martin, Douglas D. *Yuma Crossing.* Albuquerque: U of New Mexico P, 1954.

McCarthy, Cormac. *Blood Meridian or the Evening Redness in the West.* New York: Random, 1985.

McGaw, William Cochran. *Savage Scene: the Life and Times of James Kirker, Frontier King.* New York: Hastings, 1972.

McWhiney, Grady, and Perry D. Jamieson. *Attack and Die: Civil War Military Tactics and the Southern Heritage.* University: U of Alabama P, 1982.

Melendy, H. Brett, and Benjamin F. Gilbert. *The Governors of California: Peter H. Burnett to Edmund G. Brown.* Georgetown, CA: Talisman, 1965.

Mills, Jerry Leath. "Cormac McCarthy: A Great Tragic Writer." *Independent Weekly* 7.13 (1989): 9–10.

Nevin, David. *The Old West: the Soldiers.* Alexandria, VA: Time-Life, 1974.

New York Daily Tribune 1 Aug. 1849: 1.

Ober, Frederick A. *Travels in Mexico, and Life Among the Mexicans.* Boston: Estes and Lauriat, 1885.

Reid, Mayne. *The Scalp-Hunters: Or, Romantic Adventures in Northern Mexico.* London: Henry Lea, 185[ ].

Reid, Samuel C., Jr. *The Scouting Expeditions of McCulloch's Texas Rangers: Or, the Summer and Fall Campaign of the Army of the United States in Mexico 1846.* Philadelphia: Zieber, 1847.

Richardson, Rupert Norval. *The Comanche Barrier to South Plains Settlement: A Century and a Half of Savage Resistance to the Advancing White Frontier.* Glendale, CA: Clark, 1933.

Rosengarten, Frederic, Jr. *Freebooters Must Die!* Wayne, PA: Haverford, 1976.

Ruxton, George F. *Adventures in Mexico and the Rocky Mountains.* London: Murray, 1861.

———. *Life in the Far West.* Rpt. Norman: U of Oklahoma P, 1951.

Sepich, John Emil. "The Dance of History in Cormac McCarthy's *Blood Meridian.*" *Southern Literary Journal* 24 (Fall 1991): 16–31.

———. "Notes on *Blood Meridian.*" Unpublished ms. Southwestern Writers Collection. Southwest Texas State U, San Marcos; Southern Historical Collection. U of North Carolina Library, Chapel Hill.

———. "Notes Toward an Explication of Cormac McCarthy's *Blood Meridian.*" Thesis. U of North Carolina, Chapel Hill, 1989.

Smith, Ralph A. "The Comanche Invasion of Mexico in the Fall of 1845." *West Texas Historical Association Year Book* 35 (Oct. 1959): 3–28.

_____. "The Comanche Sun Over Mexico." *West Texas Historical Association Year Book* 46 (1970): 25–62.

_____. "Indians in American-Mexican Relations Before the War of 1846." *Hispanic American Historical Review* 43 (Feb. 1963): 34–64.

_____. "John Joel Glanton, Lord of the Scalp Range." *Smoke Signal*. Tucson, Westerners. No. 6 (Fall 1962): 9–16.

_____. "The 'King of New Mexico' and the Doniphan Expedition." *New Mexico Historical Review* 38 (Jan. 1963): 29–55.

_____. " 'Long' Webster and 'The Vile Industry of Selling Scalps.' " *West Texas Historical Association Year Book* 37 (Oct. 1961): 99–120.

_____. "Mexican and Anglo-Saxon Traffic in Scalps, Slaves, and Livestock, 1835–1841." *West Texas Historical Association Year Book* 36 (Oct. 1960): 98–115.

_____. "Poor Mexico, So Far from God and So Close to the Tejanos." *West Texas Historical Association Year Book* 44 (Oct. 1968): 78–105.

_____. "The Scalp Hunt in Chihuahua—1849." *New Mexico Historical Review* 40 (Apr. 1965): 116–40.

_____. "The Scalp Hunter in the Borderlands 1835–1850." *Arizona and the West* 6 (Spring 1964): 5–22.

Sonnichsen, C.L. *Pass of the North: Four Centuries on the Rio Grande—1529–1917*. Vol. 1. El Paso: Texas Western, 1968.

Wagoner, Jay J. *Early Arizona: A Panoramic History of a Frontier State*. Garden City, NY: Doubleday, 1977.

Wharton, Clarence R. *Texas Under Many Flags*. Vol. 2. New York: American Historical Society, 1930.

Winchell, Mark Royden. "Inner Dark: or, The Place of Cormac McCarthy." *Southern Review* 26 (Apr. 1990): 293–309.

Wislizenus, A. *Memoir of a Tour to Northern Mexico, Connected with Col. Doniphan's Expedition, In 1846 and 1847*. US 30th Cong., 1st sess. Misc. No. 26. Washington: Tippin & Streeper, 1848.

Witek, Terri. " 'He's Hell When He's Well': Cormac McCarthy's Rhyming Dictions." *Shenandoah* 41 (Fall 1991): 51–66.

Woodward, Arthur. *Feud on the Colorado*. Los Angeles: Westernlore, 1955.

_____. "The Great Western: An Amazon Who Made History." *Branding Iron*. Los Angeles Corral, The Westerners (June 1956): 5–8.

_____. "Side Lights on Fifty Years of Apache Warfare: 1836–1886." *Journal of Arizona History* 2 (1961): 3–14.

Young, Thomas D., Jr. "Cormac McCarthy and the Geology of Being." Diss. Miami University [OH], 1990.

"The Very Life of the Darkness"

A Reading of *Blood Meridian*

STEVEN SHAVIRO

Your heart's desire is to be told some mystery. The mystery is
that there is no mystery.
—Judge Holden (252)

He would look for spiders, and make them fight together,
or throw flies into the spider web; and then he watched that
battle with so much pleasure, that he would sometimes burst
into laughter.
—Colerus, *Life of Spinoza*

Death is a festival, a ceremony, a ritual; but it is not a mystery. *Blood
Meridian* sings hymns of violence, its gorgeous language commemora-
ting slaughter in all its sumptuousness and splendor:

> some of the men were moving on foot among the huts with torches and
> dragging the victims out, slathered and dripping with blood, hacking at
> the dying and decapitating those who knelt for mercy. . . . [O]ne of the
> Delawares emerged from the smoke with a naked infant dangling in each
> hand and squatted at a ring of midden stones and swung them by the
> heels each in turn and bashed their heads against the stones so that the
> brains burst forth through the fontanel in a bloody spew and humans on
> fire came shrieking forth like berserkers and the riders hacked them down
> with their enormous knives. . . . (156)

Everywhere in this book, death leaves behind its memorials, its trophies
and its fetishes: the scalps collected by Glanton and his men, the tree of

dead babies (57), the crucified mummy (247), the circle of severed heads (220), the eviscerated bodies of bearded men with "strange menstrual wounds between their legs and no man's parts for these had been cut away and hung dark and strange from out their grinning mouths" (153). Reading *Blood Meridian* produces a vertiginous, nauseous exhilaration. A strong compulsion draws us through this text, something beyond either fascination or horror. "What man would not be a dancer if he could, said the judge. It's a great thing, the dance" (327). Bloody death is our monotonously predictable destiny; yet its baroque opulence is attended with a frighteningly complicitous joy.

Cormac McCarthy, the solitary poet of this exultation, is our greatest living author: nomadic wanderer, lucid cartographer of an inescapable delirium. In the entire range of American literature, only *Moby-Dick* bears comparison to *Blood Meridian*. Both novels are epic in scope, cosmically resonant, obsessed with open space and with language, exploring vast uncharted distances with a fanatically patient minuteness. Both manifest a sublime visionary power that is matched only by a still more ferocious irony. Both savagely explode the American dream of manifest destiny, of racial domination and endless imperial expansion. But if anything, McCarthy writes with a yet more terrible clarity than does Melville. For he has none of Melville's nostalgia for lost—primitive or uterine—origins. The "kid" who is McCarthy's nameless protagonist knows nothing of his mother: she dies giving birth to him (3). And he scarcely knows his father any better; within the first two pages of the book he has already left home forever, "divested of all that he has been" (4). We encounter instead the monstrously charismatic figure of Judge Holden, ironic Ahab to the kid's unselfconscious Ishmael. Orphanhood is taken for granted in *Blood Meridian*; the kid, unlike Ishmael, never feels any pathos in this condition. The judge notes at one point that "it is the death of the father to which the son is entitled and to which he is heir," so that the "father dead [before the son was born] has euchered the son out of his patrimony" (145). Such a double displacement—exile so extreme that we are exiled even from the possibility, the hope and despair, of exile—characterizes the life of these wanderers in the desert. The oedipal myth of paradise lost and regained, of patrimonial inheritance and promised land, has been abolished once and for all. These travelers will feel different cravings, experience different affects. The kid's "origins are become remote as is his destiny" (4), and his only point of reference in "that hallucinatory void" (113) is the unrepresentable extremity in which the judge embraces him "like a son" (306), enfolding him forever in his "immense and terrible flesh" (333).

Blood Meridian is a book, then, not of heights and depths, nor of origins and endings, but of restless, incessant horizontal movements: nomadic wanderings, topographical displacements, variations of weather, skirmishes in the desert. There is only war, there is only the dance. Exile is not deprivation or loss, but our primordial and positive condition. For there can be no alienation when there is no originary state for us to be alienated from. Glanton's riders climb into mountainous regions or descend through narrow canyons, but they always remain in intimate contact with the superficies of the earth, with the elemental forces of ground and sky, snow and hail and lightning, water and wind and barren rock. The journey is limitless, circumscribed only by the infinite vault of "naked and unrectified night" (106), and by the open wound of the horizon, "holocaust" (105) and "distant pandemonium" (185) of the declining sun. This horizon beckons onward to all the "[i]tinerant degenerates bleeding westward like some heliotropic plague" (78). Or it emerges into violent and menacing clarity: "and where the earth drained up into the sky at the edge of creation the top of the sun rose out of nothing like the head of a great red phallus until it cleared the unseen rim and sat squat and pulsing and malevolent behind them" (44–45). In either case, the horizon is a circumference that looms ominously near, lures or threatens, and yet remains forever out of reach. As the judge warns us (thus also explaining the title of the book), "in the affairs of men there is no waning and the noon of his expression signals the onset of night. His spirit is exhausted at the peak of its achievement. His meridian is at once his darkening and the evening of his day" (146–47). Zenith and horizon continually exchange places, without mediation or delay; what is most dim, distant and uncertain abruptly appears as an inescapable fatality. *Blood Meridian* rejects organicist metaphors of growth and decay, in favor of an open topography (what Deleuze and Guattari call "smooth space") in which the endless, unobstructed extension of the desert allows for the sudden, violent and fortuitous irruption of the most heterogeneous forces: "in the convergence of such vectors in such a waste wherein the hearts and enterprise of one small nation have been swallowed up and carried off by another the expriest asked if some might not see the hand of a cynical god conducting with what austerity and what mock surprise so lethal a congruence" (153). Yet the entire book consists of nothing but such fatal encounters, lethal congruences of incompossible but converging vectors. The riders trace a fractal path upon the surface of the earth; they define an intradimensional space in which the extremities of night and day intersect, a permeable membrane for the incessant transactions of life and death. They follow the contours of an inverted circle whose circumference is everywhere and whose center is nowhere, "some maelstrom out there in the void, some vortex in that waste apposite to which man's transit and his reckonings alike lay abrogate. As if beyond will or fate he and his beasts and his trappings moved both in card and in substance under consignment to some third and other destiny" (96).

Indeed, we are consigned so utterly and irredeemably to this "third destiny," this elemental desert, that fate and will alike fade into insignificance. We are called to no responsibility, and we may lay claim to no transcendence. *Blood Meridian* is not a salvation narrative; we can be rescued neither by faith nor by works nor by grace. It is useless to look for ulterior, redemptive meanings, useless even to posit the irredeemable gratuitousness of our abandonment in the form of some existential category such as Heideggerian "thrownness" (*Geworfenheit*). We have not fallen here or been "thrown" here, for we have always been here, and always will be. Only the judge seems descended from another world (125). We are never separate from the landscape or from those other voyagers with whom we so disastrously meet and clash, for the same nomadic forces impel us all: "If much in the world were mystery the limits of that world were not, for it was without measure or bound and there were contained within it creatures more horrible yet and men of other colors and beings which no man has looked upon and yet not alien none of it more than were their own hearts alien in them, whatever wilderness contained there and whatever beasts" (138). Nothing inhuman can be alien to me. The world is infinite in novelty and variety, "a trance bepopulate with chimeras having neither analogue nor precedent," and whose "ultimate destination . . . is unspeakable and calamitous beyond reckoning" (245); and yet this world is devoid of final mystery or essential otherness, since all is composed of the one unique Spinozistic substance. We would like to believe that our destiny is lofty and singular—whether it be self-willed or decreed by a transcendent and inexorable fate—but we discover that we are merely "pursuing as all travelers must inversions without end upon other men's journeys" (121). There is finally no mystery, not even in death; if we remain puzzled as to who we are, whence we have come, and whither we are bound, this is only because, the judge explains, "[a]s the dance . . . contains complete within itself its own arrangement and history and finale there is no necessity that the dancers contain these things within themselves as well" (329). Our experience of the world's limits consists precisely in this, that we can never encounter or encompass or transgress those limits. We remain bound in a dance of perpetual immanence.

Western culture has dreamed for centuries of some act of heroic transgression and self-transformation: whether this take the Enlightenment form of rational mastery, or the romantic and mystical one of apocalyptic transfiguration. McCarthy, like Nietzsche, exposes not just the futility of the dream, but—far more troublingly—its inherent *piety*, its ironic dependence upon the very (supposed) mysteries that it claims to violate. What is most disturbing about the orgies of violence that punctuate *Blood Meridian* is that they fail to constitute a pattern, to unveil a mystery or to serve any comprehensible purpose. Instead, the book suggests that "a taste for mindless violence" (3) is as ubiquitous—and as banal—as any other form of "common sense." Scalping has been a common human practice for at least 300,000 years, as one of the epigraphs to the novel suggests. Acts of destruction are as casual, random and unreflective as acts of kindness and civility—which also occur at odd moments in the course of the narrative. The judge demonstrates this point with cynical clarity when he calmly scalps a young child after having rescued it and carried it about and played with it for three days; for all that he and his mates have just destroyed an entire defenseless village, Toadvine is scandalized (164). Toadvine is incapable even of imagining transgression; he robs and kills precisely to the extent that such acts seem to him within the normal order of things. The judge, on the other hand, transgresses only in an ironic mode: by his lights, the perversity of scalping the child after it has come to trust him is no greater than the initial perversity of rescuing it from an otherwise total holocaust. In both cases, actual transgression is impossible. Transgression is an endeavor to exhaust the world, to compel it to reveal itself: as the judge puts it, "Only nature can enslave man and only when the existence of each last entity is routed out and made to stand naked before him will he be properly suzerain of the earth" (198). Such is the self-transcending project of Enlightenment. And we might be tempted to say that whereas all the other characters kill casually and thoughtlessly, out of greed or blood lust or some other trivial cause, only the judge kills out of will and conviction and a deep commitment to the cause and the canons of Western rationality.

But the judge also knows that it is impossible to transgress when there is no Law to violate, and when there is no final accumulation of goods or knowledge to be gathered together and no ultimate boundary to be attained. We cannot deplete the world, we cannot reach the sunset. Beyond the desert, there is only more empty space, the equally daunting infinitude of the ocean, "out there past men's knowing, where the stars are drowning and whales ferry their vast souls through the black and seamless sea" (304). The judge reminds us that "more things exist without our knowledge than with it and the order in creation which you see is that which you have put there, like a string in a maze, so that you shall not lose your way. For existence has its own order and that no man's mind can compass, that mind itself being but a fact among others" (245). *Our* order is never the world's order, not even in the Nietzschean sense of an order that we impose. We mark out paths in the desert or we read the tracks of others, but we cannot thereby master futurity or compel events to our liking. For subjectivity is not a perspective upon or projection into the world, nor even a transcendental condition for our perception of the world; it is just another empirical fact, an inherence within the world like any other. There is no interiority, no intentionality and no transcendence. The radical epistemology of *Blood Meridian* subverts all dualisms of subject and object, inside and outside, will and representation or being and interpretation. We are always exiles within the unlimited phenomenality of the world, for we cannot coincide with the (nonexistent) center of our being: "the history of all is not the history of each nor indeed the sum of those histories and none here can finally comprehend the reason for his presence for he has no way of knowing even in what the event consists. In fact, were he to know he might well absent himself and you can see that that cannot be any part of the plan if plan there be" (329). And so, just as we can never possess the world (since we cannot even possess ourselves), by the same logic we can never transgress the order of the world or estrange ourselves from it—no matter how hard we try.

In the pages of *Blood Meridian*, then, there is room neither for the demonic monomania of an Ahab nor for the self-reflective detachment of an Ishmael. Or better, these types flicker only for a moment, and before we know it they have "passed all into the problematical destruction of darkness" (105). Indeed, there is something of Ahab in Glanton: "He'd long forsworn all weighing of consequence and allowing as he did that men's destinies are given yet he usurped to contain within him all that he would ever be in the world and all that the world would be to him and be his charter written in the urstone itself he claimed agency and said so . . ." (243). Glanton resolves to be equal to his destiny; without the moralistic playacting usually present in such cases, he lays claim to the absurd existential nobility of the tragic hero. Yet there's an enormous difference between what can be called Glanton's stoicism and Ahab's dualistic defiance. Glanton affirms his own agency through an identification with the whole of fate, so that it is as if he has willed even the event that destroys him. Whereas Ahab's will continues to affirm itself against the universe, even at the mortal instant when that universe consumes it into nothingness. Glanton, unlike Ahab, confirms the judge's claim that "war is at last a forcing of the unity of existence" (249). His very aggressiveness and egotism are finally nothing but a means of sacrificing himself to such unity. And his only compensation for this sacrifice is the dubious one of proclaiming his defeat as a higher victory. The judge has little respect for such consolations: "There is room on the stage for one beast and one alone. All others are destined for a night that is eternal and without name. One by one they will step down into the darkness before the footlamps" (331). The play will soon be over, and we fool ourselves if we think that we can derive from it any profits of catharsis or redemption. Glanton's heroic resoluteness does not lend any grandeur to his death; still less does it lead to any tragic recognition or transfiguration: "Hack away you mean red nigger, he said, and the old man raised the axe and split the head of John Joel Glanton to the thrapple" (275).

At the other extreme from Glanton's tragic heroism, there is something of Ishmael in the kid. He drifts from place to place, never taking the initiative, sidestepping mortal engagements and warily refusing the judge's continual seductions. The kid keeps his distance from the claims both of destiny and of agency; he offers to the world only a sort of passive resistance, a silent, obstinate rejection of all finalities and of all melodramatics. Even as he behaves as a good fellow to his comrades, and participates uncomplainingly in the most violent, barbaric actions, he seems to retain the detachment of an observer. His most typical moment is perhaps that when he watches from high in the mountains "the collision of armies remote and silent upon the plain below" (213). The kid's skeptical reserve is analogous to Ishmael's, although it arises from an utter unreflectiveness in the one case and from an exacerbated self-consciousness in the other. For we are never given any insight into the kid's inner life; apart from that manifested in the stubbornness of his refusal to commit himself, he does not appear to have any. I think it is this eerie affectlessness, rather than some more determinate quality, that leads to the kid's hesitation at certain crucial moments: such as when he does not kill Shelby (206–10), or later when he ignores Tobin's advice to launch a preemptive strike against the judge. And this blankness is also what makes the kid into an object of desire for other characters in the book. They lust after him to the precise measure of his own indifference. I am thinking here of strange scenes like that of the old hermit's advances to the kid (20), as well as the judge's disturbing interest in him: "The judge watched him. Was it always your idea, he said, that if you did not speak you would not be recognized?" (328). In fact, it is the kid's very silence and unresponsiveness that the judge singles out in him: "That feeling in the breast that evokes a child's memory of loneliness such as when the others have gone and only the game is left with its solitary participant. A solitary game, without opponent" (329). It is this indifference that irritates the will of the judge, and that he seeks to master and appropriate; this seductive child's loneliness that he needs to baptize and give (re-)birth to, as he does in the parallel case of the idiot (259). The judge reproaches the kid's refusal of tragic knowledge as much as he scorns the futility of Glanton's accession to such knowledge: "You put your own allowances before the judgements of history and you broke with the body of which you were pledged a part and poisoned it in all its enterprise. Hear me, man. I spoke in the desert for you and you only and you turned a deaf ear to me. If war is not holy man is nothing but antic clay" (307). We are left in a no-win situation: the kid's evasive blankness marks a deferral but not an exemption from the all-embracing game of war. He can refuse its communion, but not its claim to be "the truest form of divination" (249). For "[w]hat joins men together, he said, is not the sharing of bread but the sharing of enemies. . . . Our animosities were formed and waiting before ever we two met" (307). There is no retreat, no separation. The kid cannot refuse the judge's election, any more than he can live up to it. This Ishmael will not be thrown free, and will not survive the wreck.

Glanton and the kid may represent opposite poles of a dialectic, but it is a stalled dialectic, one that fails ever to advance. All these heroic or evasive stances only bring us back by circuitous routes to the immanence of the landscape and the imminence of death, that "wry and grinning tradesman good to follow every campaign or hound men from their holes in just those whited regions where they've gone to hide from God" (44). We cannot run and hide in the desert, for the desert's vastness already enfolds the shape of our destiny. "You wouldnt think that a man would run plumb out of country out here, would ye?" (285), Toadvine complains. Death stalks these vast expanses of space and time, as inevitable and unforeseen as the uncanny bolts of lightning flashing out in the darkness that repeatedly punctuate the book. There is no reserve of potentiality in *Blood Meridian*; everything is cruelly, splendidly actual. There is no transcendence, and no possibility of standing out from Being. There is no stance by which subjectivity might fold back upon itself, thereby affirming and preserving itself, or at least attenuating the shock of those multiple, fatal encounters that mark its inherence in the world: as the judge warns, "Any man who could discover his own fate and elect therefore some opposite course could only come at last to that selfsame reckoning at the same appointed time, for each man's destiny is as large as the world he inhabits and contains within it all opposites as well" (330).

This "third destiny," exceeding both will and fate, is an immanent function of the landscape itself, which means that it is also a function of writing. McCarthy's sublime prose style resonates with those of Faulkner, of Melville and of the King James Bible. And by any criterion, McCarthy's writing is as great as any of these. But still more important, I think, is the way in which the language of *Blood Meridian* caresses the harsh desert landscape, slides amorously over its surfaces. The language of *Blood Meridian* is not primarily mimetic, as in classical models of the novel; but neither is it turned inward to thought or back upon itself, as is canonically the case with modernist texts. It is rather continually outside itself, in intimate contact with the world in a powerfully nonrepresentational way. McCarthy's writing is so closely intertwined with the surfaces of the earth and the depths of the cosmos that it cannot be disentangled from them. "Books lie," says the judge, referring to the salvational fables of scripture; but the actual, material words of God—who "speaks in stones and trees, the bones of things"— these do not lie (116). The writing of *Blood Meridian* composes such an immanent, material language, a speaking inscribed in the rocks and in the sky, in the very physical body of the world: "In the neuter austerity of that terrain all phenomena were bequeathed a strange equality and no one thing nor spider nor stone nor blade of grass could put forth claim to precedence. The very clarity of these articles belied their familiarity, for the eye predicates the whole on some feature or part and here was nothing more luminous than another and nothing more enshadowed and in the optical democracy of such landscapes all preference is made whimsical and a man and a rock become endowed with unguessed kinships" (247).

In a passage such as this one, the effect of the language is the same as the effect of the light. Minute details and impalpable qualities are registered with such precision that the prejudices of anthropocentric perceptions are disqualified. The eye no longer constitutes the axis of vision. We are given instead a kind of perception before or beyond the human. This is not a perspective *upon* the world, and not a vision that *intends* its objects: but an immanent perspective that already *is* the world, and a primordial visibility, a luminescence, that is indifferent to our acts of vision because it is always passively at work in whatever objects we may or may not happen to look at. McCarthy's narrative follows the progress of the kid, and to a lesser extent of other of Glanton's men; but it is never really written from their points of view. The prose enacts not a symbolization or a hermeneutics but *an erotics of landscape*, moving easily between the degree zero of "desert absolute" (295) and the specific articulations of water, mud, sand, sky and mountains. It leaps from the concrete to the abstract and back again, often in the space of a single sentence. It observes a fractal symmetry of scale, describing without hierarchical distinction and with the same attentive complexity the most minute phenomena and the most cosmic. And its observations cannot be attributed to any fixed center of enunciation, neither to an authorial presence nor to a narrating voice nor to the consciousness of any of the characters. There is only an incessant fluid displacement, a flux of words and of visions and palpations, indifferent to our usual distinctions between subjective and objective, between literal and figurative or between empirical description and speculative reflection. The book is written "[a]s if the very sediment of things contained yet some residue of sentience. As if in the transit of those riders were a thing so profoundly terrible as to register even to the uttermost granulation of reality" (247).

Blood Meridian thus refuses to acknowledge any gap or opposition between words and things. It insists that there can be no fissure or discontinuity in the real. But if this be the case, then there can also be no separate order of signification, and questions about the adequacy or inadequacy of language to what it describes cannot even arise. Speaking of "[r]epresentations and things" (136), the judge remarks, "What is to be deviates no jot from the book wherein it's writ. How could it? It would be a false book and a false book is no book at all" (141). This is not to argue (like the philosophers decried in Plato's *Sophist*) that it is impossible to lie or to speak what is not—though as far as I can tell, everything the judge says throughout the book is in some sense true, even if the pragmatic effect of his ironies and sarcastic insinuations is to deceive his listeners. Nor is it to say that the book fatally determines the course of what happens, or conversely that it faithfully reproduces that course. It is rather to insist, in the manner of Spinoza, that the order of words and images is literally the same as the order of actions and events. The judge affirms an ontological parallelism between thing and representation, between 'being' and 'witness': "Whether in my book or not, every man is tabernacled in every other and he in exchange and so on in an endless complexity of being and witness to the uttermost edge of the world" (141). Language no less than the desert floor is a space which comprehends everything, but in which the complex intrication of heterogeneous forces fatally leads to unwelcome encounters and deadly confrontations. Words and images are inherently dangerous; they partici-pate, just as do bodies, in the "ultimate game" of war, the "testing of one's will and the will of another within that larger will which because it binds them is therefore forced to select" (249). Mimesis is not an imitation of the real so much as an aggressive and provocative solicitation of the real. The judge recalls that "he'd once drawn an old Hueco's portrait and unwittingly chained the man to his own likeness. For he could not sleep for fear an enemy might take it and deface it . . ." (141). The making of images and words is not a tranquil process of recollection and perpetuation, but a continual movement of accretion that also implies the cruelty of triage or selection. The judge duplicates the world by obsessively copying all that he encounters into his notebooks; his simulations of various objects allow him to dispense with or even destroy the originals, "to expunge them from the memory of man" (140). He complains, "Whatever in creation exists without my knowledge exists without my consent" (198). But the more that is drawn or written and that hence becomes known, the more that is thereby subjected, not to human agency or adjudication, but to "war, whose stake is at once the game and the authority and the justification" (249). The writing of *Blood Meridian* is a catastrophic act of witness, embracing the real by tracing it in gore. McCarthy's previous novel, *Suttree* (1979), ends with the admonition to flee the cruel huntsman and his hounds, "slaverous and wild and their eyes crazed with ravening for souls in this world" (471). *Blood Meridian* ignores this advice, and instead conjures the presence of those hounds, tracks them as closely as possible. For McCarthy as for the judge, writing is inevitably an act of war: deracination, divinatory affirmation, the composition and conduct of dangerous forces, and the production of an active counter-memory.

Writing, like war, is a ceremonial and sacrificial act; and *Blood Meridian* is a novel written in blood, awash in blood. Yet for all its lucidity in the face of horror, this is not a book that sets a high value upon self-conscious-ness. And for all its exacerbated sense of fatality, its tenor is profoundly anticlimactic and anticathartic. *Blood Meridian* places the reader in the position of one "who has offered up himself entire to the blood of war, who has been to the floor of the pit and seen horror in the round and learned at last that it speaks to his inmost heart . . ." (331). But there is no purgation or release in this recognition, no curative discharge of fear and pity. We are rather swamped by emotions which can find no outlet; we too are implicated in this savage spectacle. We perform acts of sacrifice—"the slaying of a large bear" (329), or of many men—not to propitiate alien gods and not to ward off distant calamities, but to confirm our own complicity with the forces that crush and annihilate us. "Is not blood the tempering agent in the mortar which bonds?" (329). The scariest thing about *Blood Meridian* is that it is a euphoric and exhilarating book, rather than a tragically alienated one, or a gloomy, depressing one. Our pulses quicken as "considerations of equity and rectitude and moral right [are] rendered void and without warrant" (250), subsumed in the trials of war. Once we have started to dance, once we have been swept up in the game, there is no pulling back.

The judge states categorically that "[a] ritual includes the letting of blood. Rituals which fail in this requirement are but mock rituals" (329). All the devastations chronicled in *Blood Meridian* occur in a ritual space and time, an Outside that helps to enforce, yet stands apart from, the social bond: "Here beyond men's judgements all covenants were brittle" (106). Glanton and his men exist only to disrupt the orderly procedures of production, conservation and trade; they "carried no tantamount goods and the disposition to exchange was foreign to them" (121). They ravage the very order upon which they parasitically feed. Their actions all fall under the rubric of what Georges Bataille calls *nonproductive expenditure*: prodigality, play, waste, recklessness, empty display and unmotivated violence. Beneath the mask of a Darwinian struggle for survival, or a Hobbesian war of all against all, or even a lust for wealth and power and honor, they sumptuously, gratuitously squander their own lives—together, of course, with those of many others—at every turn. They have no spirit of seriousness or of enterprise; they unwittingly pursue self-ruin rather than advantage. All these men—and not just the kid—are childlike in their unconsciousness, or indifference, as to motivations and consequences. According to the judge, "Men are born for games. Nothing else. Every child knows that play is nobler than work. He knows too that the worth or merit of a game is not inherent in the game itself but rather in the value of that which is put at hazard. . . . [A]ll games aspire to the condition of war" (249). Glanton and his men give themselves over to the game of war wholeheartedly, playing without taking care to preserve their stakes. Their lack of awareness is more than a match for the judge's extreme lucidity, if it is a question of reaching the point where "that which is wagered swallows up game, player, all" (249). For the clash and testing of wills in which the judge exults must end, not in the victory of one, but in the sacrificial consumption of everyone and everything. And such is finally our inmost, most secret and most horrific desire.

Blood Meridian performs the violent, sacrificial, self-consuming ritual upon which our civilization is founded. Or better, it traumatically re-enacts this ritual, for foundations are never set in place once and for all. More blood is always needed to seal and renew the pact. The American dream of manifest destiny must be repeated over and over again, ravaging the indifferent landscape in the course of its lemmings' march to the sea. Our terrible progress is *"less the pursuit of some continuance than the verification of a principle"* (337), an obsessive reiteration without advancement, for we build only to destroy. There is no escaping this ritual, no avoiding the point at which we are compelled to assume the fate we have assigned to others, by putting up our own lives as the ultimate stake. But there is also no power or knowledge to which participation in the ritual gives us access, no occult secret unveiled before an elite of initiates. We sacrifice in vain, we sacrifice to nothing. There is nothing mysterious or transfiguring or even surprising about the ritual: "The evening's progress will not appear strange or unusual even to those who question the rightness of the events so ordered. . . . We are not speaking in mysteries" (329). We all end up like the kid, violated and smothered in the shithouse; but how can we dare attach a unique significance even to this? For we are granted no marks of distinction, no special dispensation, but only the ever-renewed immanence of the dance, embodied in the grotesquely pirouetting figure of the judge, "huge and pale and hairless, like an enormous infant," who "never sleeps" and who "says that he will never die" (335). In the "light and nimble" feet of this perpetually smiling, Zarathustrian child, we may perhaps see the reason for this book's shocking *cheerfulness*. Everything in *Blood Meridian* is violence and blood, dying and destruction. But even darkness and death have their own proper vitality. As the second of the book's three epigraphs, taken from Jacob Boehme, reminds us: "It is not to be thought that the life of darkness is sunk in misery and lost as if in sorrowing. There is no sorrowing. For sorrow is a thing that is swallowed up in death, and death and dying are the very life of the darkness."

NOTES

I would like to thank a number of friends without whose input and assistance I never could have written this article. Kathy Acker introduced me to the writings of Cormac McCarthy, and especially to *Blood Meridian*. Over the last few years I have shared conversation about McCarthy and *Blood Meridian* with Leo Daugherty, who also invited me to lecture on the book before his class in post-modern literature at Evergreen State College. I have also benefited from, and at points woven into the body of this article, comments on the book made at various times by Lee Graham, Faye Hirsch, Paul Keyes, Mark Lester and Laurie Weeks.

WORKS CITED

McCarthy, Cormac. *Blood Meridian or the Evening Redness in the West*. New York: Random, 1985.

_____. *Suttree*. 1979. New York: Vintage, 1986.

Gravers False and True

Blood Meridian as Gnostic Tragedy

Leo Daugherty

I want to argue here that gnostic thought is central to Cormac McCarthy's *Blood Meridian*. I will go about this by discussing four of its characters—the judge, the kid, the graver and the mysterious man of the epilogue—and the particular sort of world they inhabit. I am aware at the outset of the difficulties involved in establishing a relationship between any two things (in this case *Blood Meridian* and Gnostic thought) when some readers may have a working knowledge of only one of them (in this case, I hope, the novel). While it is impossible to provide more than an introductory sketch of Gnosticism here, I believe that its dualistic core can be simply and briefly shown, and that it can then be understood well enough to make clear its connections with McCarthy's book.

I. The Gnostics

No one knows exactly how or when Gnosticism originated, but it is generally agreed that it came about as yet another answer to the question, How is it that the world is experienced as so very evil and that so many people's central response to it is alienation? The Gnostic answer took two basic forms, the Syrian-Egyptian and the Iranian, the latter of which probably stemmed from Zoroastrianism and found its principal exponent in Mani (215–277 AD). Because *Blood Meridian* exemplifies the latter, I will use it almost exclusively here.[1]

In the beginning, there was a "pleroma," a condition of perfection and thus of literal plenitude, in the divine realm. This realm was made up of God and the lesser divinities, themselves called aeons. Then, somehow, this unity was sundered, either from within or without. In the Iranian version it was riven from without, by some sort of opposing "dark force." (This presupposes, as Hans Jonas has noted, some yet more primal dualism ["Gnosticism" 338].) In the words of one scholar of this (Manichean) version: "All existing things derive from one of these two: the infinite light of spiritual goodness or the bottomless darkness of evil matter, coexistent and totally opposed to each other" (Greenlees 167). A state of affairs ensued which is termed the "crisis in the pleroma," one result of which was the "falling" or "sinking" of some of the aeons, including (in Mani's system) "primal man." Of these, some became the archons (lords), who took charge of the various lower realms. The characteristics most typically found in them are judgment and jealousy, and their "creative" energies are spent in satisfying their "ambition, vanity, and lust for dominion" (Jonas 338).

One of the archons' works was the creation of the world. A second was the creation of man, who would contain some of the original divine substance. Their motive for making human beings is unclear, but Jonas argues convincingly that it was either simple envy and ambition, or the more calculating "[motive] of entrapping divine substance in their lower world by the lure of a seemingly congenial receptacle [the body] that will then become its most secure bond" (339). As Robert Grant has noted, "The Gnostic, like the Platonist, regarded his body as a tomb" (327). To him, it is *this*, then, that is the *imago Dei* of Genesis, and in Manicheanism the *imago* is that of the original fallen "primal man." Yet the spirit within humans is not from the archons. Rather, it is from the great original god of the pleroma, and it is imprisoned *in* humans *by* the archons—in Mani's version through a violent victory of the archons over the real, good god of the pleroma—and the result, on the earth, is obviously a state of affairs in which the good and the light are eternally trapped inside the evil and the dark.

The spirit imprisoned within matter is called *pneuma*—the "spark of the alien divine," in the familiar Gnostic phrase—and its presence naturally causes some humans to *feel* alienated, although they are for the most part comatose. The spirit within is, however, capable of learning, and the alienation it feels is its clue that there is indeed something to be learned. In the various Gnostic systems, knowledge is the key to extrication. It is thus a central task of the archons to prevent the human acquisition of liberational knowledge at all costs. To this end, they have established *heimarmene*—Fate—which is, in Jonas's words, a "tyrannical world rule [which] is . . . morally the law of *justice*, as exemplified in the Mosaic law" ("Gnosticism" 339).

Humans are comprised of flesh, soul and spirit. Of these, the first two are from the archons and the third is from the original, good god. This god has nothing to do with the world the archons made, and is in fact as alien to it as the spirit of humankind. But he feels something akin to incompleteness, and he is thus moved to "call his spirit home." He does this by means of messengers, who go into the world with the "call of revelation." This revelation is the "facts of the case"—the knowledge necessary to enable humans to overcome the world and return to their true home with him. God's revelational messenger "penetrates the barriers of the [lower spheres, including the world], outwits the archons, awakens the spirit from its earthly slumber, and imparts to it the saving knowledge from without" (340). These salvational Gnostic envoys—those in possession of *gnosis*—called (and still call) themselves "pneumatics." Their work necessarily entails assuming "the lot of incarnation and cosmic exile"; moreover, in Mani's system, the revelator is "in a sense identical with those he calls—the once-lost parts of his divine self— [thus giving rise] to the moving idea of the 'saved savior' (*salvator salvandus*)" (340).

Manichean Gnosticism is easily confused with nihilism, as the latter is commonly understood. The reason is that the Gnostic god, being totally not of this world, generates no *nomos*, no law, for either nature or human activity. The law, instead, is the law of the archons, and justice is theirs as well. And so is vengeance—the "vengeance that is mine." God's only activity with respect to matter is his attempt, via his suffering-servant pneumatic messengers, to rescue the spirit within humans— the truth of them—*out* of matter. So, while Jonas is right in arguing that Gnostic "acosmism" makes for the worldly *appearance* of nihilism, the mere fact that the Gnostic god has a rescuing function makes Gnosticism and nihilism differ importantly (Jonas, *Gnostic* 332). In Gnosticism, because of this difference, there is conflict and drama. Its human drama takes place within and is a microcosm of its larger cosmic drama which pits spirit against matter, light against darkness and the alien god (and the alien pneumatic spirit within sleeping humankind) against the archons. It is precisely a war. For humans, it is a war against the archons' *heimarmene*, but this is merely part of the larger war in which the fate of the original god is the primal stake. Mani taught that the cosmic drama amounts to "a war with changing fortunes [in which] the divine fate, of which man's fate is a part and the world an unwilled byproduct, is explained in terms of . . . captivity and liberation . . . " (Jonas, "Gnosticism" 341). And in his teachings, the primal man, the "knightly male figure, the warrior, assumes the role of the exposed and suffering part of divinity" (341).

With respect to this warrior-knight, Wilhelm Bousset, who was perhaps the most esteemed nineteenth-century authority on Gnosticism, held that he represents god in the form of a hero

> who makes war on, and is partly vanquished by, darkness. He descends into the darkness of the material world, and in so doing begins the great drama of the world's development. From [god] are derived those portions of light existing and held prisoner in this lower world. And as he has raised himself again out of the material world, or has been set free . . . so shall also the members of the primal man, the portions of light still imprisoned in matter, be set free. (156)

The practicing Gnostics naturally saw themselves as such heroes, as such messengers of god or "primal men." And in this fact, Bousset concludes, is to be found the obvious meaning of the primal man figure in some Gnostic strains, including Mani's; for it provides a simple (and self-serving) answer to the question, "How did the portions of light to be found in the lower world, among which certainly belong the souls of [us] Gnostics, enter into it?" (156).

So, whereas most thoughtful people have looked at the world they lived in and asked, How did evil get into it?, the Gnostics looked at the world and asked, How did *good* get into it? This was of course a very sensible question, and remains so. After all, the Satan of Roman Catholicism, the Orthodox Church and the Protestant Reformation is a strikingly domesticated, manageable, partitioned-off personification of evil as the Gnostics saw evil. They saw it as something so big that "evil" is not really an applicable term—because it is too small. For them, evil was simply everything that *is*, with the exception of the bits of spirit emprisoned here. And what they saw is what we see in the world of *Blood Meridian*.

II. The Archon and His World

Early in *Blood Meridian*, the reader comes upon this passage: "The survivors . . . slept with their alien hearts beating in the sand like pilgrims
exhausted upon the face of the planet Anareta, clutched to a namelessness
wheeling in the night" (46). Anareta was believed in the Renaissance to
be "the planet which destroys life," and "violent deaths are caused" when
the "malifics" have agents in "the anaretic place" (OED entry, "anareta").
Because McCarthy has not placed a comma after "pilgrims," it is likely
that his simile includes the entire remainder of the phrase; yet it is easily
possible to read the passage *as if* a comma were present, thus producing
the reading: *this* is Anareta. Either way, the implication is clearly that our
own Earth is Anaretic.

And in *Blood Meridian*, the Earth is the judge's.

Even so, on our own evil planet Judge Holden's power is not yet complete,
since his will is not yet fulfilled in its passion for total domination. He is
working, as he implies to Toadvine, to become a full "suzerain"—one who
"rules even where there are other rulers," whose authority "countermands
local judgements" (198). Yet this was also necessarily true of the Gnostic
archons, just as it was true of the Old Testament Yahweh, whom they saw
as evil. And, like those archons, Holden also possesses all the other characteristics of Yahweh as the Gnostics saw him: he is jealous, he is vengeful,
he is wrathful, he is powerful and—most centrally—he possesses, and is
possessed by, a will. And he is enraged by any existence or any act outside that will. At one point, he places his hands on the ground, looks at
Toadvine, and speaks:

> This is my claim, he said. And yet everywhere upon it are pockets of
> autonomous life. Autonomous. In order for it to be mine nothing must
> be permitted to occur upon it save by my dispensation. (199)

In Holden, the stressed archonic element is of course *judgment*. Yet, like
Yahweh, he judges things simply according to the binary criterion of their
being inside or outside his will. In one of the passages most crucial to an
adequate understanding of *Blood Meridian*, he tells David Brown, "Every
child knows that play is nobler than work," that "Men are born for games"
and that "all games aspire to the condition of war for here that which is
wagered swallows up game, player, all" (249). We are reminded here of
the novel's epigraph from Jacob Boehme: "It is not to be thought that the
life of darkness is sunk in misery and lost as if in sorrowing. There is no
sorrowing. For sorrow is a thing that is swallowed up in death, and death

and dying are the very life of the darkness." Indeed, *war is the ultimate cause of unity*, involving as it does the "testing of one's will and the will of another within that larger will [i.e., war itself] which because it binds them is therefore forced to select. War is the ultimate game because war is at last a forcing of the unity of existence. War is god" (249).

And it is the warrior judge's work to achieve dominion—to be the realized territorial archon of *this* Anaretic planet—through becoming the totalizing victor in all conflicts, real and perceptual, involving his will. The corollary is to show no mercy to those others whose wills have led them to be outside one's own: as Holden tells the kid late in the novel, "There's a flawed place in the fabric of your heart . . . . You alone reserved in your soul some corner of clemency for the heathen" (299). And because the kid *has* shown them mercy, the judge must *not* show *him* any—and does not. Ultimately, a person serves the god of war, as Holden tells Tobin, in order to be "no godserver but a god himself" (250).

III. The Name of the Gun

The Earth is the judge's, and, when he names his gun, the judge makes ironic comment upon the fact that not only is the earth his, but also that it is an anti-pastoral, anti-Arcadian world.

The gun's name is *Et in Arcadia Ego* (125).

This is a familiar late Renaissance proverb, dating back at least to Schidoni (c. 1600). It was a commonplace memorial inscription for tombs and representations of tombs, it was scrawled as graffiti under pictures of skulls, and it was conventionally employed by painters such as Poussin and Reynolds as a verbal/visual icon. It means, "Even in Arcadia there am I [Death]." The more interesting, least sentimentalizing pastoral poets had stressed this all along, of course, and had accordingly positioned death prominently in their Arcadias—Marguerite of Navarre in her *Heptameron*, as well as Shakespeare in *Love's Labors Lost*, for example, and most importantly Sidney in the seminal *Arcadia*.

Blood Meridian centers upon what can be reasonably thought of as a fraternity of male shepherds who kill the sheep entrusted to them. One of the shepherds is the kid, who feels the "spark of the alien divine" within him through the call of what seems to be conscience. He thus "awakens" a bit, attaining in the process a will outside the will of his murdering shepherdic subculture and the archon who runs it. The kid reminds us here of Huckleberry Finn, who, in the crucial act of saving his friend Jim from slaveholder justice, similarly defies the will of a pernicious subculture, but who is judged only by his own cultural conscience, saying to himself at the novel's turning point, "All right, then, I'll go to hell." Both these boys are a little bit awakened by the spark of the divine, and both extend acts of fraternal mercy when they are "not supposed to." In the Mark Twain world, Huck gets away with it; in the McCarthy world, the kid is killed by the judge for it in an outhouse. The kid has "awakened," but he is not progressed sufficiently in wisdom much beyond mere awakening and thus has no chance at survival, much less at the victory of Gnostic liberation.

Even so, it would be a gross understatement to call *Blood Meridian* a "pastoral tragedy," or even to term it "anti-pastoral." The point of the gun's name is not that because of its appearance in the landscape, or by synechdoche the judge's appearance, death has been introduced into an idyllic Arcadia: the entire novel makes clear (primarily through the judge, who continuously emphasizes the point in his preachments) that the human world is, and has always been, a world of killing. This is surely the point of the book's third epigraph, a quote provided by McCarthy from a 1982 news release: "Clark, who led last year's expedition to the Afar region of northern Ethiopia, and UC Berkeley colleague Tim D. White, also said that a re-examination of a 300,000-year-old fossil skull found in the same region earlier shows evidence of having been scalped." Rather, I would argue that the name suggests the judge's awareness of, and his enthusiastic endorsement of, the reality that the world has been a place of murder ever since the first victorious taking of a human life by another human. The judge's name *Et in Arcadia Ego* stands not for his gun and not for himself, but rather for murderous humankind on this very real killing planet.

Blood Meridian is a study of power relations within what, to the habituated expectations of our "received culture," ought by all rights to have been a pastoral setting. But McCarthy's long-meditated observations, coupled with his reading of the relevant southwestern history, have led him to other conclusions, and he extrapolates from what he knows of the Glanton gang's exploits to make a narrative about a world-program seemingly set up by something like a gnostic grand demiurge and enjoyed by him as proprietor, with earthly power being that of judgment sprung from will (the judge's judgment, the judge's will, both perhaps signifying the author's as-above-so-below—and *vice-versa*—notions), untempered by mercy and wisdom: this is Yahweh's programmatic power (as the Gnostics saw it), exercised by his archonic overseer. A good "alien" god exists somewhere, as is always the case in Gnosticism, and he is the god of the epilogue who put the fire in the earth and part of himself in the souls of humans, including the kid—to which we will return. But: with respect to these southwestern doings on this southwestern set, so what?[2]

IV. The False Graver

Midway through *Blood Meridian* the kid asks Tobin, the ex-priest, the obvious and paramount question about Judge Holden: "What's he a judge of?" The ex-priest cautions the kid to be quiet: "Hush now. The man will hear ye" (135).

The question goes unanswered for a long time, and when it finally *is* answered—in the kid's feverish dream—it comes in a passage which is at once the most difficult in the book and yet absolutely necessary to understanding it adequately:

> The judge smiled. The fool was no longer there but another man and this other man he [the kid] could never see in his entirety but he seemed an artisan and a worker in metal. The judge enshadowed him where he crouched at his trade but he was a coldforger who worked with hammer and die, perhaps under some indictment and an exile from men's fires, hammering out like his own conjectural destiny all through the night of his becoming some coinage for a dawn that would not be. It is this false moneyer with his gravers and burins who seeks favor with the judge and he is at contriving from cold slag brute in the crucible a face that will pass, an image that will render this residual specie [the judge, as explained in the previous paragraph] current in the markets where men barter. Of this is the judge judge and the night does not end. (310)

On first reading, the passage seems impenetrably perverse. It is clearly outside the judge's will for the forger to succeed in contriving a face that will pass, an image that will render this residual specie current in the markets where men barter, whereas it appears to us as more likely that this *would* be the judge's will. And it is clearly outside his will for the night to end, for the dawn to come, and this too has to strike us as odd, since the dawn being spoken of is one in which the engraver's counterfeit coin, which he quite reasonably believes the judge wishes him to succeed at producing, would "pass"—with the judge thereby presumably profiting. But the judge keeps judging its likeness of him inadequate. The reason is that the judge doesn't want a victory based on any currency (even his own counterfeit currency) in any "marketplace." The point is that he is a warrior—one who wants only war and the continuous night of war—in *opposition* not only to "true coinage" but to *any* coinage involving him. The "markets where men barter" exist, of course, but the judge believes them derivative, not primary—derivative of the war culture, which is the true culture upon which the markets (themselves only arenas for decadent symbolic war *games*) depend. (This view is presented in small in the brief picture of the "sutler" presented early in the novel [44]. A sutler is a peddlar to an army, following along behind it, in McCarthy's image, like any debased and predatory camp-follower: a predator upon predators.)

Yet it is to the judge's advantage to foster the delusion that he wishes to create a new civilizational order, because this is a goal toward which he can encourage people to work at their various professions and trades—people like this graver. "Of this is the judge judge and the night does not end." Yes: because if he ever judges his own likeness "passable," thus allowing the transformation of war (which for him is god, as we know) into the merely symbolic, "civilized" competition of money-based conflict, he loses, there being little or no blood, and therefore no ultimately unifying victory, in symbolic warfare.

Another way of saying the same thing is that, just as the ascetic Gnostics thought it the wisest course not to "play the game" of the creator and his archons (Jonas, "Gnosticism" 341), so this archon will not play the (to him, "safe") money-changing game of marketplace humans as a means to defeating, dominating and destroying them. For him, *all* human coinage is counterfeit, and any victories won with it would just be meaningless counterfeit victories—solving, settling and signifying nothing.

It is helpful here to remember an earlier passage in which the judge debates a "Tennessean named Webster." In that passage the judge makes the familiar argument that many people in many cultures intuitively know that accurate portraiture "chain[s] the man to his own likeness," thus weakening him and perhaps killing him. The judge himself obsessively draws likenesses from nature, he says, in order to "expunge them from the memory of man." Webster counters that "no man can put all the world in a book," no matter what his goals for trying to do so might be—"No more than everthing drawed in a book is so." "My book or some other book," answers the judge: "Whether in my book or not, every man is tabernacled in every other and he in exchange and so on in an endless complexity of being and witness to the uttermost edge of the world" (140–41). The word to notice here is *exchange*. The judge refuses to be tabernacled in any other man. He refuses to be part of the exchange system.

What is the judge judge of? He is judge of all attempts—including those of patronage-seekers—to place him *within* that system, and he thus judges all attempts inadequate. It is not merely that he positions himself outside all tabernacles filled with "money-changers"; rather, it is that he positions himself outside all temples, period—to stand beyond that "outermost edge of the world" of which he speaks to Webster.[3]

V. The Man of the Epilogue

In the dawn there is a man progressing over the plain by means of holes which he is making in the ground. He uses an implement with two handles and he chucks it into the hole and he enkindles the stone in the hole with his steel hole by hole striking the fire out of the rock which God has put there. On the plain behind him are the wanderers in search of bones and those who do not search and they move haltingly in the light like mechanisms whose movements are monitored with escapement and pallet so that they appear restrained by a prudence or reflectiveness which has no inner reality and they cross in their progress one by one that track of holes that runs to the rim of the visible ground and which seems less the pursuit of some continuance than the verification of a principle, a validation of a sequence and causality as if each round and perfect hole owed its existence to the one before it there on that prairie upon which are the bones and the gatherers of bones and those who do not gather. He strikes fire in the hole and draws out his steel. Then they all move on again. (337)

When I first read *Blood Meridian*, I took the walking, digging, fire-striking man of its epilogue as somehow standing for the judge as some manner of (Nietzschean? evil Promethean?) culture-making force, with the mass of humanity blindly following along after him in a line—an interpretation which a little "close reading" shortly caused me to abandon. My attempts at reinterpreting it—with the help of others—then led to my first glimpses of what I am arguing here to be the novel's Gnostic, and perhaps even specifically Manichean, features. I now believe that *Blood Meridian* exemplifies the rare coupling of Gnostic "ideology" with the "affect" of Hellenistic tragedy by means of its depiction of how power works in the making and erasing of culture, and of what the human condition amounts to when a person opposes that power and thence gets introduced to fate.

The epilogue pictures a brutal contrast between a man who is very much alive and a host of other people who are effectively (or perhaps even actually) dead, and the picture it paints is one based directly on the sort of machine of which the watch or clock is the most familiar example. This is what the words "escapement" and "pallet" refer to. And the idea is that the alive digger and the dead wanderers are all *moving* in the way that such a machine moves. The wanderers move "haltingly" because they are "cogs in the wheel," it is suggested, groping forward in tick-tock fashion, just as the digger goes forward in the pursuit of his continuance in tick-tock fashion himself (digging and walking, digging and walking), even though *they* have no holes to dig or fire to strike. The idea appears to be that the vast majority of people, moving one by one through space (and presumably time), cross this track, this "evidence," of fire struck out of the earth, but that these people go neither backward to try to trace its source nor forward to follow its lead. They just stumble over it—and either fail to notice it at all or experience a dull moment of bemusement or puzzlement because of it. (And, as we are talking about a writer and his book here—and an uncommonly erudite writer at that—it is worth noting that the other prominent use of the escapement device is in the typewriter, where, activated by the struck keys, it controls the horizontal movement of the carriage.)

The natural question to ask is, What is the connection between the man of the epilogue and the main narrative body of *Blood Meridian*? To this I have two answers. The first is a fairly obvious corrective to my initial feeling that the man somehow represents the judge, while the second is a reflection upon the significance of the first for studies of McCarthy. The first is that the man provides a "structural" element which is absolutely necessary to the novel's Gnostic world-view, but which is nowhere to be found in the characters who figure in its primary story: he is the revealer or "revelator" of the divine, working to free spirit from matter—the pneumatic (albeit corporeal) messenger, in possession of *gnosis*, who is in service to the good "alien god." This reading is, I think, clearly supported (if not indeed mandated) by the imagery of his striking and freeing bits of fire, imprisoned in the earth, which come from God; by the fact of his solitary, ascetic and superior nature and work (set in clear opposition to other people's nature and work, themselves the "sleepers" of Manichean thought); and by the Gnostic context provided by the novel proper, which not only implies his existence but mandates his eventual appearance. The "continuance" of which the digging man is in "pursuit" is the ongoing work of making his way back to the good, alien god—and of freeing and revealing imprisoned bits of holy fire in the evil world of the archons and all their sleeping inmates as he goes.

My second answer is more provisional. Even so, it will likely strike a good many readers as curious, irrelevant, outright wrong or all of the above.

I think McCarthy may be showing us in the epilogue, in parable form, his reading of himself as writer—particularly in opposition to others. I think he goes so far as to make of himself a "presence" at the end—he has always been, after all, something of a Stendhalian editorialist as a narrator—affirming among other things that he is a particular, rare sort of "supply-side" producer of very serious stories: a solitary obsessive who, in his alienation from this Anareta world, this killing planet, and in his fidelity to the real god, has a "can do no other" (because Called) *purpose*, and who cares not a whit for the "market." ("Selling a book is the job of the publisher," the reclusive author said in the mid-1980s, in response to questions about his unwillingness to do the usual interviews and promotional work [Morrow 52].) If there were a "god of this world," such a sense of artistic purpose might be usefully termed *mithectic*, with the artist doing his part to help his god out—to make the sun come up for the tribe by sitting and facing east every morning, for example, because it has been given to him as his calling to do this as the work of his life. But when there is *no* "god of this world," the artist-as-solitary obsessive is truly solitary and thus truly obsessive throughout his sentence here.

If this is so, then McCarthy has carried the romantic conception of the artist-as-creator/progenitor (itself derived from strains in the Italian Renaissance, in part Neoplatonist) to a new apotheosis based on an opposing premise. In McCarthy, the idea of the world-creating artist retains much of the romantic one—particularly its notion of the *stance* of the artist on earth—but everything is changed by virtue of the fact that *this* artist reflects and serves neither the Old Testament Yahweh nor some other good god of this world. Rather, he is inextricably bound to, and reflective of, the good "alien god" who did not make the world, is not in charge of it and is no part of it—except for the "spark of original divinity" residing in people, waiting to be awakened (by the Call) and then nurtured to the most of those persons' capacities. I think this has been a logical step for artists since Nietzsche—whom McCarthy has certainly read and read well—although Nietzsche, no Gnostic, would not have approved of the theology. And if I am right, it would actually be an understatement to call McCarthy an "elitist" for having taken it, because he has actually gone about as far as Nietzsche himself went while he still had a grip—and that was a ways.

All of which is just to say: The man in the epilogue, as he moves over the landscape digging holes and striking his God's fire in them, is the exact antithesis of the false "graver" of the kid's dream who seeks the judge's favor through a different sort of line-drawing. And just as the judge (although unbeknownst to the graver) does not want to "pass" in the civilized world, but wants only war, victory and then more war in the unending night of fallen matter, so the man of the epilogue cares nothing for playing and winning in the judge's world (for to win is to lose there just as much as to lose is to lose), but wants only the "pursuit of his continuance" in the service of what he takes to be the good and right way to go. Neither the man nor the judge will enter the exchange system.

VI. Gnostic Tragedy and Enchantment

Finally, how could it be so exhilarating and so obviously good for us to read such an excessive, doom-obsessed, bone-chilling novel of blood? How could such a thing be so oddly exuberant and elicit such a pleasurable response? The answer, I think, directly demonstrates how, on the level of what we used to so unembarrassedly call the "human condition," Gnosticism is not really so far from Hellenism (to which it has often been opposed) after all. I think *Blood Meridian* elicits the same human responses as Greek tragedy, the reason being that its archon, Holden, plays the same role as the original untamed Fates (in *The Oresteia*, most notably), who judge and avenge, or who sometimes just do whatever they want. In the Western tradition, they have been steadily domesticated—from Fates to Eumenides to Fortune to Chance to Lady Luck. But if Fates stay Fates, then the just-doing-one's-best, divine-spark protagonist has got to lose, through no fault of his or her own, and it has always been bizarrely energizing, bracing, "cathartic" and joy-producing to feel the delirious pity and fear when the protagonist takes his or her heroic bloodbath at the end—to read it and weep.

Students of Gnosticism agree that its version of Fate (*heimarmene*) is central to its system, and scholars of literature know that it is not that unusual to find writers working with Gnostic materials. Yet I know of no writers in English save McCarthy who have seen the potential for human tragedy in those materials when Fate is placed front and center—as it must be if Gnosticism is to be Gnosticism—and who have then proceeded to make the tragedy. (This is why *Blood Meridian* is so much more powerful in its effect than either other Gnostic narratives or mere pastoral tragedies.) And, while it could be argued that the kid is no "tragic hero," it seems clear enough that some tragic heroes do not really fill any formulaic bill, most notably Antigone; all that's needed is a dumb kid possessed of a spark of the divine who's outside the will of some Yahweh or other and meets his or her fate at said nemesis' hands at the end. The *peculiar* thing, really, is that it strikes us Americans in the 1990s as so outlandishly shocking to find one of our writing countrymen not only refusing to water down the tragic vision, but embracing it with open arms.

McCarthy's greatness lies most centrally and most obviously in the fact that, in "progressing over the plain," he has become our finest living tragedian. And part of genuine tragic enchantment is the unrepressed gaity which both results from and then informs cosmic alienation in the greatest tragedians and their characters. In 1604 London, a long forgotten storyteller known only as "An. Sc., Gentleman," implied that the secret of *Hamlet*'s fineness is that in Shakespeare "the comedian rides when the tragedian stands on tiptoe."[4] There are precious few writers of whom one could say this, but one can say it of the writer of *Blood Meridian*. In major consequence of his mastery of the high tragedian's art, Cormac McCarthy has become the best and most indispensable writer of English-language narrative in the second half of the century.

NOTES

I owe many of this essay's insights into Gnosticism, and particularly into the claim that Holden is an "archon," to Lee Graham, who is completing her master's thesis on McCarthy at the University of Washington, and I am also grateful to her for reading the paper through various drafts and giving me suggestions for revision. The essay originated as a series of letters to Edward Abse and Ginnie Daugherty, doctoral students respectively at the University of Virginia (anthropology) and The New School for Social Research (sociology), who had asked for my thoughts on the question "What's the epilogue to *Blood Meridian* all about?" Some of the essay is unaltered text from those letters. For general and particular inspiration, I also want to thank McCarthy lovers Steven Shaviro of the University of Washington, Tom Maddox of The Evergreen State College, Robert L. Bergman, MD, and—last but not least—David Browne, who in circumstances not to be believed first introduced me to McCarthy.

[1]The best short introduction to Gnostic thought is probably Jonas's entry in *Encyclopedia of Philosophy*: two other useful, accessible starting places are provided by Bousset and Grant. Pagels has stirred renewed interest in Gnosticism during the last decade with her deservedly celebrated work, but Jonas's *Gnostic Religion* remains the magisterial study—and is uncommonly readable for scholarship in esoteric thought. Giovanni Filoramo's recent *A History of Gnosticism* (Cambridge, MA: Blackwell, 1990) is indispensable. Greenlees gives a clear, if perhaps too enthusiastic account of Manicheanism in the introduction to his

edition of Mani. Excellent recent translations of several of the more important Gnostic gospels are provided by Meyer. Last, I am aware of no previous source which points out that the oldest mention of the Gnostic strain discussed in this essay may be Philolaus (by some classed as "Presocratic"), Fragment 13, for which see Wheelwright.

[2]My rhetorical "So what?" could equally be asked by those who would maintain that Gnosticism is, or amounts to, nihilism. The difference is that Gnosticism is strongly redemptionist. And my reading of *Blood Meridian*—particularly its epilogue—causes me to conclude that it is redemptionist as well, in precisely the same way and for precisely the same reasons, and that those who consider McCarthy a nihilist are off the track, although it is not difficult to see how they got there.

[3]McCarthy's fascination with coin-makers and their connection with fate (through the images they fashion) continues. Edwin T. Arnold has been kind enough to point out—and to share with me—a passage from an advance copy of *All the Pretty Horses* in which another young man in his teens, John Grady Cole, has related to him a parable of a coiner in circumstances which make it clear that the parable speaks centrally to both his present situation and his destiny. My inference is that McCarthy sees in coins and their makers compelling symbols of dualism and the difficulties (even the ambivalences) inherent in deriving unity from it: the authentic versus the counterfeit, the image on the slug versus the naked slug itself, the two sides of the coin, and of course—as in *Blood Meridian*—the symbolic (currency and coinage itself) versus the real (in the judge's sense).

[4]An. Sc. was once thought by some to be Anthony Scoloker, but this is just a wild (and unlikely) guess. The quote comes from *Daiphantus, or The Passions of Love* A2. With further reference to McCarthy's rare gift for combining tragedy with comedy: Bell points out that the author was originally named "Charles" and that his family renamed him "Cormac" for the fifteenth-century Irish king (xii). This king built Blarney Castle (c. 1446), but I have not noticed that anyone else has stumbled onto the fact that the true Blarney Stone there has for centuries had "Cormac McCarthy" inscribed upon it. "Blarney" supposedly derives from the king's gifts for cheerful, persuasive eloquence, although he was generally reckoned a "wise, melancholy man."

WORKS CITED

Bell, Vereen M. *The Achievement of Cormac McCarthy*. Baton Rouge: Louisiana State UP, 1988.

Bousset, Wilhelm. "Gnosticism." *Encyclopaedia Britannica*. 1911 ed.

Filoramo, Giovanni. *A History of Gnosticism*. Cambridge, MA: Blackwell, 1990.

Grant, Robert M. "Gnosticism." *Dictionary of the History of Ideas*. New York: Scribner's, 1973.

Greenlees, Duncan, ed. *The Gospel of the Prophet Mani*. Madras, India: Adyar, 1956.

Jonas, Hans. *The Gnostic Religion: The Message of the Alien God and the Beginnings of Christianity*. 2nd ed. Boston: Beacon, 1963.

_____. "Gnosticism." *Encyclopedia of Philosophy*. London: Macmillan, 1972.

McCarthy, Cormac. *Blood Meridian or the Evening Redness in the West*. 1985. New York: Ecco, 1986.

Meyer, Marvin W., ed. and trans. *The Secret Teachings of Jesus: Four Gnostic Gospels*. New York: Random, 1984.

Morrow, Mark. *Images of the Southern Writer*. Athens: U of Georgia P, 1985.

Pagels, Elaine. *The Gnostic Gospels*. 1979. New York: Vintage, 1981.

Sc., An. *Daiphantus, or The Passions of Love*. London: T.C. for William Cotton, 1604.

Wheelwright, Philip, ed. *The Presocratics*. London: Macmillan, 1966.

All the Pretty Horses

John Grady Cole's Expulsion from Paradise

GAIL MOORE MORRISON

Winner of the 1992 National Book Award and the 1992 National Book Critics Circle Award for fiction, Cormac McCarthy's sixth novel, *All the Pretty Horses*, simultaneously recapitulates and transcends many of the themes, situations, structures and characters of his earlier work, even while it is remarkably different from them. Like *Blood Meridian*, *All the Pretty Horses* is a western, although it is considerably gentler in tone and imbued with an archetypal aura of romance. Nonetheless, it is firmly grounded in the details of time (1949–1951) and place (west Texas in and around San Angelo, southeast to San Antonio, southwest to Langtry and Pumpville, farther south to various locations in the Mexican border state of Coahuila, and farther south still to Zacatecas), and topography (mountains, mesas, marshes, deserts, rivers). And, like its immediate predecessor, *All the Pretty Horses* is infused with the tensions of conflicting and competing cultures (the Anglo, the Comanche, the mestizo, the Mexican, the Spaniard) and economies (the agrarian-pastoral and the industrial-commercial, the legal and the illegal).

Like virtually all of McCarthy's work to date, *All the Pretty Horses* is permeated with a sense of loss, alienation, deracination and fragmentation.

The novel opens on 13 September 1949, the funeral day of John Grady Cole's maternal grandfather, whose death John Grady clearly understands portends the loss of the family ranch. And, although he is technically a boy, only sixteen, he recognizes that he is "like a man come to the end of something" (5). The last of his grandfather's line with its generations-deep commitment to the land, he is certainly as powerless to protect it against foreign encroachment—twentieth-century technology and the oil interests to which his often absent actress mother sells it—as was the Comanche nation he envisions as he rides out along their ancient war trail under a "bloodred and elliptic" sun "under the reefs of bloodred cloud" after his grandfather's funeral, "with the sun coppering his face and the red wind blowing out of the west." He hears "the low chant of their traveling song which the riders sang as they rode, nation and ghost of nation passing in a soft chorale across that mineral waste to darkness bearing lost to all history and all remembrance like a grail the sum of their secular and transitory and violent lives" (5). The comparison to the defeated and eradicated Comanche is made explicit by John Grady's divorced, dying father during their last horseback ride together:

> The last thing his father said was that the country would never be the same.
> People dont feel safe no more, he said. We're like the Comanches was two hundred years ago. We dont know what's goin to show up here come daylight. We dont even know what color they'll be. (25–26)

And, like the Comanche, the dispossessed John Grady, rejected by mother and girlfriend, will ride south shortly after Christmas on a quest of his own into a world of passion and greed, of primal ferocity and violence, to confront the codes and customs of another civilization which he is ill-equipped to understand and where his undefeatable adversaries turn out surprisingly to be two passionate and impassioned Mexican women.

While *All the Pretty Horses* looks backwards to *Blood Meridian*, which occurs some one hundred years earlier, for an abbreviated historical frame of reference to a changing land and dying people and for its western setting, it also shares with this and others of McCarthy's novels reliance on the central structuring principle of the journey. Most of McCarthy's novels, despite their apparent episodic organization, involve both metaphoric and literal journeys which bring their voyagers inevitably into a series of conflicts and confrontations with themselves as well as with the various communities intersected by their wanderings. And, in most of these novels, the central characters' journeys, however random in time and place they may be, are apparently rooted in dysfunctional families and troubled filial relationships. *Suttree* is the most extended development of the journey as metaphor for the exploration of the duality of the human soul, of the search for self, and of its apparently successful reintegration. The title character remains the most self-aware of McCarthy's troubled protagonists, the narrative point of view most intimately his. Nonetheless, the journey motif also informs *The Orchard Keeper*, where the fatherless John Wesley grows to manhood under the tutelage of two surrogate fathers, one of whom has actually murdered his real father; *Outer Dark*, where incestuous siblings Rinthy and Culla wander through a Dantean landscape in their dual quest, Rinthy for her child, Culla for Rinthy; *Child of God*, where Lester Ballard's search for community disintegrates into serial murder and a macabre quest for his own peculiar brand of romance; and *Blood Meridian*, where "the kid," under the tutelage of Judge Holden, his surrogate ﾐﾐﾐﾐﾐ"her," wanders through the desert more or less committed to horrific violence and destruction.

All the Pretty Horses is, as reviewers have noted, more conventionally plotted than its predecessors.[1] This assessment perhaps both underestimates the structural sophistication of the novel and testifies to the fact that in the earlier novels the unusual characters and their dark and unconventional behaviors—which encompass murder, infanticide, incest, necrophilia, suicide and cannibalism—distract readers from McCarthy's reliance on archetypal structural devices, including the journey and quest motifs, their apparently episodic, occasionally picaresque progression notwithstanding. It is difficult, for example, to think of any more classical plot device than the circularity of *Outer Dark*, which ends where it began, opening with the birth of a child and closing at the "grave" of the same child, or of *Suttree* with its city-country-city movement, from civilization into the wilderness and back again.

But *All the Pretty Horses* is set in a world of comparative normalcy, which is not to say that it is any less dominated by evil, any more controlled by rationality, logic or divine purpose, than that of its predecessors. John Grady Cole may no better understand the rapaciousness of the world, the divisions of the human heart or the power struggle that occurs behind the thick walls of the Hacienda de Nuestra Señora de la Purísima Concepción than John Wesley, Suttree or "the kid" comes to understand the circumstances of his own destiny. But John Grady confronts them with a courage, strength of character and grace that seem to emanate from an unwavering commitment to a set of significant values he has internalized, even when he might not have been expected to do so, given his youth, his upbringing or his inexperience.

For this novel is fundamentally a *Bildungsroman*, a coming of age story in the great tradition of Hawthorne, Twain, Melville and James, that archetypal American genre in which a youthful protagonist turns his back on civilization and heads out—into the forest, down river, across the sea or, as in John Grady's case, through desert and mountain on horseback—into the wilderness where innocence experiences the evil of the universe and risks defeat by it.[2] This initiation tale also is imbued with the uniquely American variation on the theme of the fall from innocence into experience so aptly explored by James in particular, but also by Hawthorne and Twain, in which the American naif with his straightforward, unsophisticated notions of right and wrong, his code of honor and his simplistic conception of good and evil, is challenged by the moral relativism of an older, more complex civilization to deepen that vision. McCarthy does not provide us with the characteristic Jamesian "center of consciousness" to explicate the conflicts experienced, to elucidate the lessons learned through an extended narrative of "psychological realism." Instead, character revelations are, for the most part, oblique and understated, implied through terse, sparse dialogue, inferred from specific actions and reactions. Landscape remains, in *All the Pretty Horses*, a central character and a characterizing agent.[3] Thus the lessons John Grady learns from his descent into Mexico and his rejection by his Mexican beloved in the very heart of that country remain elusive. His journey portrays him not solely as a modern day horse-taming cowboy, although his skills in this regard are the stuff of which legends are made, but as an unlikely knight errant, displaced and dispossessed, heroically tested and stubbornly faithful to a chivalric code whose power is severely circumscribed by the inevitable evil in a hostile world.

One reviewer has criticized the novel for John Grady Cole's larger than life heroic qualities[4]: his horsemanship, his physical stamina, his prowess with chess pieces and knife, his capacity to endure excruciating pain, his ability to doctor himself and others, his kinship with the land. By contrast to McCarthy's other protagonists, John Grady is clearly more hero than anti-hero. However, while all these attributes serve him well, they do not ensure that he will prevail. At novel's end, he returns to the cattle ranch virtually empty-handed, albeit one horse richer, after his Mexican odyssey; he has not won Alejandra and in fact appears to have seriously compromised her by alienating her from her father. Although he was the seduced as much as the seducer, their love is powerless against the irrevocable opposition of father and grand-aunt. Ultimately, the sixteen-year-old has no recourse other than to accept Alejandra's rejection, apparently promised to her aunt in exchange for the purchase of her lover's freedom from the prison into which her wrathful father has cast the unexpectedly dangerous usurper. Equally important, John Grady fails to protect one of his traveling companions, a thirteen-year-old runaway named Jimmy Blevins, for whose death he feels responsible and in expiation for which he risks his own life to recover the magnificent horse for which Jimmy was prepared to die.

By novel's end, when he returns to his own time and place and, briefly, to the now sold cattle ranch, John Grady's fall from innocence into experience encompasses sexual experience as well as betrayal in love and expulsion from paradise, his hands are bloodied with the self-defensive murder of a fellow prisoner in the purgatory of the Mexican prison, and his conscience is troubled by his passive acquiescence to Jimmy's "eye-for-an-eye" execution. He left a boy and returns a man, but it is a poignant and sobering rite of passage that leaves him still adrift in time and space. If it was the boy who bid goodbye to his maternal grandfather in the novel's second scene, in its penultimate scene it is the man who attends a second funeral, this time "Abuela's," or "Grandmother's," the surrogate mother who had worked for his family for fifty years. Her death severs the last remaining emotional tie he has to the ranch, his father having died while John Grady was in Mexico. His tears for Abuela are shed as well for the boyhood now behind him and for the somber vision of what is to come:

> he said goodbye to her in spanish and then turned and put on his hat and turned his wet face to the wind and for a moment he held out his hands as if to steady himself or as if to bless the ground there or perhaps as if to slow the world that was rushing away and seemed to care nothing for the old or the young or rich or poor or dark or pale or he or she. Nothing for their struggles, nothing for their names. Nothing for the living or the dead.[5] (301)

The novel's final scene evokes two early scenes. Just as he rode down the Comanche war path at sunset following his grandfather's funeral, after Abuela's funeral he rides out again, across the oil fields around Iraan, Texas, and past the sadly reduced few descendants of tribes such as the mighty Comanche, who are camped in wickiups on the western plains. The images closely link the two scenes: John Grady rides, leading

Blevins' wonderful bay, into a red desert under a "bloodred sunset" with "the sun coppering his face and the red wind blowing out of the west" as "their long shadows passed in tandem like the shadow of a single being. Passed and paled into the darkening land, the world to come" (302).[6] Marvelously compressed, the juxtaposition of the two scenes evokes the history of a defeated and decimated people (and links John Grady with them through the image of the sun "coppering" his face). It chronicles the despoiling of the land to which he no longer has any ties, and implies through the color imagery ("bloodred," "darkening") an ominous future for the land and its peoples alike.

Yet it is not insignificant that John Grady leads behind him Blevins' horse, and it is the image of the horses moving into the wind that links this scene with another early in the novel which tempers the pessimism of the novel's closing pages. Shortly after his grandfather's funeral, John Grady asks his mother to lease the ranch to him. She dismisses the notion that he could run the ranch as "ridiculous" (15) and ends the conversation by leaving her son sitting alone at the dining room table studying an oil painting of horses that had "been copied out of a book" (15–16):

> They had the long Andalusian nose and the bones of their faces showed Barb blood. You could see the hindquarters of the foremost few, good hindquarters and heavy enough to make a cuttinghorse. As if maybe they had Steeldust in their blood. But nothing else matched and no such horse ever was that he had seen and he'd once asked his grandfather what kind of horses they were and his grandfather looked up from his plate at the painting as if he'd never seen it before and he said those are picturebook horses and went on eating. (16)

The painting adumbrates precisely the central horse business of the Hacienda de Nuestra Señora de la Purísima Concepción where in an ironic double entendre on his estate's name Don Hector Rocha y Villareal has conceived a breeding strategy to produce a superior cutting horse by crossing his quarter horse mares with a thoroughbred stallion, "well muscled and heavily boned for his breed" (126). The horses in the painting appear to John Grady to embody precisely the same thing: Spanish stock crossed with the bloodline of Steeldust, the most celebrated Texas quarter horse stallion of one hundred years earlier. This legendary bay stallion, bred and foaled in Kentucky, was transported to Texas where he had a long and distinguished career in quarter racing, much of which is now impossible to trace.[7] In the tradition of Don Quixote and Tom Sawyer in *Huckleberry Finn*, John Grady is given a miraculous opportunity to bring the "picture-

book horses" to life and arrives at the hacienda only just enough ahead
of Rocha's imported chestnut stallion to have begun to cull out the mares
and train them.[8] Against this background, if Blevins' remarkable and presumably Texas-bred bay horse is associated with Steeldust in John Grady's
mind, then the motivation for his incredible "rescue" of the animal becomes
clearer. Although the animal is never specifically identified as stallion or
gelding, his legitimized possession of it at novel's end may suggest he now
has at his disposal the means and knowledge to bring his "picture-book
horses" into being on his own terms.[9]

John Grady is, of course, banished from the hacienda because Señor Rocha
is not interested in a similar experiment in crossbreeding between his
daughter Alejandra and the Texas import. Like the native mares, Alejandra
is described as being small and slight. She rides a black Arabian mare,
another ancient breed technically different from but customarily associated with the North African Barb. John Grady is master of all he rides, with
or without saddle or bridle, half-man, half-horse. His identification with
the stallion, "dripping and half crazed" (129) from its tryst with a mare,
is symbolic of his own sense of potency and vital energy: "Soy coman-
dante de las yeguas, he would say, yo y yo sólo. Sin la caridad de estas
manos no tengas nada. Ni comida ni agua ni hijos. Soy yo que traigo las
yeguas de las montañas, las yeguas jóvenes, las yeguas salvajes y ardien-
tes" (128).[10] Alejandra challenges both his authority and his mastery with
her own skill as horsewoman: she insists on riding the lathered stallion
bareback and does so with ease, revealing that her earlier appearances in
prim and proper riding hat and habit on the gaited Arabian are image and
not reality. Ultimately, she is as wild and passionate as the native mares,
a creature of the lake and lagoons, of the night and darkness, dark-haired
and dark-horsed. When she comes to John Grady's bed in the bunkhouse
on nine consecutive nights, she is more overtly the aggressor in the consum-
mation of their romance and, in the end, she is its most insistent destroyer.

This doomed romance is the third major plot line in the novel. Along
with the Jimmy Blevins subplot and the marvelously detailed business of
horse herding, breaking and breeding, it, like the others, is also subsumed
within the allegorical framework of the novel's carefully crafted initiation
motif. The novel's four chapters divide the book into distinctive but inter-
related sections: (1) the long *andante* movement of the journey south, on
horseback, through an increasingly sterile and incomprehensible wasteland,
a false purgatory that foreshadows the false redemption that follows; (2)
an *allegro* pastoral interlude in an edenic paradise, rife with fertility of

landscape and horse and the promise of Eve, the site of temptation for body as well as for spirit; (3) the *staccato* expulsion into purgatory of the newly fallen naif whose education in the dissonances of life's injustices, chaos and confusion has only just begun; and, finally, (4) the rendering of judgment, the component parts of which include the failed quest to regain paradise, retribution and a reintegrative odyssey home.

The movement of the first and fourth sections is generally linear; the movement of the second and third sections generally circular. The uninitiated, untested boy descends southward, discovering and formulating his code of conduct as he moves into a brave new world—heaven in Chapter II at La Purísima, hell in the prison in Chapter III—that is Blakean in its divisions and also reminiscent of Melville in the malevolent and omnipotent presence of evil. Tempted in the garden by Eve, expelled by the vengeful father and defeated by the wily serpent (in the guise of Alejandra's godmother), the fallen Adam, now with blood on his hands, rides "through a grove of apple trees gone wild and brambly and he picked an apple as he rode and bit into it and it was hard and green and bitter" (225–26).[11] Initiated into the "truth" of a hostile universe where "the wildness about him" is matched by "the wildness within" (60), John Grady has experienced the duality of man's nature, including his own. He has experienced first hand the fact that the chaos and anarchy, the irrationality and senselessness, of the world are perfectly capable of triumphing over love, loyalty, truth, law, justice, honor and idealism. As he ascends homeward, traveling into the dark northern wind across a landscape briefly covered with snow, then drenched by a symbolically cleansing, purifying rain, he displays against all odds a heroic capacity to accomplish his quixotic rescue of his horses, a quest undertaken as a matter of principle, as a reaffirmation of the traditional values and principles of honor, loyalty, courage and constancy in direct response to Dueña Alfonsa's refrain, "there is nothing to lose" (240). As a sphinx-like voice of moral authority at the novel's philosophical center, Alfonsa has experienced the overwhelming defeat of such principles, and in her despairing and embittered idealism sees in John Grady, not their embodiment, but the false and revolutionary hope of their re-enacted betrayal.

The first chapter is the novel's longest and most leisurely. It occupies almost one-third of the book's three hundred pages and begins by chronicling the severing of ties with John Grady's family and community, depicting the innocent's forced expulsion from an edenic childhood which adumbrates the guilty initiate's loss of paradise later on. Then it details the arduous journey south into Coahuila. While on the surface the journey may be a quest for such a paradise as young horsemen dream of—"Where do you reckon that paradise is at?" (59)—on a symbolic level it involves in essence the stripping bare of the human soul to its simple, most elemental level to test its integrity and determine its reason for being.[12] When John Grady and Rawlins cross the Rio Grande, they literally strip naked, unmasking. The landscape becomes progressively wilder and more barren: roads, trucks and stores give way to desert and mountain. The animals that they hear or fear become progressively more ferocious: coyote, wolf, lion. The food that they eat becomes increasingly more primitive: first purchased restaurant food, then canned goods, followed by food offered and prepared by others, to food hunted and cooked by themselves, first a rabbit, then a buck. The people they encounter become increasingly savage: the kindly family who worry about Blevins' embarrassment, the rough "zacateros" who ask about missing relatives, the migrant traders, the rootless waxmakers who try to buy the half-naked Jimmy, "el rubio" (75), whose blondness makes him doubly alluring, and finally the horse thieves of Encantada, where Rawlins accurately predicts, "Somethin bad is goin to happen" (77). There Jimmy mindlessly, carelessly, kills a man, an "officer of the state" (228) according to Dueña Alfonsa, in attempting to retrieve his ,tolen pistol.

As these reductions of each boy to the elemental, untamed, isolated and independent self occur, the interplay among John Grady, Rawlins and Blevins suggests what John Grady's moral stance will be. Rawlins' function as foil in the novel serves to illuminate John Grady's character. Rawlins' growing irritation, intensifying complaints, and eventually his ill-disguised but well-grounded fear—"You ever think about dyin?" (91) he asks—lead John Grady to question his loyalty: "You aint fixin to quit me are you?" (91). Rawlins has, after all, the home of his childhood to return to, so his quest lacks the seriousness of purpose of John Grady's. Rawlins' emotionalism contrasts with his friend's stoicism: his realism, which recognizes Jimmy Blevins as a dangerous force of chaos and anarchy, highlights John Grady's idealism and his sentimentality about the innocence of childhood. But Rawlins' judgments are grounded in clichés and conventions, and John Grady typically reacts against or ignores Rawlins' advice. For example, early in Chapter I, Rawlins comments about Mary Catherine's rejection, "She aint worth it. None of em are" (10), to which John Grady responds, "Yes they are" (10). Later Rawlins remarks that "[a] goodlookin horse is like a goodlookin woman. . . .

They're always more trouble than what they're worth. What a man needs is just one that will get the job done" (89) to which John Grady merely responds, "Where'd you hear that at?" (89). Rawlins' fundamental lack of sympathy for Blevins—his rudeness, his ridicule, his reluctance to ride to his rescue—all stand in marked contrast to the almost chivalrous responses of John Grady to women and to the younger boy alike. He assumes responsibility for Blevins because it is the noble and right thing to do; although he is powerless to control the senselessness and irrationality of the universe in which they must exist, he refuses to abandon Jimmy, despite his very powerlessness and Rawlins' demonstrable lack of support. Rawlins is a voice for non-engagement and convention, for self-interest and safety. He is ultimately the voice of childhood and so is sent home, bloodied, but little wiser for his adventure. Although John Grady's incredible skills with horses are not displayed in action until the novel's second and fourth chapters, by the end of the novel's first chapter, the interplay of characters, as well as the action proper of the plot, have established his essential value system as a positive one and have elucidated the revelation that

> What he loved in horses was what he loved in men, the blood and the heat of the blood that ran them. All his reverence and all his fondness and all the leanings of his life were for the ardenthearted and they would always be so and never be otherwise. (6)

For "the ardenthearted"—for Jimmy, for Alejandra, for himself, for Blevins' horse—he will risk much, for he is a man of action, of passion, of character and of honor, but he will nonetheless fail to attain paradise, although he will penetrate to the inner sanctum of its power through his confrontation with Dueña Alfonsa.

The novel's fourth and final chapter, its second longest, mirrors the first in its depiction of the severing of relationships and its account of the even more arduous return to Texas, since John Grady is now physically as well as psychologically wounded. Given the controlling initiation theme, this is an appropriate structural strategy which is subtly but masterfully handled. It carries with it the implicit comparison of the boy John Grady was to the man he has become. In the fourth section, for example, the ties which John Grady now severs are those in which he has a considerably deeper emotional investment, with Alejandra, with the fertile horse country, with the horses themselves. The first chapter begins, although it gradually darkens, with a boyish exuberance, a light-hearted adventure quest where pastures are literally and figuratively greener and still feed cattle and horses rather than the "great primitive birds welded up out of iron" (301) of the Texas oil fields. By contrast, in the fourth chapter, the journey home is marked by a seriousness of purpose, one of its goals retribution, another judgment on both himself and others.

John Grady's rescue of "all the pretty horses" that had been stolen from the three American boys by the Mexican authorities who are ostensibly pledged to uphold the law is simultaneously his retribution for Jimmy Blevins' death and his penance for his failure to prevent it. If in the novel's first chapter the promised land lies just over Coahuila's Sierra Encantada, that land of false enchantment has been stripped by novel's end of its magic. Its refinement and civility have been revealed as thin veneer, and its moral code exposed as distorted and subverted.

The novel's journey south is mirrored, then, in the return journey north. Many of the specific episodes in the novel's first chapter are elegantly balanced by similar scenes in its last chapter to heighten our sense of the new self emerging from the maëlstrom of John Grady's initiation into the world of experience. This structural device functions as an understated but nonetheless dramatic and highly controlled method of characterization and also to set his code of traditional values in opposition to the moral anarchy which threatens it at every turn.

The novel is framed by thirty and fifteen pages at beginning and end respectively, and these sections structurally balance each other with parallel episodes. As the novel opens, a series of brief vignettes depict John Grady disassociating himself from family, friends and community by judging them, especially his mother and girlfriend, to establish his independence before he heads off into the literal and figurative wilds of northern Mexico. By novel's end, after he emerges from the wilderness, several brief episodes depict his reintegration into the community and his willingness to be judged by it, formally in a court of law, and more informally through the paternal wisdom of the judge. The novel begins and ends with the funerals of Grandfather and Abuela and with brief encounters with John Grady's grudgingly loyal but ultimately unsympathetic friend and traveling companion Lacey Rawlins. John Grady's futile visit to a lawyer to ascertain whether he can do anything about the sale of the family ranch by exploring his father's right of title foreshadows his later more successful appearance in court where the judge grants him title to Blevins' horse. His visit to the judge's home, where he seeks paternal judgment as to the merits of his actions as well as absolution, echoes meetings early in the novel with his own father who urged his son to temper his harsh judgment of his mother and forgive her for her abandonment of him.

Other details reflect and refract against each other in the inverted movements of the novel's first and last chapters. John Grady's trip to watch his mother perform on stage in San Antonio is a tensely silent effort to understand her rejection of the ranch, of his father, of himself. It parallels his return trip to the hacienda and his extended conversation with Dueña Alfonsa, Alejandra's surrogate mother, whose rejection of him is even more ruthless, more complex. His father's brief account of his own failed marriage—"She liked horses. I thought that was enough" (24)—and the chasm between the aspiring actress and the cowboy-gambler play out in miniature the larger conflict of class and culture in which John Grady finds himself embroiled with the exemplary horsewoman Alejandra. John Grady's bitter farewell to his former girlfriend, Mary Catherine, who has rejected him in favor of another boy, foreshadows his despairing but more compassionate separation from Alejandra, who can better cope with the loss of his love than with the loss of her father's, although the extent to which her father's wealth, status and power are implicated in her decision remains unclear.

The journeys themselves are also carefully juxtaposed through the structural counterpointing of their component episodes. The horseback ride south with John Grady's friend Lacey Rawlins and the runaway Jimmy Belvins is mirrored in John Grady's more somber return northward with their now riderless horses. In each instance a posse follows in hot pursuit, but by novel's end it is John Grady himself rather than Blevins who is the object of the pursuers' murderous intent. John Grady's rejection of the Mexican wax workers' offer to buy Jimmy adumbrates his meeting with the "men of the country" who take the captain, the agent of Jimmy's murder, away from him, probably to execute him for crimes against the people, a judgment to which John Grady now acquiesces. The boys' casual conversation about the Del Rio radio station foreshadows John Grady's visit to the Rev. Jimmy Blevins, a Del Rio radio evangelist whose name the boy seems to have appropriated to hide his identity. Blevins' tall tale about his family's inherited affinity for being struck by lightning is balanced by John Grady's telling of his own story to a group of children in the mode of a tragic fairy tale or romance. Finally, almost at journey's end in Chapter I, Rawlins shoots a spikehorn buck; John Grady notices matter-of-factly merely that "it lay dead in its blood" and "its eyes were just glazing," but otherwise the boys' conversation revolves around the "hell of a shot" that killed it (90). Contrast this episode to the parallel scene of John Grady's killing a small doe toward the end of his journey

homeward. The act has profoundly deepened in meaning and recapitulates
John Grady's rites of passage:

> When he reached her she lay in her blood in the grass and he knelt with the
> rifle and put his hand on her neck and she looked at him and her eyes were
> warm and wet and there was no fear in them and then she died. He sat watch-
> ing her for a long time. He thought about the captain and he wondered if he
> were alive and he thought about Blevins. He thought about Alejandra and he
> remembered her the first time he ever saw her passing along the Ciénaga road
> in the evening. . . . He remembered Alejandra and the sadness he'd first seen
> in the slope of her shoulders which he'd presumed to understand and of which
> he knew nothing and he felt a loneliness he'd not known since he was a child
> and he felt wholly alien to the world although he loved it still. He thought that
> in the beauty of the world were hid a secret. He thought the world's heart beat
> at some terrible cost and that the world's pain and its beauty moved in a rela-
> tionship of diverging equity. . . . (282)

Just as the style of this passage echoes Hemingway's, John Grady is like a
number of Hemingway's young protagonists in that he finds that his destiny
is strangely but inevitably linked to war and revolution. Only in his case it is
a war long since past, and not contemporaneous with the action proper of the
novel: the Mexican Revolution of 1911–1913. His rejection by Alejandra,
to the extent that it is explained, is mysteriously rooted in the power of the
seventy-three-year-old Dueña Alfonsa, whose monologue reveals her obsession with the life and times of the failed idealist of the revolution, the mar-
tyred Francisco I. Madero, and his family. These have become not only the
emotional center of her life but the essence of Mexico since their martyrdom
precipitated a bloody revolution that lasted for forty years, virtually Alfonsa's
entire adult life. The novel implies that the revolution in a sense is unending;
the essential nature of human existence is an unending dialectical tension between law and lawlessness, order and anarchy, realism and idealism, heroism
and cowardice, paradise and purgatory, the hacienda and "el campo."

John Grady's final rite of passage is his immersion in the anarchy of that
revolution through the justification and defense of her life which Alfonsa
shares with him as the ultiamte explanation for his failure to claim Alejandra. This device is strongly reminiscent of the monologue which Miss Rosa
Coldfield delivers to the twenty-year-old Quentin Compson in Faulkner's
Absalom, Absalom! The two spinsters share a number of important characteristics, including their obsession with the central male figure in their tales,
each of whom is master of a vast estate, author of a grand but failed design,

soldier and revolutionary. Each man is also executed ignominiously. Each young woman is both attracted and repelled by the "failed idealist," by Sutpen and by Francisco Madero respectively. Like Miss Rosa, Dueña Alfonsa feels compelled to justify herself and her actions across time to her youthful auditor. As it was said of Miss Rosa that she never forgave "the final and complete affront which was Sutpen's death" (14), so it could also be said that Alfonsa never recovered from the "death" of her relationsh with Francisco's brother, Gustavo, or from the horror of the Maderos' executions. In her monologue, as in Miss Rosa's, Alfonsa reveals her outrage at her own sense of her powerlessness, inferiority and missed opportunities. In justifying herself, she nonetheless manages, unwittingly, to condemn herself. Both women are dominated by strong fathers who espouse compelling and destructive principles, the girlhood of each is hopelessly decimated by the holocaust of revolution, and in the sterility of her old age, each labors to craft an explanation and a defense for her own attitudes and behaviors.

It is as if all the images of blood in the novel—the bloodred clouds, sun, desert and wind; the blood of the dispossessed Indians; the blood pounding through the veins of horse and cowboy; Alejandra's virgin blood; the spilled, sacrificial blood of Jimmy, the boy in prison, the captain, the doe and, ultimately, John Grady's own—coalesce in the central metaphor of the Mexican revolution, whose violence and madness become for Alfonsa the ultimate truth, the essential destiny: "the ruin of a nation. . . . How it was and how it will be again" (231). Ironically, the hacienda and Alfonsa herself, then as now, are distanced from the realities of the revolution, the poverty, lawlessness and anarchy across the land which are all too apparent during John Grady's journey. Even while she espouses intellectually the revolution's reformist idealism of empowering the people, spreading agrarian reform and landing the landless, on the Hacienda de la Purísima Concepción, it is as if the revolution never were, as if it remained only the purest conception of an empty ideal.

Alfonsa is both a radical and a reactionary. On the one hand she rebels against the suppression of women and paternal authority, refusing marriage and rejecting a conventional marriage for her great-niece. She has espoused the reformist causes of the Maderos, in her seventeen-year-old idealism, although they run counter to the traditional interests of the landed aristocracy of which she and the Maderos are members and which seems to have managed to preserve its way of life. But she is sent safely out of the line of revolutionary fire to Europe where she is checkmated by being not only unable to rebel against her father but also unable to forgive him for her deportation. Her frustration is reflected in her vision of the world as a "puppet show"

(231). And if she has been in her youth a puppet, so now in her old age she becomes the puppeteer who pulls the strings of her great-niece's life. What is left her is to live vicariously through Alejandra, who "is the only future" (239) she contemplates, whose name echoes her own. Without scruple, she bends the girl to her will and changes her destiny by taking advantage of the opportunity to save John Grady's life. She buys his way out of prison in exchange for Alejandra's promise to reject his offer of marriage.

The fact that Alejandra is precisely the same age Alfonsa was when Francisco and Gustavo returned from Europe and her "life changed forever" (234) is ominous. Alfonsa's life was perhaps inspired by the Maderos' revolutionary fire, which literally loosed anarchy and chaos across the land and in short order upon themselves, but her life was also ruined by it. She was exiled from country, friends and family, and the lessons learned from that experience, while admirable in their stoicism, are nihilistic. Embittered, she has watched the idealism of the reformers destroy the "brave and good and honorable men" (236) who fueled the revolution because they could not channel that idealism or control it. The legacies of the revolution—a failure given the apparent changelessness of La Purísima and the poverty, corruption and lawlessness of the land beyond—to Alfonsa are reduced to the "bonds of grief," the "closest bonds we will ever know" in the "deepest community of sorrow" (238). The only certainty in the defeated dreams of the revolutionary world is the one constant of history, "greed and foolishness and a love of blood and this is a thing that even God—who knows all that can be known—seems powerless to change" (239). In repeating history—in pulling the strings of Alejandra's life and in effecting the expulsion of John Grady much as she expelled Gustavo—Alfonsa is ostensibly confident that she knows best the lessons of time and history. But Alfonsa may simply be deluding herself as to her motivations with respect to her great-niece.

For ultimately, as the novel is at great pains to show, John Grady is not the gentle dreamer, the failed idealist, although he is neither without ideals nor without gentleness. He is a man of action capable of negotiating the troubled terrain of the wilderness, even of mastering it occasionally. But he is also like the quixotic hero of the revolution, Madero, in that he possesses both a capacity for self-deception, believing that he can achieve the impossible, as well as the charisma of leadership, the ability to persuade others that he can achieve the impossible. That is both his promise and his threat, and therein lies the source of his rejection. Alfonsa protests that she rejects him not because he is "young or without education or from another country" (240). In actuality she may see in him the real revolutionaries of her youth, the Zapatas, Obregóns, Villas and, in her native state of Coahuila, Pablo Gonzalez, for whom her destroyed aristocrats, Francisco and Gustavo, were too conservative, not radical enough. The paradoxical achievement inherent in their own personal failure as leaders was to inspire the real revolution in which, according to one account, "a vehement desire to regenerate everything asserted itself, an impulse to transform the whole social fabric of Mexico in its diverse aspects."[13] This desire burned bright for the next forty years and is still reflected in the "men of the country" who emerge as agents of justice and retribution on John Grady's journey home.

It is possible, then, that Alfonsa sees in John Grady a manifestation of the betrayers who initially supported the Maderos and then turned against them, the men of the land who are not landed, the idealists who dared dream, who aspired above their class, looked outside their station, who possessed the strength and courage and merit to upend the world if but a smidgin of power, or a single ideal, were granted to them. But ultimately her sympathies do not lie with the revolutionaries who subverted the dream into a bloody reality, illustrated most dramatically in the account of the murder of Gustavo Madero. She tells John Grady:

> In the end we all come to be cured of our sentiments. Those whom life does not cure death will. The world is quite ruthless in selecting between the dream and the reality, even where we will not. Between the wish and the thing the world lies waiting. (238)

Hers is a grim and to some extent unjust vision, rooted in the nature of existence as she has experienced it, or watched from afar. It recognizes John Grady's inherent worth but rejects his danger, misinterprets his motives, discounts his heartfelt offer of marriage. More importantly, it takes no risks, for it is passive and sterile at its core. When Alejandra accedes to this vision—"I cannot do what you ask, she said. I love you. But I cannot" (254)—then John Grady realizes that his banishment from the empty garden, and his participation in the inner and outer wildness, are complete:

> He saw very clearly how all his life led only to this moment and all after led nowhere at all. He felt something cold and soulless enter him like another being and he imagined that it smiled malignly and he had no reason to believe that it would ever leave. (254)

But John Grady does not fall prey to existential despair in an irrational and indifferent world. Nor does he withdraw from that world in bitterness, in unforgiving judgment, in self-pity as he might have, as he did in fact early in the novel in his immaturity. Instead, there is something in the history lesson Alfonsa shares with him which galvanizes him to action. The rescue of his and Rawlins' horses, as well as Belvins' horse, seems certainly to be an impassioned response to Alfonsa's "there is nothing to lose" (239). John Grady's losses and disappointments cannot help but be placed in perspective by contrast with the horrifying account of the destruction of Alfonsa's beloved, a man of ideals and principles but, at least by contrast with his brother, also a man of action and practicality and hence linked with John Grady across the distances of time and place. Gustavo's courage and stoicism in the face of violence, his fortitude in pain, his ultimate assumption of responsibility and the dignity with which he bears the consequences of his actions are all ultimately reflected in the events of John Grady's homeward journey, the naif no longer, but a man considerably deepened and enriched by the experience.

NOTES

[1] For example, in his thoughtful review in the *New York Times Book Review*, Madison Smartt Bell notes that "where 'Suttree' and 'Blood Meridian' are deliberately discontinuous, apparently random in the arrangement of their episodes, 'All the Pretty Horses' is quite conventionally plotted." For this reason, and because of the "presence of a plainly sympathetic protagonist," the novel is "probably the most accessible of Mr. McCarthy's six novels, though it certainly preserves all his stylistic strength" (9).

[2] For Richard Ryan in his review in the *Christian Science Monitor*, the novel is merely "a conventional coming-of-age novel," "woefully meager literature." By contrast, Irving Malin in his review in *Commonweal* sees the novel as resembling "[o]n one level . . . the traditional initiation we find in *Huckleberry Finn* or, for that matter, in Faulkner's *The Reivers*. (The novel seems particularly 'American' because of its underlying structure; it is our kind of *adolescent picaresque*.) But on a second (and deeper) level it is an occult narrative of the ultimate meanings—if there are any—of these adventures. There are echoes of a religious quest, a trip to discover the Holy Grail."

[3] Alan Cheuse writes appreciatively of the important use of landscape in "A Note on Landscape in *All the Pretty Horses*."

[4] In his review in the *Los Angeles Times Book Review*, Richard Eder complains that John Grady "is simply too good at everything" and compares him to "Parsifal" (13).

[5] This passage, as well as the earlier ride through the snow, echoes James Joyce's story "The Dead" in *Dubliners*: "His soul swooned slowly as he heard the snow

falling faintly through the universe and faintly falling, like the descent of their last end, upon all the living and the dead" (288). It also recalls in a more general way the prayer to nothingness in Hemingway's "A Clean, Well-Lighted Place": "It was all a nothing and a man was nothing too" (32).

[6] The end of the novel echoes in a number of important details—the young man headed west, the workers, the wind, the clouds, the red sunset, the blood imagery, the interplay of light and shadow, the evocation of a lost people—the ending of *The Orchard Keeper*:

> He sat there for a while, rubbing his foot abstractedly, whistling softly to himself. To the west a solid sheet of overcast sped the evening on. Already fireflies were about. He put on his shoe and rose and began moving toward the fence, through the wet grass. The workers had gone, leaving behind their wood-dust and chips, the white face of the stump pooling the last light out of the gathering dusk. The sun broke through the final shelf of clouds and bathed for a moment the dripping trees with blood, tinted the stones a diaphanous wash of color, as if the very air had gone to wine. He passed through the gap in the fence, past the torn iron palings and out to the western road, the rain still mizzling softly and the darkening headlands drawing off the day, heraldic, pennoned in flame, the fleeing minions scattering their shadows in the wake of the sun.
>
> They are gone now. Fled, banished in death or exile, lost, undone. Over the land sun and wind still move to burn and sway the trees, the grasses. No avatar, no scion, no vestige of that people remains. On the lips of the strange race that now dwells there their names are myth, legend, dust. (246)

[7] According to Wayne Gard in *Fabulous Quarter Horse: Steel Dust*, Steel Dust was a yearling stallion in 1844 and became one of the foundation sires of the most popular strains of quarter horses. Standing between fifteen and sixteen hands high, weighing 1100–1200 pounds and thus larger than the average quarter horse, he was exceptionally well-muscled. His demand as a sire greatly increased after 1855 when he defeated Monmouth at age twelve. However, his racing career ended that same year when he injured his shoulder, probably as a result of his growing blindness, at the beginning of a match with Shiloh, another of the great quarter horse foundation stallions. Steel Dust was still standing at stud in April of 1864 and is thought to have lived until age thirty or thirty-two. Rocha's stallion is described similarly: he "stood sixteen hands high and weighed about fourteen hundred pounds and he was well muscled and heavily boned for his breed" (126). One of the notable attributes passed to his get and transmitted through generations by Steel Dust was a very prominent jaw. In justifying to Rawlins the worth of some of the hacienda's horses, John Grady remarks of one, "That's a good horse. Look at his head. Look at the jaw on him" (99). This may link Steel Dust explicitly to the first stage of the breeding enterprise at La Purísima. Señor Rocha had already established a program to breed quarter horses after the war, importing American sires of the "Traveler-Ronda" (101) quarter horse line (descendants of both Steel Dust and Shiloh) to cross with native mares, presumably descendants of the Andalusians ridden by the Spanish conquistadores.

[8]The brief account of the illiterate Antonio's being sent to Kentucky for the stallion is reminiscent of Faulkner's tale of the three-legged horse's English groom, old Negro and child in *A Fable*; they display a similar and amazing resourcefulness in a foreign world (153–58).

[9]In *Cities of the Plain,* the final volume of the Border Trilogy, there is no mention of Blevins' wonderful horse; though John Grady continues to work as a horse trainer on McGovern's ranch in New Mexico, the later novel does not fulfill the promises tentatively held out for John Grady's future at the end of *All the Pretty Horses.*

[10]"I am commandant of the mares, he would say, I and I alone. Without the charity of these hands you have nothing. Neither food nor water nor children. It is I who bring the mares from the mountains, the young mares, the wild and ardent mares."

[11]While the biblical story of *Genesis* is the most overt, other mythic substructures resonate throughout the novel, including the Greek (the *Odyssey*; the story of the Golden Fleece; the descent of Orpheus into the underworld to rescue Eurydice), the Arthurian quest for truth and the holy grail and the Bible's story of Job. All of these imbue the novel with its timeless, archetypal quality and, despite its wonderful humorous moments, invest it with a tragic dimension.

[12]For Irving Malin, the plot is, for the most part, merely an excuse to look for "epistemological answers," and the novel will "assume its place as an example of the great religious novels written by any American."

[13]Martín Luís Guzmán, "Foreword," *The Eagle & the Serpent.* While I have not attempted to identify sources for the novel, it clearly relies on historical materials, especially for Dueña Alfonsa's account of the martyrdom of the Maderos, sometimes to as close a degree as John Emil Sepich has demonstrated for *Blood Meridian* in his article " 'What kind of indians was them?': Some Historical Sources in Cormac McCarthy's *Blood Meridian*" in this volume. For example, Alfonsa's account of the execution of Gustavo Madero (237) strongly echoes its telling by Stanley R. Ross in *Francisco I. Madero: Apostle of Mexican Democracy*:

> . . . Gustavo was taken by car to the Ciudadela. . . .
>
> The President's brother was forced with blows and pushes to the door leading to the patio. Bleeding, his face distorted by blows, his clothes torn, Gustavo tried to resist that frenzied, drunken mob. . . . Holding desperately to the frame of the door he appealed to that sea of faces reflecting the madness of mob violence. Referring to his wife, children, and parents, he pleaded with them not to kill him. His words were greeted by jeers and laughter. One of the crowd pushed forward and, with the mattock from his rifle or the point of a sword, picked out the prisoner's good eye. The blinded Gustavo uttered a single mournful cry of terror and desperation. After that, he made no more sounds, but covering his face with his hands turned toward the wall.
>
> The mob laughed and jeeringly referred to the victim as a "coward" and a "whiner" and as "Ojo Parado." Prodding and sticking him with mattock and sword points and dealing him blows with fists and sticks they forced him to the patio. Gustavo moved, stumbling, without uttering a word. An assailant pressed a revolver to his head. The hand holding the weapon was unsteady and slipped, and the shot tore Gustavo's jaw

away. He was still able to move a short distance, falling, at last, near the statue of More-los which, inappropriately, was silent witness to this scene. A volley of shots was fired into the body. One of the crowd fired yet another shot into the body explaining drunkenly that it was *coup de grâce*. The assassins proceeded to sack the body, and Gustavo's enamel eye was extracted and circulated from hand to hand. (313)

Many, although not all, of the salient facts concerning the Maderos appear in Ross's work, and McCarthy may also have consulted the primary sources cited by Ross as well.

WORKS CITED

Bell, Madison Smartt. "The Man Who Understood Horses." *New York Times Book Review* 17 May 1992: sec. 7: 9+.

Cheuse, Alan. "A Note on Landscape in *All the Pretty Horses.*" *Southern Quarterly* 30.4 (1992): 140–42.

Eder, Richard. "John's Passion." *Los Angeles Times Book Review* 17 May 1992: 3+.

Faulkner, William. *Absalom, Absalom!* New York: Modern Library, 1964.

———. *A Fable.* New York: Modern Library, 1966.

Gard, Wayne. *Fabulous Quarter Horse: Steel Dust, The True Account of the Most Celebrated Texas Stallion.* New York: Duell, Sloan and Pearce, 1958.

Guzmán, Martín Luís. *The Eagle & the Serpent.* New York: Knopf, 1930.

Hemingway, Ernest. "A Clean, Well-Lighted Place." *The Snows of Kilimanjaro and Other Stories.* New York: Scribner's, 1964. 29–33.

Joyce, James. "The Dead." *Dubliners.* New York: Modern Library, 1954. 224–88.

Malin, Irving. "A Sense of Incarnation." *Commonweal* 119 (25 Sept. 1992): 29.

McCarthy, Cormac. *All the Pretty Horses.* New York: Knopf, 1992.

———. *The Orchard Keeper.* New York: Random House, 1965.

Ross, Stanley R. *Francisco I. Madero: Apostle of Mexican Democracy.* New York: Columbia UP, 1955.

Ryan, Richard. "Galloping Fiction." *Christian Science Monitor* 84 (11 June 1992): 13.

Sepich, John Emil. " 'What kind of indians was them?': Some Historical Sources in Cormac McCarthy's *Blood Meridian.*" *Perspectives on Cormac McCarthy.* Ed. Edwin T. Arnold and Dianne C. Luce. Jackson: UP of Mississippi, 1993. 121–141.

The Road and the Matrix:

The World as Tale in *The Crossing*

DIANNE C. LUCE

Like *All the Pretty Horses* (1992), *Blood Meridian* (1985), and *Outer Dark* (1968), *The Crossing* is a road narrative, but more than in the earlier novels *The Crossing* employs the road as metaphor for the life journey or the narrative of a life. "En realidad la vía del mundo no es fijada en ningún lugar. . . . Nosotros mismos somos nuestra propia jornada. Y por eso somos el tiempo también" (In reality the way [or road] of the world is not fixed in any place. . . . We ourselves are our own day's journey. And therefore we are time as well), the gypsy tells Billy near the end of the novel (413–14). *The Crossing* focuses on the course of life, sequential and linear, causative, perhaps fated and yet surprising, as narrative plot—as story. And McCarthy is concerned with the role or function of story in human experience of life, not only our own stories, our autobiographies, but our biographies of others, our witnessing.[1] These concerns are manifested in the folk ballad or *corrido* (literally, the running or the flowing) associated with Boyd, and in the many stories told Billy by the people whose paths cross his on his journeys in Mexico. The three longest tales told to Billy—by the priest at Huisiachepic, by the blind revolutionary and his wife, and by the gypsy in charge of the wrecked airplane—create eddies in the flow of his own tale, still pools in which the forward course of his own life lulls and he becomes audience to other lives parallel and tangential to his own. There are also many briefer "tales" embedded in Billy's narrative: encounters in which minor characters tell partial tales, parables, or just the morals of their stories—interpreting or foretelling life to the young man who approaches the end of his road in *The Crossing* claiming that most of what he has heard is fraudulent (418) and that life has "but one reality and that was the living of it" (380). These include Don Arnulfo's "tale" of the wolf and its place in the matrix of the world; the prophecies, warnings, and interpretations of his own life offered Billy by indians, fortunetellers, and the horse factor Gillian, and which he almost always rejects; the tale within a tale of *I Pagliacci* enacted by the traveling opera company, and the diva's related tale of the murder of the theatrical mule; the local philosopher's comments on the mapping of reality and the role of the map-maker; the tale of the killing of the *jefe* popularly circulated after Boyd's wounding, and which prefigures the *corrido*; the "tale" of Boyd held to by the Mexican girl in contention against Billy's own tale of him; Quijada's account of Boyd's fate; the tale of the American who has hired the *gitano* and who explicitly contradicts his tales of the airplane. Stripped of these tales, the road narrative of Billy's life is a greatly diminished thing. Even so, there are the tales that reach closure within the open-ended narrative of Billy's young manhood, the sub-plots or major movements within his own story, all of which involve great loss and which evoke the exquisite sadness of the book: the doomed enterprise of Billy's attempt to return the wolf to the mountains of Mexico, the deaths of his parents, Boyd's brief ride to heroic stature and early death, the fall from grace of the opera diva, which Billy only infers because he cannot bear to witness her debasement, his successful but largely empty enterprise of recovering and interring Boyd's bones in New Mexico.

The Crossing is indeed a matrix of intersecting stories, partial or complete, often competing, with varying relationships to truth, cutting across and interwoven with the apparently simple linearity of the road narrative of Billy's life. The novel suggests alternately that the events of his life flow in a continuous thread from the hands of the weaver god (149)[2] or that they come to him seemingly by chance in the course of the road he runs, or through some logic of the road itself. But ironically Billy has attempted to plot his own course even as a child. The novel begins with his mapping the world for his baby brother and telling him stories about their future: "He carried Boyd before him in the bow of the saddle and named to him features of the landscape and birds and animals in both spanish and english. . . . [H]e would lie awake at night and listen to his brother's breathing in the dark and he would whisper half aloud to him as he slept his plans for them and the life they would have" (3). And Billy continues intermittently to journey with such intentionality until he reaches closure on one of the goals he sets for himself: to recover Boyd's bones. Billy attempts what almost everyone attempts, to script his own life. But each destination he sets for himself in pursuit of his sense of rightness or justice—returning the wolf to Mexico, recovering his father's horses, retrieving Boyd's bones—brings unforeseen consequences and calamitous loss. He learns, as one of the locals debating the merits of map-making points out, that "plans were one thing and journeys another" (185).

In an image analogous to the road metaphor, these sudden turns of fortune seem to flow on the rivers Billy attempts to cross or to ride along: the wolf is taken from him after his failed attempt to cross a river; Boyd is shot on the banks of a river; Billy's last memento of his father, the horse Niño, is stabbed nearly mortally and Boyd's bones are walked in near the river along which the gypsies transport the remains of the second airplane. In his first story of the airplane, the *gitano* offers Billy an image of a drowned man afloat on the river that encapsules this notion of man's life borne upon the rushing flume of events and yet endowed with the illusion of intentionality:

> a drowned man shot out of the cataract upriver like a pale enormous fish and circled once facedown in the froth of the eddywater . . . as if he were looking for something on the river's floor and then he was sucked away downriver to continue his journey. He'd come already a long way in his travels by the look of him for his clothes were gone and much of his skin and all but the faintest nap of hair upon his skull all scrubbed away by his passage over the river rocks. . . . [W]hen he passed beneath them they could see revealed in him that of which men were made that had better been kept from them. . . . He circled and gathered speed and then exited in the roaring flume as if he had pressing work downriver. [408–09]

Though Billy's own choices in some sense "lead" to his griefs, the events of his life bear him along in directions entirely contrary to his intentions, and he is no more responsible for his losses than is the heretic hermit for the deaths of his parents and little boy, the revolutionary for his blinding at the hands of a madman, or the pilot's father for the death of his son. This is so despite Billy's desire to make sense of his experience by assuming guilt and despite his intermittent attempts to escape unforetold disaster by drifting, which he always does for a period of months or years after each defeat. Such drifting constitutes his abdication of the authoring of his own life in response to his recognition of the limits the world places on his will,[3] a commitment to the road or the flow of experience without autobiographical narrating to give it shape, direction or meaning. Billy's experiences raise the question of action in the face of unexpected, specifically unforeseeable and yet inevitable loss, and at times for him life becomes mere motion, having no meaning beyond the living of it from moment to moment, from one experience of pain and thwarting to the next. When Billy contemplates the gypsies, he infers they have concluded that "movement itself is a form of property" (410); but the *gitano*'s extended story is designed specifically to offer Billy an alternative to his despair by validating the narrative acts that could give meaning to his life and to his terrible losses. As the priest has told Billy, "All is telling" (155).

Having absorbed (and perhaps transformed) the old pensioner's deathbed assertions that "Ultimately every man's path is every other's" and that "There are no separate journeys" (156–57), the priest says that all tales are one. In the sense that all lives encounter moments of grace, reflecting the primary gift of life, and losses unexpected in their particulars though generally predictable, prefiguring the protagonists' ultimate deaths, this is undeniably so. The priest's tale and the blind revolutionary's tale focus primarily on the survival of great loss and narrate their protagonists' attempts to make meaning of their bereavements. As such, they comment aptly on Billy's own losses, but he takes no comfort from their stories nor from the information that such grief is universal. He does listen respectfully, and he finds the blinded man's wife, who has narrated much of his tale, "very beautiful" (294). Both tales, of course, are narrated by witnesses, and thus comprise figurative tales within tales; to differing degrees, the tales told of the old heretic and the blind man are presented as portions (subplots) of the incompletely told tales of their narrators. The priest comments explicitly on the role of witnessing others' lives as a solution to the problem of living one's own—as a way of breaking out of the relentlessly linear road narrative of one's life and connecting into the larger matrix of the world by witnessing and being witnessed (154). The idea is echoed and extended in the *gitano*'s tale of the old photos collected by his father and the lessons he drew from them: "as the kinfolk in their fading stills could have no value save in another's heart so it was with that heart also in another's" (413). This matrix of witnessing, in which individuals' tales encompass and are embedded in one another's, and in which we are our lives not only as we live them from day to day but also as we are tabernacled in the hearts and memories of others who participate in creating the meaning of our lives, validates story as life itself even where particular stories may be seen as lies or fiction.

Although Billy denies or ignores the assertions about him or his course of action made by several minor characters throughout the novel, McCarthy's treatment of the "truth" of narrative is concentrated in the latter sections, after Boyd has died and Billy is told he has two brothers: the one who is dead and the other who lives (369), presumably in the *corrido*. Billy, of course, denies that he has two brothers and has no inkling of what the palm reader might mean; he remains true to his solipsistic view of his brother as he alone has witnessed him, although he eventually makes concession to the Mexicans' view when he restores their shrine to Boyd after he exhumes his brother's bones from his Mexican grave, and he admits to Quijada late in the novel that maybe he has not known Boyd at all, and that Boyd might actually have known Billy himself better (387). The *gitano* tells Billy that the past "is always this argument between counterclaimants" (411), and this is so not only of the three tales the gypsy tells of the airplane but of many of the novel's minor tales as well. The *gitano*'s narrative, however, is the primary locus of McCarthy's treatment of the authority of competing narratives and the complex relationship of experience, witness, and tale. Together with the earlier diva's tale, it comments on the role of fiction in our lives and on the validity of our lives as fictions.

When Billy sees the opera company perform in Hacienda de San Diego, he watches with interest but feels he understands little of what they enact— a dynamic that in fact characterizes Billy in all his encounters after the death of the wolf. Significantly, he guesses that as they perform the play, "The company was perhaps describing some adventure of their own in their travels" (219), a notion suggested to him by his observation that the mules and caravan that carry the company on their road tour are themselves in the opera, costumed or decorated for their parts. The work performed is Leoncavallo's *I Pagliacci*[4] (*Punchinello*), a two-act opera of the realistic *verismo* school, set at the intersection of two roads in a village in Calabria, and which itself concerns a traveling company of *commedia dell'arte* performers. Its prologue announces that the events to be enacted actually occurred, suggesting that art imitates life. But the opera also depicts the converse, as the second act of the opera, the comic play-within-a-play, burlesques the first act, which introduces the real tensions among the players. After hearing a warning in Act I that his wife Nedda is planning to run off with her lover, and enraged that she will not reveal the identity of the man, the jealous husband Canio confuses the comic play and painful reality during their performance of a similar situation in Act II. He kills Nedda on stage as well as her lover Silvio when Silvio finally recognizes that he is witnessing more than the comedy and comes to her aid. *I Pagliacci* itself, then, is a play-within-a-play in which the fiction impacts reality and reality is transformed to, represented in, or masked by fiction.

McCarthy's use of *I Pagliacci* extends this reciprocal matrix even further, adding more layers to Leoncavallo's tale. In *The Crossing* the opera about a traveling comedy troupe is enacted by a traveling opera caravan which performs in a small village in Mexico. McCarthy's scene describing the gathering of the inhabitants of Hacienda de San Diego parallels that describing the convening of the villagers in Calabria, and Billy himself reflects the uncomprehending audience in *I Pagliacci* who gather to see a comedy and only slowly realize they are witnessing something quite the reverse.[5] In a grimly comic twist on the tragi-comic realism of *I Pagliacci*, the Mexican opera company too enacts violence within its own troupe in the second act of its story as witnessed by Billy. When he and Boyd find the caravan broken down by the road, the diva tells him that one of the company, the drunken *arriero* (muleteer) Gaspar, has murdered one of their "dramatic mules" (226) on the road by cutting its throat (as Canio has threatened Nedda when demanding the name of her lover) and has also assaulted Rogelio as he tried to protect the mule (as Silvio tried to come to Nedda's aid). Gaspar emerges from the wagon as they converse, and when Billy asks the diva why the punchinello or clown (Pagliacci) kills her in the opera, she looks to Gaspar for an answer. Billy thinks it is because he is jealous (Billy has correctly inferred that the man killed in the opera is "perhaps his rival" [219]); but Gaspar says it is because he knows the secret that "en este mundo la mascara es la que es verdadera" (in this world the mask is that which is true[6]; 229).

Gaspar's comment implies not only the blurring of the lines between art and reality, but that in some way art or what is performed is the thing itself, or at least can be taken for it. His assertion resonates with the experience of the American boys in Mexico, particularly Boyd, who becomes the outlaw and hero that he and Billy imagine they will temporarily enact to retrieve their father's horses or to rescue the girl. But the languorous primadonna rejects this notion that we are what we enact: she claims that she cannot fully participate in operatic passions night after night; in her performances she makes "a study of smaller things. . . . the attitude of the head. The movement of a hand" (229–30). She claims that the *arriero* is wrong because he is "only a spectator in these matters. He cannot see that for the wearer of the mask nothing is changed. The actor has no power to act but only as the world tells him. Mask or no mask is all one to him" (230). Nevertheless, though he is no player in the company, Gaspar is an actor: he has enacted the very violence that he has seen rehearsed repeatedly in the opera company's arena. Like the priest who initially "chose to stand outside the critical edifice of his own church" and thus "sacrificed his words of their power to witness" (152), the diva has found an illusion of safety by reserving her passion—as Billy himself increasingly does. She voices a kind of fatalism in her vision of life as scripted.[7] And yet the final "act" of her story in *The Crossing*, when Billy next sees her faded wagon in a carnival sideshow in Madera (375–378), in a scene that recalls to him the wolf's exhibition in the "shabby circus" (104), suggests that her withholding of passion has afforded her no protection from the unexpected nor from loss. Her warning to Billy about long journeys, borne of her ideas about the difficulty and unwisdom of sustained passion, is prophetic for both:

> The road has its own reasons and no two travelers will have the same understanding of those reasons. . . . Listen to the corridos of the country. They will tell you. . . . The shape of the road is the road. There is not some other road that wears that shape but only the one. And every voyage begun upon it will be completed. [230]

Shaped by being killed as Nedda/Columbine night after night, the diva's fatalistic focus on the road itself, analogous to Billy's idea that life consists only in the linear flow of experience, discounts the rich matrix of passion and value that McCarthy suggests is life itself and is achieved in the intersections of human *jornadas*, in the dynamic tales we create of ourselves and others, tales which alone formulate meaning and value as we witness and are witnessed by one another. Billy's skepticism about the truth of the tales he hears, his devotion to the road alone even while he denies that he is "un hombre del camino" [414] and to the evidence only of his own experience leads to his inner rejection of all tales, analogous to his rejection of faith in life and other men. Although he partially rejects the diva's view of life as scripted when he claims that "it was true that men shape their own lives," he echoes her when he continues, "it was also true that they could have no shape other for what then would that shape be?" (380).

The priest has argued that only God can be "true" witness to the life of man—either to the road he travels to the end and the shape of that road, or to the whole meaning of that individual's life. But he nevertheless affirms that witnessing, tale-telling, is man's essential act: "In the end we shall all of us be only what we have made of God" (158); and *The Crossing* implies, too, that we are what we make of ourselves and others.[8] Myth, parable, philosophy, fiction, it matters not; in the end, the priest hints, the meaning of our lives that can be known and of value to us as we live is the meaning we put there by exercising our human gift for storytelling or narrating. This idea seems central to the Border Trilogy, especially as it focuses on Billy. It recurs in the epilogue of *Cities of the Plain* when the storyteller tells Billy, "The events of the waking world . . . are forced upon us and the narrative is the unguessed axis along which they must be strung. It falls to us to weigh and sort and order these events. It is we who assemble them into the story which is us. Each man is the bard of his own existence" (283). McCarthy was thinking about the role of narrative in our lives and had done some reading in Hegel that seems to have influenced his ideas at least by Fall 1991, when he traveled by train from Washington D.C. to New York City with Douglas Wager, artistic director of Arena Stage, to accept a Kennedy Center award for New American Plays for *The Stonemason*. Wager recalls that during their three hour trip McCarthy talked about "how narrative is basic to all human beings, how even people who are buried alive go over their life stories to stay sane. Verification of one's story to someone else is essential to living . . .; our reality comes out of the narrative we create, not out of the experiences themselves" (Arnold, *Stonemason* 121). At this time, it was likely that McCarthy had substantially completed his drafting of *All the Pretty Horses*, which was published the following spring, and was beginning to turn his attention to *The Crossing*.

When the *gitano* asks Billy which of the three stories of the airplane he wishes to hear, Billy asks for the "true history" (404). In response, the *gitano* gives him all three as he boils leaves to heal the gravely wounded Niño, Billy's father's horse (literally, his father's "little boy"). Clearly the *gitano*'s intention is to heal both *niños*, and his stories seem invented for that purpose as he ponders his words before he tells each segment of his tale. His compatriots, who figure in the tales of the airplanes, listen as though they do not know what will come next, "[a]s if they themselves were only recent conscriptees to this enterprise" (406), and the American who follows behind the gypsies says that the tale is a fabrication (418). The *gitano*'s story responds specifically to two comments Billy makes early in his own very brief account of what has brought him to this pass: his preference for the true story and his information that he is carrying the bones of his brother. The tales of the airplanes sought and retrieved from the Mexican mountains at the behest of the grieving father of the pilot parallel Billy's own grieving journey to retrieve Boyd's bones, as the airplane the gypsies tow on the float echoes the bones Billy draws behind him on the travois. The tales of the two planes, "counterclaimants," raise the question of authenticity, and it may well be that the gypsy invents the "sister" (405) airplane to counter what he intuits lies behind Billy's request for the truth. For Billy has earlier denied having two brothers, one dead and one alive, as he has denied the girl's view of his brother and the truth of the *corrido,* and yet his act of retrieving the bones implicitly credits Quijada's tale of Boyd's end and his Mexican grave. In this instance, because Boyd does evoke his passion, Billy acts upon what he believes may be a fiction. The *gitano*'s tales comment on both the futility and the paradoxical necessity of Billy's act, and finally they hint an alternative to the retrieval of bones.

Recalling the priest's assertion that all tales are one, the *gitano* tells that before the expedition the two lost planes shared "a single history. Whether there be two planes or one. Whichever plane was spoken of it was the same" (404). When the first plane is swept away by the river, the *gitano* argues, the replacement of one plane by the other neither authenticates the surviving one nor invalidates its identity. Rather, he shifts the grounds of their consideration so as to call into question the value or authenticity of any artifact:

> A false authority clung to what persisted, as if those artifacts of the past which had endured had done so by some act of their own will. Yet the witness could not survive the witnessing. In the world that came to be that which prevailed could never speak for that which perished but could only parade its own arrogance. It pretended symbol and summation of the vanished world but was neither. [410–11]

The pilot's father, like Billy, wants to retrieve the only artifact of his son that he can tangibly possess, not as a memento, the *gitano* has concluded, but so that he can gain control of its story:

> as long as the airplane remained in the mountains then its history was of a piece. Suspended in time. Its presence on the mountain was its whole story frozen in a single image for all to contemplate. The client thought and he thought rightly that could he remove that wreckage from where it lay year after year in rain and snow and sun then and then only could he bleed it of its power to commandeer his dreams. [405–06]

The father's wish reflects Billy's motives for some of his most passionate acts; his taking the wolf to Mexico, his shooting her and burying her in the mountains, his efforts to reclaim his father's horses, and his retrieving Boyd's bones all are attempts to rewrite their stories to allay his desires and grief. But though the *gitano* affirms that such an act may promise to be psychologically freeing, he quietly adds that "La historia del hijo termina en las montañas" (406). The story of the son still ends in the mountains regardless of the compensatory images his father may reconstruct. And the stories of the wolf, Billy's parents, and his brother still end in their deaths. The *gitano* says that the artifact "had no real power to quiet an old man's heart because once more its journey would be stayed and nothing would be changed" (406).

And yet the *gitano* affirms "the history that each man makes alone out of what is left to him" (411) over artifact and over the elusive "true" history that the priest says only God can know and that the *gitano* says God does not reveal even if the accidents of this world in some way enact His will. The *gitano* pointedly tells Billy with his cargo of bones that

> the world was made new each day and it was only men's clinging to its van-
> ished husks that could make of that world one husk more.
>   La cáscara no es la cosa. [The husk is not the thing; 411]

Billy changes the subject, asking for the third story, but the *gitano* tells him that the third story is the story constructed by the witness and survivor, the pilot's father or, he implies, Billy himself. This too is problematic, for these tales made of records and memories cannot approach the thing itself: "Memories dim with age. There is no repository for our images. The loved ones who visit us in dreams are strangers. To even see aright is effort." We strive to construct a story out of "Bits of wreckage. Some bones. The words of the dead. How to make a world of this? How live in that world once made?" (411).

The *gitano* appears to have finished his stories, and the gypsies treat the horse and prepare to leave; but when the *gitano* looks again towards Boyd's bones and back at Billy, and Billy responds, "Estoy regresándole a mi país" (I am returning him to my country; 412), the gypsy resumes his third story about the stories we make of memory and artifact. He centers this tale around the discarded photographs or tintypes collected and displayed by his father: artifacts of past lives meaningless now because of the deaths of those in whose hearts these men and women had value.

The interaction of memory, imagination and artifact is a recurring theme in McCarthy's work, dating from his very first story, "Wake for Susan" (1959), in which the protagonist constructs a story of a long dead girl out of the artifact of her gravestone and the concerns of his own life.[9] McCarthy's first novel, *The Orchard Keeper,* may be read as John Wesley Rattner's partly imagined reconstruction of his childhood as he contemplates the gravestone of his dead mother; and the historical story enacted in his screenplay, *The Gardener's Son,* is presented as an imaginative transcendence of the "false authority" of the historical records that document the life of Robert McEvoy. The screenplay specifically evokes still photographs as artifacts of the dead that represent and yet falsify them—as the *gitano* says of photos, "All past and all future and all stillborn dreams cauterized in that brief en-capture of light within the camera's closet" (412–13). In *The Gardener's Son,* Robert's sister Martha claims that memory, as frail as it is, serves bet-ter than photos. The screenplay suggests that collective memories of coun-terclaimants may come closer to "the thing" than does any single view and that an imaginative and compassionate reconstruction may be best of all. In *Suttree,* photographs of Suttree's dead relatives or of Mother She prompt him to varying sorts of imaginative "story"-making (126–30; 279), as does the abandoned house associated with Suttree's family (135–36).

In all these works, artifacts prompt the imaginative recovery of the past, but as McCarthy's career has progressed he has increasingly suggested in his works that artifacts also misrepresent the vanished world they pretend to symbolize and summarize. In *Blood Meridian,* for instance, Judge Holden's sketching of birds he has killed, or of historical artifacts which he then de-stroys, eradicates and replaces the thing itself. In McCarthy's unpublished filmscript "Whales and Men," which, as I show below, dates from about the same time as his initial work on the Border Trilogy and which has plot par-allels with the story of Billy and the wolf and thematic parallels with all of *The Crossing,* Peter Gregory speaks of his meditations at seventeen, when he had lost his father and brother, become very ill with measles, and expected to lose his eyesight:

> I began to see all symbolic enterprise as alienation. Every monument a false idol. Language had conditioned us to substitute our own creations for those of the world. To replace the genuine with the ersatz. The living with the dead. [58]

The *gitano* tells Billy that as he contemplated the fading photos collected by his father he came to see that "Every representation was an idol. Every like-ness a heresy. In their images they had thought to find some small immor-tality but oblivion cannot be appeased" (413). All value is in the heart. But if the hearts in which value resides are mortal, the value of a life seems des-tined to die, if not with that life then with the hearts of those who treasure it. This is why the *gitano* finds the web of meaning created as hearts witness and are witnessed by one another, "a terrible and endless attrition" (413), for the matrix of meaning achieved in human connectiveness itself appears con-strained by the linearity of the road. The threads that flow from the hand of the weaver god, however intricately interwoven in the web of life, flow from his hands forever into history. Or so it appears to the individual who journeys into the world and is borne on its current, passing through and observing the passing of others.[10]

But the gypsy's parable is finally not so nihilistic, for this man of the road ultimately rejects as illusion the linearity of time and of the road, and affirms the matrix of meaning and value, the concept of the world as tale. His storytelling itself constitutes that affirmation, as he weaves his tales to succor the young stranger he finds broken down in the road with his terrible burden. The *gitano*'s stories assert the meaninglessness of artifacts, and yet both as cautionary tales and as expressions of good will, they are themselves meaningful. He concludes by adding that "what men do not understand is that what the dead have quit is itself no world but is also only the picture of the world in men's hearts. He said that the world cannot be quit for it is eternal in whatever form as are all things within it" (413). The world itself is an eternal tale in which, as the priest says, all is telling. The dead may drift out of our individual sub-plots in the tale that is the world, they may quit our illusion of that world, but they are eternally in the living tale, living the tale: "Pensamos . . . que somos las víctimas del tiempo. En realidad la vía del mundo no es fijada en ningún lugar. Cómo sería posible? Nosotros mismos somos nuestra propia jornada. Y por eso somos el tiempo también" (We think that we are victims of time. In reality the way of the world is not fixed in any place. How could this be possible? We ourselves are our own day's journey. And therefore we are time also; 413–14). If the world is a tale, as both the priest and the *gitano* concur, then none of us ever quits it.[11] We are embedded in it, and our time is a manifestation of that tale and of us. As the diva and the priest have said, no one can know the shape of the road he himself travels; but we can and do witness the journeys and departures of others. To construct tales of others and of ourselves, not still artifacts but moving images of the living world that embody the value that is in our hearts, is to connect with life: it is, perhaps, to fulfill that aspect of human nature that is in God's image—to imitate Him in His weaving the matrix. The old pensioner in his questioning has already answered Billy's complaints that the *corrido* and many other tales he hears are false: "For what is deeply true is true also in men's hearts and it can therefore never be mistold through all and any tellings. . . . If the world was a tale who but the witness could give it life? Where else could it have its being?" (154).[12]

At the end of Section I, when the wolf has died, Billy has a vision of her that comes close to embodying and comprehending the *gitano*'s implicit advice to participate in the life of the world through narrative acts that create meaning and value. Billy imagines the wolf

> running in the mountains, running in the starlight where the grass was wet and the sun's coming as yet had not undone the rich matrix of creatures passed in the night before her. Deer and hare and dove and groundvole all richly empaneled on the air for her delight, all nations of the possible world ordained by God of which she was one among and not separate from. [127]

To the wolf, the matrix of the world present and past is made real through her rich sense of smell, and she can be lured only by that matrix. McCarthy's unpublished and unproduced filmscript, "Whales and Men," set primarily in 1984 and focused on a group of men and women who are transformed by their vision of the whale and their doomed enterprise of attempting to save several, shares the environmental vision of *The Crossing*.[13] The screenplay also anticipates McCarthy's use of the matrix metaphor in *The Crossing* in its references to "a matrix, a mother field, existing outside of time" (58), to "the whale who strings the world together" (25), to the "living web" of whale beings exquisitely sensitive to one another's experience (120), to the "net of life and time" in which both whales and men are caught up (94), as well as in the tapestry of crossings finally envisioned by the curious but analytical and initially disaffected doctor John Western:

> I know that one life can change all life. The smallest warp in the fabric can tilt all of creation to run anew. Choice is everywhere and destiny is only a word we give to history. . . . I think of them out there at night on their endless reachings. As if their crossings and recrossings stitched the world together. . . .[129]

In "Whales and Men," McCarthy evokes wonder at the whale's auditory sensitivity similar to Billy's awed acknowledgement of the wolf's olfactory acuteness. Guy Schuler describes his recognition that blue whales, who like all whales have little to do but "contemplate the universe" (23), "were sending and receiving signals the entire width of the Pacific Ocean. . . . I had a sudden realization of their natures on a level I'd never even imagined" (91). He elaborates:

> The world the whale inhabits is above all else a world of sound. . . . It's not just another way of looking at the world. It is the world. Perceived with an immediacy that is foreign to us. When we describe something we see, we translate visual images into sounds and then speak them. But the whale sees with sound in the first place. [93–94]

For wolves and whales, the matrix of the world in which they are embedded is comprised of and accessed through physical sense. The comparable physical sense for humans is usually assumed to be eyesight, as the pensioner's initial despair at his blinding attests. But eyesight is curtailed by physical and temporal proximity in ways that the wolf's sense of smell or the whale's sense of hearing transcends, nor does it provide man an immediate apperception of the world sufficient to compensate for his tendency to replace the world with language. The blind pensioner comes to the realization that "En este viaje el mundo visible es no más que un distraimiento. . . . Ultimamente sabemos que no podemos ver el buen Dios. Vamos escuchando. Me entiendes, joven? Debemos escuchar" (In this journey the visible world is no more than a distraction. . . . Ultimately we know that we cannot see the good Lord. We go listening. You understand me, young man? We should listen; 292). Beyond this, he says that after his blinding he came to understand that the world itself is not perceptible through eyesight:

> He said that it was not a matter of illusion or no illusion. He spoke of the broad dryland barrial and the river and the road and the mountains beyond and the blue sky over them as entertainments to keep the world at bay, the true and ageless world. He said that the light of the world was in men's eyes only for the world itself moved in eternal darkness and darkness was its true nature and true condition and that in this darkness it turned with perfect cohesion in all its parts but that there was naught to see. He said that the world was sentient to its core and secret and black beyond men's imagining and that its nature did not reside in what could be seen or not seen. [283]

And his final admonishment to Billy is to remind him that "because what can be touched [and seen] falls into dust there can be no mistaking these things for the real. At best they are only tracings of where the real has been. . . . Perhaps they are no more than obstacles to be negotiated in the ultimate sightlessness of the world" (294).

The Crossing suggests that rather than any physical sense, the human capability for narrative—not for language, which is another kind of artifact, but for formulating the tale that carries our past, gives meaning to our present, and right intention to our future—is our primary means of accessing and perhaps communicating the thing itself: the world which is a tale. For McCarthy, "the thing itself" carries connotations of truth, ultimate essence, the sacred heart of things that inspires reverence, and he implies that humans access the thing itself only by transcending the obstacles posed by artifact, language, and physical sense in moments of spiritual insight that constitute a direct and immediate apperception of the "world as given." The pattern first surfaces in *The Gardener's Son*, where the Timekeeper says of old records and photographs that "They aint the thing" (5). In "Whales and Men" Peter Gregory expresses his concern that we do not live "in the world as given" but rather in a "linguistic model of the world." He continues, "Everything that is named is set at one remove from itself. Nomenclature is the very soul of secondhandness. . . . [T]he name is not the thing and we experience nothing" (57). However, for the whale with its direct apperception, "the name and the thing are the same" (94), Guy Schuler says. Eric, the young man hired by John Western to sail his ship, says that John is only interested enough in yoga to analyze it, and Guy responds, "Which is not the same thing." Eric adds, "Not the reverend thing itself," and the two repeat this mantra when they mention Fibboniaci numbers and Eric points out that numbers too are human constructs: "We're the ones doing the counting. They're our numbers. A number's not the thing. . . . The reverend thing" (80–81). In *The Crossing,* these references to the thing itself are even more frequent and are of central importance. In addition to those in the passage from the blind pensioner just cited, Don Arnulfo says that men "see the acts of their own hands or they see that which they name and call out to one another but the world between is invisible to them" (46). The *gitano* says "La cáscara no es la cosa" (The husk is not the thing; 411); and Billy demonstrates that he has heard the *gitano* when he says, near the end of his life in *Cities of the Plain,* "[A map of your life] aint your life. A picture aint a thing. It's just a picture" (273). Later in the epilogue, the storyteller picks up and extends Billy's idea: "This life of yours is not a picture of the world. It is the world itself and it is composed not of bone or dream or time but of worship" (287). The priest in *The Crossing* says of the relationship of the world men perceive in temporal events to the all-encompassing eternal world itself: "The events of the world can have no separate life from the world. And yet the world itself can have no temporal view of things" (148); and he says of the heretic that "By his arrogance he had engaged the living thing" (152). Similarly, the blind pensioner tells Billy that the world itself encompasses both good and evil, and further, that

> while the order which the righteous seek is never righteousness itself but is only order, the disorder of evil is in fact the thing itself. . . . This [righteous] man of which we speak will seek to impose order and lineage upon things which rightly have none. He will call upon the world itself to testify as to the truth of what are in fact but his desires. [293]

At its truest, narrative is equivalent to spiritual insight into the world itself: a vision that is not related to eyesight, but that penetrates to the black mystery at the core of things.[14]

In McCarthy's works, the wolf and the whale, with the immediacy of their perception of the world, are not only instancings of the thing itself ("The wolf is made the way the world is made" Don Arnulfo tells Billy [46]), but also models of beings more harmoniously attuned to the heart of things than are humans.[15] In "Whales and Men," all the characters find ways to renew their connectedness with life and the enterprises of men as a result of their experience with the whales; but Billy's vision of the wolf at the end of Section I is fleeting, and he never achieves a comparable one again in this novel even though it is clear he is innately capable of them. His even briefer vision of the diva bathing, which causes him to feel that "the world which had always been before him everywhere had been veiled from his sight" and that "nothing was the same nor did he think it ever would be" [220], has no real effect in his life, coming as it does just days before the wounding of Boyd and his abandonment of Billy, when "the enmity of the world was newly plain to him" [331]).[16] And Billy's "troubling" dream of wolves, in which he once more sees them in moonlight as he had in the opening pages of the novel, and they touch him and their breath "smelled of the earth and the heart of the earth," is a wish to return to the time before his parents' death when such vision into the heart of things was possible for him—a wish that even his dream confounds when Boyd whispers that their parents will not wake (295–96). Near the end of his life, in *Cities of the Plain,* Billy tells the epilogue's storyteller about dreams that "I aint thought about em at all. I've just had em" (277), confirming that his adult life has been characterized by suppression of vision and denial of his potential for understanding. However, the narrative voice of *The Crossing* extends Billy's vision of the wolf at the end of the first section, comprehending the world as Billy cannot, in a passage that anticipates the *gitano*'s tale and prefigures Billy's enterprise with Boyd's bones. Billy lifts the wolf's head and the narrator comments that he

> held it or he reached to hold what cannot be held, what already ran among the mountains at once terrible and of a great beauty, like flowers that feed on flesh. What blood and bone are made of but can themselves not make on any altar nor by any wound of war. What we may well believe has power to cut and shape and hollow out the dark form of the world surely if wind can, if rain can. But which cannot be held never be held and is no flower but is swift and a huntress and the wind itself is in terror of it and the world cannot lose it. [127]

The Crossing is the story of a boy who discovers too early and too crushingly what cannot be held and whose spirit suffers a grievous wound. His innate capacity for narrating the world, participating in its vast matrix, which we see in his boyhood storytelling for his beloved brother and in his visions of the wolf in Section I, is never restored in this novel and only partly and temporarily so in *Cities of the Plain*, in which Billy at seventy-eight tells the storyteller/dreamer of the epilogue, "I think you just see whatever's in front of you" (269). The old indian who tells him he is an orphan warns him to stop his wandering and to return to the company of men: "He said that the world could only be known as it existed in men's hearts. For while it seemed a place which contained men it was in reality a place contained within them and therefore to know it one must look there and come to know those hearts and to do this one must live with men and not simply pass among them" (134). The indian sees and foresees that Billy will spend much of his life "just passin through" as Billy has told the young *hacendado* who commandeers the wolf (119) and will tell the priest at Huisiachepic (141). *Cities of the Plain* bears this out, picking up Billy's life at twenty-eight, when he has settled at the Cross Nines Ranch in New Mexico because, "[y]ou need to find you a hole at some point" (19) but more truthfully because the ranch owner Mac's wife has died and because John Grady Cole, who reminds him so much of his brother Boyd, is there. When John Grady dies and Billy yet again suffers the loss of his "brother," he becomes irrevocably committed to the road.

Billy seems deaf to the indian's view that "he contained within him a largeness of spirit which men could see and that men would wish to know him and that the world would need him even as he needed the world for they were one" (134). He responds only—and falsely—that he is not an orphan. After his doomed attempt to return to his home, Billy seems confirmed in his course of alternately seeking futilely to hold what cannot be held (but cannot be lost) and "passin through." Unlike Boyd, he will not trust or connect with those he meets in Mexico, and the brothers' loss of their parents has created a breach between them that Billy cannot heal and Boyd has not cared to mend. Billy makes no attempt to rescue the diva from her depraved circumstances as he earlier attempted to rescue the she-wolf and the young Mexican girl,[17] and he angrily refuses to see her in that situation (377). (Similarly, in *Cities of the Plain* he warns John Grady not to try to rescue Magdalena from her bondage to Eduardo and he suppresses his compassion for Magdalena, regarding her and her sisters as "Goddamn whores" [261].)[18] Billy's attempts to enlist in the armed services come to stand for his only sustained effort to live among men in *The Crossing*, and this enterprise is doomed, too, because of the newly-discovered or newly-developed flaw in his heart. Significantly, the doctors find that his vision is excellent, while his heart is damaged, suggesting that his shortcoming is more in courage than in the capacity for understanding. After interring Boyd's remains, Billy wanders from job to job for several years, and the narrative itself finds nothing of value in his life to chronicle. His driving away the grotesquely pathetic dog, "Repository of ten thousand indignities and the harbinger of God knew what," who howls as if "some awful composite of grief had broke through from the preterite world" (424), is a cowardly disavowal of his connectedness to the matrix of the world that includes horror and loss and grief—a more explicit instance of the fear of pain that causes Billy to turn away from the sight of the opera singer become an exhibit in a profane sideshow. In *Cities of the Plain*, Billy will tell John Grady, "When you're a kid you have these notions about how things are goin to be . . . . You get a little older and you pull back some on that. I think you wind up just tryin to minimize the pain" (78).

Billy's impulse, too late, to call the crippled dog back to him after the explosion of the atomic bomb at the Trinity Site,[19] the import of which he vaguely intuits, is a small sign that his capacity for life and the right valuing of it has not been utterly extinguished.[20] But the book's final image of Billy picks up the road metaphor with its connotations of wandering, avoidance and entrapment within the illusion of linear time-boundness,[21] leaving Billy crumpled in the road ambiguously in defeat or in supplication[22] in dire contrast with the opening scene of *The Crossing* where Billy and Boyd ride joyfully into their future life in New Mexico, and even with the final image of John Grady's manfully setting off to make a new life at the end of *All the Pretty Horses*.[23]

More affirmative is the novel's ending with the rising of the "right and godmade sun" (426) to make the world anew despite man's enactment of a destructive false dawn, suggesting that the tale of the world continues to unfold, flowing from the hands of the weaver god in a web which enfolds and contains man's desires and tantrums, "Not chaos itself . . . outside of that matrix" (149).[24]

ACKNOWLEDGEMENTS

In addition to specific debts detailed in the notes to this paper, I wish to express my gratitude to two individuals who read this work in early stages and offered their suggestions. Edwin T. Arnold has been a gracious collaborator for many years, and in all my work on Cormac McCarthy I have benefitted from his conversation and encouragement. This study would not have taken its current shape without his generous sharing of materials, insights, and worthy opposition. Gail M. Morrison, with her first-hand knowledge of Mexican Spanish, gave me invaluable assistance with my translations and made several helpful suggestions for revisions.

NOTES

[1] See Georg Guillemin for a Bakhtinian reading of this aspect of the novel. Guillemin argues, "The textual whole of *The Crossing* invites interpretation as not just a circle of stories, but a thematization of the *circulation* of stories as the sharing of experienced negative materiality [of death]. The novel does not simply revitalize old-fashioned storytelling—though it does that, too—but it illustrates how death remembered allegorically (i.e., in stories) and collectively (i.e., through the act of storytelling) modifies the very void of individual death informing these allegories" (93).

[2] The heretic's notion of the weaver god is of a deity "much occupied. . . . Weaving the world. In his hands it flowed out of nothing and in his hands it vanished into nothing once again. Endlessly. Endlessly. So. Here was a God to study. A God who seemed a slave to his own selfordinated duties. A God with a fathomless capacity to bend all to an inscrutable purpose. Not chaos itself lay outside of that matrix" (149). McCarthy's notion of the weaver god is partly borrowed from Herman Melville. In the first of the "research newsletters" that film-maker Richard Pearce sent to the Alicia Patterson Foundation when he and McCarthy were working on *The Gardener's Son* in 1975 is quoted the passage from Chapter 102 of *Moby-Dick*:

> Nay—the shuttle flies—the figures float from forth the loom; the freshet-rushing carpet for ever slides away. The weaver-god, he weaves; and by that weaving is he deafened, that he hears no mortal voice; and by that humming, we, too, who look on the loom are deafened; and only when we escape it shall we hear the thousand voices that speak through it. For even so it is in all material factories. [*Moby-Dick* 374; newsletter 8]

Melville's emphasis on man's deafness within the material factory is perhaps echoed in the blind pensioner's admonition that we should listen (292), and McCarthy's novel stresses more than this isolated passage from Melville that though there are obstacles, man can perceive the matrix while in the material factory, because the factory itself is not outside the matrix. It is possible that McCarthy contributed this quotation from *Moby-Dick* to Pearce's newsletter. As early as 1969 he had mentioned Melville as one of the "gutsy" writers he most particularly admired (Jordan 6).

[3] Billy over-learns from his devastating experiences what the Dueña Alfonsa strives to make John Grady understand in *All the Pretty Horses*: "Between the wish and the thing the world lies waiting" (238).

[4] The opera was first identified by Betty W. Morris (214).

⁵As witnesses, the audience plays an important role in *I Pagliacci*. Often their reactions are in ironic counterpoint to the real drama of love and betrayal, but they also
recognize the genuine emotion expressed by Canio as Pagliacci and Nedda as
Columbine when they break out of the dialogue of the comedy and communicate as
the conflicted lovers they are. For instance, when Nedda tries to cover their confrontation by resuming the lines of the comedy, calling Canio Punchinello, he insists,

> No! Punchinello no more! I am a man again,
> With aching heart and anguish deep and human,
> Calling for blood to wash away the stain,
> Thy foul dishonor, thou shameless woman!
> No! Punchinello no more! . . .
> What have I now, but a heart that is broken?

The women in the audience, still believing that they are witnessing a play, exclaim,

> Sweet gossip, ah, it makes me weep,
> So true it all is seeming. [385]

⁶A free translation, "The play (or masquerade) is the thing," might make more
explicit the allusion to *Hamlet* (III.i; 919). The situation enacted in the *commedia
dell'arte* performance elicits Pagliacci/Canio's self-destructive and violent reaction
just as the situation enacted in Hamlet's play "The Mousetrap" elicits Claudius'
guilty self-revelation (III.ii.). McCarthy often uses his Spanish for just such subtle
effects (as when he switches into Spanish to evoke the metaphor of life as journey
carried in the words *jornada* or *viaje*).

⁷Guillemin points out that "To the observer listening to the story of a life, the person's death indeed defines the story and therefore the life remembered, until the
agency of a sentient fate may be quasi-logically deduced, while, actually, the notion
of fate originates in the retrospective discursivity of storytelling which, in turn, is
grounded in mortality. Progressive (i.e., 'correct') chronicling of events, by comparison, will reduce death to man's accidental, if inevitable destiny, and what could be
truer and more banal than the statement that man's fate is death?" (95). The diva's
sense of fate results from such hindsight. The story she enacts over and over is one
whose ending in death she already knows. It is impossible for her to sustain the illusion that, as Nedda, she is traveling to an unknown end.

⁸In *Cities of the Plain,* one of the more heartening scenes is when Magdalena, fugitive from the hospital, encounters a woman on the road who offers to take her in so she
will not have to return to the White Lake brothel. When Magdalena declines, the woman
takes her face in her hands and studies it "as if to remember her. Perhaps to read at second hand the shapes of the roads that had led her to this place. What was lost or what
was ruined. Whom bereft. Or what remained" (211). She offers to bear witness to Magdalena's life. In the book's epilogue, the storyteller and McCarthy both challenge us to

do the same for each of our brothers: "Do you love him, that man? Will you honor the path he has taken? Will you listen to his tale?" (288–89).

⁹See my forthcoming study, " 'They aint the thing': Artifact and Hallucinated Recollection in Cormac McCarthy's Early Frame-Works," *Myth, Legend, Dust: The Landscapes of Cormac McCarthy, Volume I: Cormac McCarthy's Appalachia*, ed. Rick Wallach.

¹⁰In "Whales and Men," Peter Gregory says of a photograph album of his family and their ancestral house in Ireland:

> I find old photographs a bit unsettling. They do seem to accuse somehow. They're not like paintings. They're a more successful illusion. There are photos here of my great great grandparents going back a hundred and thirty years. They were taken in front of the house and in the photographs the house is exactly the same. It has not changed at all. Well, I think you get my point. I find it . . . The fact that we are sequential beings in a sense. [. . .] That their most enduring reality—and mine—should take the form of a small square of tin or cardboard. Like a form of taxidermy, really. [. . .] It's just unnatural in some way. [46]

Later Peter's friend John Western writes in his log:

> [The whale] sees with sound. What does that mean? That it cannot be preserved, yes. It vibrates and is gone. . . . It's not just that the sea is hostile to monuments. It's the other thing. The state of immediacy. . . . [T]he whale has no need for monuments because the whale has no history. It's not the other way around. . . . What we are talking about is the whale's perception of time. . . . Our history . . . really exists only in the individual memory and is lost with that memory forever. We perceive it to be a summation, a communal enterprise, and it is not. . . . What is experienced is broken down into parts it was never even made of. We have no faith in being because we have fractured it into history. And this is the way we live. In archives of our own devising. Among sketches and bones. [96]

Similarly, Don Arnulfo tells Billy:

> men wish to be serious but they do not understand how to be so. Between their acts and their ceremonies lies the world and in this world the storms blow and the trees twist in the wind and all the animals that God has made go to and fro yet this world men do not see. They see the acts of their own hands or they see that which they name and call out to one another but the world between is invisible to them. [46]

¹¹The storyteller in the epilogue of *Cities of the Plain* tells Billy, "I doubt that our journey can be lost to us. For good or bad" (269). And he relates that the traveler in his dream "saw that a man's life was little more than an instant and that as time was eternal therefore every man was always and eternally in the middle of his journey, whatever be his years or whatever distance he had come" (282).

¹²John Grady seems to hold to this intuition more consistently than Billy is able to. In *Cities of the Plain* he tells Magdalena how he used to ride on the old Comanche trail "and the ghosts of the Comanches would pass all about him on their way to the

other world again and again for a thing once set in motion has no ending in this world until the last witness has passed" (205).

[13]This undated screenplay was most likely composed in the middle 1980s, and was certainly not finished any earlier than 1986. The script ends after the marriage of John Western's girlfriend Kelly McAmon to his friend Peter Gregory, the birth of their first child, and the conception of their second—perhaps two or three years after the main action of the screenplay, which is set in 1984. James Lilley has shared with me that Barry Lopez' *Arctic Dreams*, referred to in the screenplay, was published in 1986, which demonstrates at least that McCarthy was doing some work on the screenplay after the appearance of Lopez' book. And of course, the whole may have been composed in 1986 or later, but the best hypothesis seems that it dates from sometime in the period from 1984 or '85 to 1987, between McCarthy's most intensive work on *Blood Meridian* (1985) and *All the Pretty Horses* (1992). In *Blood Meridian*, McCarthy makes reference to a horse standing on the Pacific shore, watching "out there past men's knowing, where the stars are drowning and whales ferry their vast souls through the black and seamless sea" (304). "Whales and Men" has many more philosophical affinities with *The Crossing* than does the screenplay "Cities of the Plain," which depicts the doomed love of John Grady Cole for a young prostitute in Juárez, and casts Billy in the peripheral role of his less quixotic friend. "Cities of the Plain" apparently dates from the early 1980's; without naming it, McCarthy's interviewer, Richard B. Woodward, described the screenplay in 1994 and indicated that it had existed "for more than 10 years" (40).

[14]McCarthy's concept of the reverend thing itself likely has its roots in a wide array of readings in philosophy and literature. While he does not directly discuss what McCarthy calls "the thing itself," Edwin T. Arnold's forthcoming article, "McCarthy and the Sacred: A Reading of *The Crossing*" is suggestive of its affinity with the thought of the mystic Jacob Boehme, especially as McCarthy embodies it in the wolf which is "at once terrible and of a great beauty" (*Crossing* 127). *Moby-Dick* is another obvious influence. Ishmael sees "the image of the ungraspable phantom of life" (14) in the ocean and, it becomes apparent, in the whale—like the wolf both terrifying and mercilessly hunted.

[15]*Cities of the Plain* suggests that the horse, too, has such direct apperception of the world. Old Mr. Johnson tells John Grady that the horse sees things on the desert at night that humans cannot. When John Grady presses him to explain, Johnson finally says, "I aint talkin about spooks. It's more like just the way things are. If you only knew it" (124).

[16]The enmity of the world is equally plain to John Grady Cole. In *All the Pretty Horses*, he leaves the grave of his *abuela* holding out his hands "as if to slow the world that was rushing away and seemed to care nothing for the old or the young or rich or poor or dark or pale or he or she. Nothing for their struggles, nothing for their names. Nothing for the living or the dead" (301). In *Cities of the Plain*, when John Grady tells Billy that all one can do is use his best judgment as a guide, Billy re-

sponds, "Yeah. Well. The world dont know nothin about your judgment." John Grady replies, "I know it. It's worse than that, even. It dont care" (219).

[17]The screenplay "Cities of the Plain" adumbrates this contrast between John Grady and Billy. John Grady is passionately committed to rescuing the young prostitute he loves from the Juárez brothel where she is held a prisoner, while Billy cautions him to reserve his emotion and declines to consider the plight of the prostitutes he hires. It is interesting to speculate that the novels' infinitely more complex stories of these two young men grew partly out of McCarthy's decision to flesh out the background experiences of the ardent-hearted John Grady and the broken-hearted and emotionally reserved Billy.

[18]McCarthy emphasizes the connection between Magdalena and the diva—and even, more faintly, the wolf—when Magdalena is being carried to the river and her death and she narrowly misses having an epileptic seizure. She has a vision of herself "on a cold white table":

> She sat upright on the table and threw back her head as if she would cry out or as if she would sing. Like some young diva remanded to a madhouse. [225]

[19]James Campbell has pointed out that Billy is in southern New Mexico in "July of that year [1945]" (*The Crossing* 422), and that the false dawn he sees is the nuclear explosion at the Trinity Site that occurred on July 16, 1945 (16). In private conversation, Campbell has also informed me that McCarthy's descriptions of the flash of light and the reactions of the animal-life are drawn from the published accounts of witnesses of the Trinity explosion.

[20]In *Cities of the Plain* Billy laconically tells John Grady parts of his story, and he risks loving this younger man who stands for his brother and who, as the epilogue's storyteller says, "stands in the dock for us until our own time [death] come and we must stand for him" (288). Billy's pledge to care for John Grady's puppy recalls his protection of the wolf and his summoning the misshapen dog in *The Crossing*, reinforcing the idea that his capacity for vision and compassion have not been eradicated but merely suppressed.

[21]*Cities of the Plain* is not a road novel, but one of uneasy, tenuously-achieved domesticity. There the associations of the road are transformed and heightened in the many images of corridors (like *corrido,* a word implying running or flowing): at the White Lake, the hospital, the morgue, the police station. All suggest entrapment, impersonality, and the constriction of the West. Even the corridor leading from the ranch house kitchen back to Mac's office and bedroom hints of the narrowing of the world the protagonists inhabit.

[22]See Edwin T. Arnold's discussion of the ambiguity of the novel's ending in his forthcoming "McCarthy and the Sacred: A Reading of *The Crossing*." Arnold makes a strong and provocative case that McCarthy associates the nuclear explosion with Jacob Boehme's concept of *schrack*—the soul-shaking flash of insight, but also

comments on the ways in which it remains ambiguous whether Billy achieves *schrack* or misses the opportunity.

[23]In *All the Pretty Horses*, the opening depicts John Grady Cole in the context of his valued but endangered home and family, whereas the end shows him riding into a dubious "world to come" (302), having told his friend Lacey Rawlins that he no longer knows where his country is (299). This first novel of the Border Trilogy, itself a road novel, anticipates the images of linearity associated with the road in *The Crossing* when in its first pages John Grady views his dead grandfather lying in state and then rides out into the night, where he sees a train

> boring out of the east like some ribald satellite of the coming sun howling and bellow-
> ing in the distance and the long light of the headlamp running through the tangled
> mesquite brakes and creating out of the night the endless fenceline down the dead
> straight right of way and sucking it back again wire and post mile on mile into the dark-
> ness after where the boilersmoke disbanded slowly along the faint new horizon and the
> sound came lagging and he stood still holding his hat in his hands in the passing
> ground-shudder watching it till it was gone. [*ATPH* 3–4]

The speeding train, running on its linear track into view and out, with its faint after-traces and its delayed aural report, is comparable to the *gitano*'s image of the man borne upon the rushing flume of the flooded river into sight in a moment of brief illumination and out again, or to the old heretic's sudden image of himself as a single thread in the ever-flowing tapestry created by the hand of God.

[24]Several readers have associated the novel's reference to the "right and godmade sun" rising "once again, for all and without distinction" (426) with the *vanitas* theme of Ecclesiastes and Hemingway's use of it in *The Sun Also Rises*. Those who do, often see the ending as nihilistic. Edwin T. Arnold rightly points out, however, that the passage echoes Matthew 5:46:

> That ye may be the children of your Father which is in heaven; for he maketh his sun
> to rise on the evil and on the good, and sendeth rain on the just and the unjust.

Arnold comments: "This is Christ's description of the common grace of God, offered 'without distinction' to all" ("Sacred"). Obviously, I see Matthew as the primary allusion in McCarthy's passage, with its emphasis on imperturbable, enduring, and "godmade" order. Even Ecclesiastes, with its emphasis on human weariness and dissatisfaction, recognizes the eternalness of the world:

> A generation goes, and a generation comes,
>   but the earth remains for ever. [1:4]

But in Ecclesiastes are expressed a dichotomy between the material world and the eternal, and a rejection of earthly life; whereas in *The Crossing*, McCarthy posits a more integrated matrix that one possessing "largeness of spirit" (134) may recognize. The priest's observation that "Every word we speak is a vanity. Every breath taken that does not bless is an affront" (158) may comprise an oblique criticism of Ecclesiastes' lament about the vanity of the world and of its complaint that omits to bless.

WORKS CITED

Arnold, Edwin T. "Cormac McCarthy's *The Stonemason*: The Unmaking of a Play." *Southern Quarterly* 33.2–3 (Winter-Spring 1995): 117–129.

_____. "McCarthy and the Sacred: A Reading of *The Crossing*." *Writing on the Border: Essays on Cormac McCarthy's Fiction*. Ed. Robert Brinkmeyer and James Lilley. (Forthcoming.)

Campbell, James. "'Seeking Evidence of the Hand of God in the World': Transforming Destruction in *The Crossing*." *Proceedings of the 2nd Annual International Conference on the Emerging Literature of the Southwest Culture*. El Paso: U of Texas at El Paso, 1996. 13–17. (Privately distributed).

Guillemin, Georg. "*Et In Arcadia Ego*: On Violence and Death in the Novels of Cormac McCarthy." M.A. thesis. Ludwig-Maximilian-University [Munich], 1995.

Jordan, Richard. "'Just Write' Says Successful Author." *Daily Beacon* [U of Tennessee] 28 Jan. 1969: 6.

Leoncavallo, Ruggiero. "I Pagliacci." *The Authentic Librettos of the Italian Operas*. New York: Crown, 1939. 363–387.

McCarthy, C. J., Jr. [Cormac]. "Wake for Susan." *The Phoenix* [U of Tennessee *Orange and White* Literary Supplement] Oct. 1959: 3–6.

McCarthy, Cormac. *All the Pretty Horses*. New York: Vintage, 1993.

_____. *Blood Meridian or the Evening Redness in the West*. New York: Vintage, 1992.

_____. *Cities of the Plain*. New York: Knopf, 1998.

_____. "Cities of the Plain." Unpublished ts. Cormac McCarthy collection, Southwestern Writers Collection, Albert B. Alkek Library, Southwest Texas State U, San Marcos.

_____. *The Crossing*. New York: Vintage, 1995.

_____. *The Gardener's Son: A Screenplay*. Hopewell, NJ: Ecco, 1996.

_____. *Suttree*. New York: Vintage, 1992.

_____. "Whales and Men." Unpublished ts. Cormac McCarthy collection, Southwestern Writers Collection, Albert B. Alkek Library, Southwest Texas State U, San Marcos.

Melville, Herman. *Moby-Dick: An Authoritative Text*. Ed. Harrison Hayford and Hershel Parker. New York: W.W. Norton, 1967.

Morris, Betty W. "A Matrix of the Southwest in *The Crossing*." *Proceedings of the 2nd Annual International Conference on the Emerging Literature of the Southwest Culture*. El Paso: U of Texas at El Paso, 1996. 211–217. (Privately distributed).

Pearce, Richard Inman. Research newsletter, [c. 7 Apr. 1975]. Richard Inman Pearce Collection. South Caroliniana Library. U of South Carolina.

Woodward, Richard B. "Cormac McCarthy's Venomous Fiction." *New York Times Magazine* (19 April 1992): 28–31+.

The Last of the Trilogy:

First Thoughts on *Cities of the Plain*

EDWIN T. ARNOLD

We have come to the end of something magnificent. With *Cities of the Plain*, Cormac McCarthy brings to a close the work that has consumed him for the past decade and more. The Border Trilogy is destined to engage us in speculation and debate for years to come. Indeed, it seems intended that way. Each volume joins in the larger pattern, to be sure, but each also maintains its essential uniqueness, and each will, no doubt, find its supporters and detractors. *All the Pretty Horses* is the romantic adventure, a modern *bildungsroman* set on a foundation of philosophical and ontological speculation. *The Crossing* delays the expected continuation of the adventure started in the first book by repeating the basic broad narrative with completely new characters; moreover, it inverts the structure by making the adventure story of secondary importance to the metaphysical and theological meditations that form the beating heart of the novel. A much denser, more demanding work, *The Crossing* is a painful and exhausting and finally devastating narrative whose purpose seems almost a corrective to those popular readings of the first book. With *Cities of the Plain*, McCarthy shifts again. He brings together the protagonists of the first two novels, returns to the romance of John Grady Cole's story but tempers it with Billy Parham's sadder, fatalistic view of the world. Some will view *Cities of the Plain* as a lesser work, and certainly it is more constricted than either of the first two volumes, whose protagonists are initially large of heart as they move from one place to another, into and out of Mexico. This is a diminished world McCarthy creates in *Cities of the Plain,* a post-war West suffering through its final mockeries and subtractions, a world hard pressed for heroics and depending instead on simple decency. Neither John Grady nor Billy has been spared by these diminishments. But *Cities of the Plain* is also a necessary work, the one towards which the first two have journeyed in all their richness, and it is not without its moments of quiet splendor. It may, in fact, prove ultimately to be the wisest of the books and, in its cumulative effect, the one that in retrospect will move us the most deeply.[1]

The Screenplay and the Novel

In his April 1992 *New York Times Magazine* article "Cormac McCarthy's Venomous Fiction," Richard B. Woodward explained that *All the Pretty Horses* (then about to be published) was the first volume of a projected trilogy and that "the third part has existed for more than 10 years as a screenplay. [McCarthy] and [film director] Richard Pearce have come close to making the film—Sean Penn was interested—but producers always became skittish about the plot, which has as its central relationship John Grady Cole's love for a teen-age Mexican prostitute" (40). A copy of what appears to be a late version of this screenplay can be found in the Cormac McCarthy Collection at Southwest Texas State University.[2] Certainly this version of John Grady's story is extremely close to corresponding John Grady episodes as they are related in the novel *Cities of the Plain.*

In the screenplay, neither John Grady nor Billy is given a family name, but both are obvious prototypes for the characters in the novel. The time is designated as the Fall of 1952. As Woodward noted, John Grady is the central figure; Billy is an important secondary character but has nothing like the stature he obtains in the book. Like the book, the screenplay begins in La Venada, the Juárez brothel where John Grady first sees the young prostitute Magdalena with whom he falls in love. (As becomes common in the western novels, McCarthy employs Spanish—with English translations provided as intended subtitles—for verisimilitude, most often in the scenes between John Grady and Magdalena.) In subsequent scenes, the screenplay establishes John Grady's position at the McGovern ranch, where he works with Billy, Oren,

Troy, J C, and other cowboys. Uncle John, McGovern's elderly father-in-law, described as "doddering, vacant-eyed" ("Cities" screenplay 9), and the cook Socorro also live on the ranch. As in the novel, John Grady is hurt while trying to break a horse and has to be stopped when he stubbornly and recklessly attempts to saddle and ride the horse again on his own. "Said he was fixin to ride his horse if people would mind their own damn business," according to Billy (24), who is alarmed by the younger man's insistence. John Grady later returns to Juárez to learn more about Magdalena, but she no longer works at La Venada. In his search, he talks with a streetwise twelve-year-old shoeshine boy and becomes acquainted with a blind pianist and his young daughter. With the help of a taxi driver, he encounters a pimp named Manolo, who tells him that the girl—"She is seventeen years old. She is the epileptica. There is only one" (37)—has been moved to another, more exclusive brothel, the White Lake. "It's the fanciest whorehouse in Juarez," Billy tells him. "You better stay out of The White Lake, son. It aint no place for a cowboy" (40). Taking an advance on his next month's pay from Mr. McGovern, John Grady visits the White Lake and buys Magdalena for the night. "There are now scenes of their lovemaking, very romantic, at once sophisticated and naive," McCarthy writes. "A certain clumsiness, not without humor to them. These scenes end with her head on his chest and a look of sadness on her face" (55).

The White Lake is run by a man named Eduardo; his assistant and henchman is a villainous character named Tiburcio, described as "a sinisterlooking invert" (52). They become suspicious of John Grady's attentions to Magdalena, and Eduardo tells Tiburcio to keep an eye on both of them. Now in love, John Grady determines to buy the girl outright from Eduardo. To do so, he sells his horse and pawns his grandfather's pistol and holster, his heritage, and then engages Billy to act as agent since he knows Eduardo would never do business with John Grady himself. Against his better judgment— "Son, you dont even know how crazy you are. You dont know those people," he warns him (81)—Billy goes to the White Lake and offers Eduardo two thousand dollars for Magdalena. When Eduardo as expected refuses, John Grady determines to help her escape and to bring her across the border to America. Mr. McGovern agrees to let him fix up an old adobe house away from the ranch as a home for his bride. While combing through a wrecking lot looking for replacement windows for the house, John Grady is offered a dog by the yardman. The puppy, drawn forth from under the porch, is the last male of the litter, "big and ungainly with huge feet," and John Grady pays five dollars for him. "He'll make ye a good watchdog now," the yardman tells him. "His mama's just a crackerjack" (117).

Finally John Grady is ready to attempt the rescue from the White Lake. He meets one last time with Magdalena and tells her that on the following Wednesday she must go to the café "in la calle Noche Triste" (124). There she will be met by Ramón Gutierrez, the taxi driver, and he will take her across the border where John Grady will be waiting.[3] Magdalena hesitates. "I know you say that you can forget what I have been but I wonder do you know your own heart?" she asks (126), but she agrees to the plan. On her return to the White Lake, a funeral procession passes before her and the spinning spokes of the wagon wheels cause her to have an epileptic seizure and she later finds herself in a hospital. Sneaking out, she walks fearfully through the night streets before reaching the brothel. There Eduardo accosts her: "What do you think? That you have brought some special dispensation into this house? That you are touched by God?" he demands. "Well, regardless of what you believe, I can assure you that I believe no such thing. To me you are just a whore with a sickness. A gonorrea [sic] of the soul. . . . Who do you think would want you? A crazy whore. Who?" (129–30).

The next Wednesday Magdalena leaves the White Lake as planned. John Grady has told her to take nothing, but she is unable to leave her religious icon, a wooden santo. Later, when Josefina, the "old one-eyed criada" (134), enters the room, she immediately notes the missing santo and hurries off to tell Tiburcio. At the café, Magdalena is met by a driver other than Ramon and, after some uncertainty, goes with him. He drives her away from the bridge leading to America and onto an old road running alongside the river. The sun shining through the trees and the flickering pickets of a fence they pass cause the girl to begin another seizure, and it is in this unbalanced state that she sees Tiburcio coming toward the car to kill her.

When Magdalena fails to appear at the prearranged site, John Grady goes in search of her in Juárez. At the morgue he sees her body, its throat cut. "Do you know her?" he is asked (140), and he shakes his head in denial. The screenplay then quickly moves to its inevitable ending. John Grady "strolls along like an automaton" (142) on his way to the White Lake. He calls Eduardo out into the alley behind the bordello by breaking into his car and sounding the horn. "I come to kill ye," he tells the man. "No," Eduardo replies. "If you had come to kill me I would be already dead. . . . You have come to die" (143). John Grady takes out his hunting knife, Eduardo his switchblade, and they begin to circle. Eduardo lectures John Grady during the fight. "You see my friend, it was not my doing that brought her to ruin. It was yours. . . . The head must rule the heart, my friend. Where the mind lacks strength cheap sentiment is always ready to enter and take possession of his house. Once lodged there it is no easy matter to dislodge him. And so the mind becomes weaker and weaker until . . . the simplest truths become obscured. As in your case, my friend. Who cannot see that the most elementary fact concerning whores. (He feints) Is that they are whores" (144). Eduardo proves his superior skill with the knife and John Grady is badly cut, especially across the stomach; nevertheless, he is determined, and in his pain "his eyes show even more resolution." Eduardo continues to instruct. "In his dying perhaps he will even see that it was his commitment to death that brought him here. That it was death he sought. And that it was always so. Even from the very beginning. For we will devour you, my friend. You and all your pale empire" (145). Finally the boy is cut to pieces, "his midsection spilling out his intestines" (146), and it is only by ignoring his wounds and welcoming the blade that he is able to catch Eduardo off guard and kill him by burying the hunting knife through the bottom of Eduardo's jaw and up into his mouth and brain. "The point of the blade must be somewhere just behind Eduardo's eyes," McCarthy writes (146).

As John Grady staggers from the alley behind the White Lake, the shoeshine boy sees and runs after him. He leads John Grady through a "wasteland of rubble" (148) to a shack made from a packing crate and then goes to call Billy at McGovern's ranch. When Billy arrives, John Grady is near death. John Grady speaks of Magdalena:

> I laid here all night worryin about her. You know we talked that time about where people go when they die. I just believe you go somewhere. I seen her layin there on that table. I thought if it's like the preacher says then maybe she wont go to heaven. I was wonderin if I ought to ask God to forgive me for killin that son of a bitch. I mean this may sound ignorant but if she aint in heaven than [sic] I aint interested in goin there. Does that sound crazy? I reckon it does. Bud, when I seen her layin there I didnt care if I was alive or dead. [153]

He then asks Billy to redeem his grandfather's gun: "You keep it. It belonged to my daddy and his daddy and I want somebody to have it" (153). He also asks Billy to care for the puppy he bought for Magdalena. Billy leaves to get the boy water, and when he returns, he finds John Grady dead. "He drags John Grady out of the crate and picks him up in his arms and starts across the lot with him. He is crying. A gray dawn and the ragged shape of Juarez behind him." "Goddamned whores," Billy cries as he carries John Grady's body. "Goddamned fucking whores" (156).

This, then, is the story which began the trilogy, the ending towards which all else has been aimed. What to do with it as a film? As read in this screenplay, it seems rather thin and incomplete, and one can see why, despite a number of good scenes and intriguing characters, it never made it to the screen. Without the background provided by the yet unwritten books, both John Grady and (especially) Billy at times come close to caricature, although one must keep in mind that screenplays can often seem flat and simple in reading. As a film, *Cities of the Plain* might very well have achieved that sense of loss and diminishment and bittersweet regret found in such western films as *Monte Walsh* (based on the novel by Jack Schaefer, author also of the classic western *Shane*) or Sam Peckinpah's *Ride the High Country* and *The Ballad of Cable Hogue*. As a picture of cowboy life at the end of an era, the screenplay does provide convincing moments both comic and wistful. Among these are scenes in the barn and the ranch house kitchen where the men talk together, as both authentic cowboys and as cowboys who are fully aware of the popular image of cowboys and do not hesitate to appropriate that image for exaggeration and humor; a hunting scene in which John Grady, Billy, and others listen to stories of Pancho Villa and the revolution while the dogs run a mountain lion through the hills; several horse scenes, including Oren's wonderful explanation of how a horse sees and thinks; quiet moments between John Grady and Mr. Johnson as the old man contemplates how his life has fallen away from him. All of these episodes can also be found in the novel, revised and elaborated and made part of the whole.

Other ideas in the screenplay are expanded or reconfigured in the novel in fascinating ways. John Grady's understanding of horses is central to the screenplay, but the subplot involving the horsetrader Wolfenbarger is absent, as is the masterful set piece of the horse auction (106–15). The puppy John Grady buys from the yardman evolves into that taken by John Grady and Billy from the den underneath the huge rock following the wild dog hunt (153–77). The hunt itself stands as the central and highly problematic action in the novel, situated between John Grady's hard-headed attempts to break the horse at the beginning and his determined fight to the death with Eduardo at the end. Although it is a great action episode, described and paced with all of McCarthy's controlled artistry, the almost unconscious brutality of the characters makes us confront their motive to violence as effectively as anything in *Blood Meridian*. The maestro's character is expanded from screenplay to novel (he appears rather abruptly in the book, causing one to wonder if McCarthy confused the story lines while transferring screenplay episodes to the book), as is Eduardo, who is also made a more complex figure through his love for Magdalena. During the knife fight in the novel, Eduardo again lectures John Grady, but there is less a sense of performance and a greater suggestion both of cynical wisdom and even of regret in his words:

> In his dying perhaps the suitor will see that it was his hunger for mysteries that has undone him. Whores. Superstition. Finally death. For that is what has brought you here. That is what you were seeking. . . . Your kind cannot bear that the world be ordinary. That it contain nothing save what stands before one. But the Mexican world is a world of adornment only and underneath it is very plain indeed. While your world—he passed the blade back and forth like a shuttle through a loom—your world totters upon an unspoken labyrinth of questions. And we will devour you, my friend. You and all your pale empire. [253]

Though Eduardo's dialogue may still strike readers as overly portentous (it might have worked better heard on film rather than read from the page), he represents a philosophical view of the world often posited in McCarthy's writings, one which characters like John Grady hope to resist.[4]

The most striking difference between the screenplay and the novel, however, is Billy Parham. "Billy" in the screenplay is primarily an older companion to John Grady. He plays much the same role Lacey Rawlins enacts in *All the Pretty Horses,* a voice of common sense, of caution, of reserve. Billy is something of a comic misanthrope in the screenplay who warns John Grady away from love and marriage, and his feeling toward women is best illustrated by his anguished, angry cry in the very last lines: "Goddamned whores. . . . Goddamned fucking whores" (156). He primarily blames Magdalena, not Eduardo, for his friend's death. Anyone reading the screenplay after knowing Billy from *The Crossing* would be justified in wondering if these two "Billys" should indeed be considered the same character, for the young, melancholy Billy Parham of *The Crossing* initially seems worlds apart from the garrulous, folksy cowboy we find here. The novel's "Billy" also seems at first disconnected from the Billy of the previous book, although near the end of *The Crossing* we do find a Billy beginning to adopt the mannerisms of the character introduced in the first scenes of *Cities of the Plain.* "I just got to jabberin," Billy tells the American horseman he meets on his way home from Mexico with his brother Boyd's body. "I been more fortunate than most. There aint but one life worth livin and I was born to it. That's worth all the rest" (*C* 420). These are lines more suitable to the manifestation of Billy in *Cities of the Plain,* both screenplay and novel, than to the Billy Parham we have come to know in most of *The Crossing.* As *Cities of the Plain* continues, however, McCarthy reveals to us that earlier Billy, and one might argue that the novel becomes, in fact, more Billy Parham's story than John Grady Cole's, that in creating the background histories to these two characters, McCarthy found himself pulled closer to the older, wounded man than to the young, impulsive boy. And perhaps this explains why John Grady's story is so little changed from screenplay to novel, while the additions to Billy's are ultimately more profound and provide the novel its soul.

John Grady and Billy

Among the reservations a reader might have about the John Grady story is that it seems such a replay of the boy's experiences some three years earlier as recounted in *All the Pretty Horses*. Once again he is characterized by his skill with horses, his innate courage and dignity, his sense of honor. Once again he falls heedlessly in love with a Mexican girl (the lovely, headstrong daughter of a wealthy landowner in *Horses*; the beautiful, doomed prostitute in *Cities*). Once again he engages in a vicious knife fight in which he kills his opponent. It is possible that in establishing John Grady Cole's background in *All the Pretty Horses*, McCarthy cannibalized his own script and then found himself unable or unwilling to revise the concluding narrative even though he had already used much of the same material. McCarthy seems in general, however, to have had the overall plan of the trilogy in mind for some time, and he never wavered from carrying it to its tragic conclusion. "You haven't come to the end yet," McCarthy told Richard Woodward in 1992 when Woodward questioned the relatively benign atmosphere of *All the Pretty Horses*. "This may be nothing but a snare and a delusion to draw you in, thinking that all will be well" ("Venomous" 40).

In retrospect, *All the Pretty Horses* seems a much darker book than Woodward and other readers realized at the time, and the bait in the snare is John Grady's supposed invulnerability. He is so smart, so good-hearted, so masterful at everything he tries that we tended to overlook the self-destructive qualities that were to be found in his character even in the first novel. After Alejandra tells him she cannot marry him, "He felt something cold and soulless enter him like another being and he imagined that it smiled malignly and he had no reason to believe that it would ever leave" (*ATPH* 254). Shortly thereafter, drunk and beaten, he foresees images associated with his own death, as we will later discover in *Cities of the Plain*: "He saw a vacant field in a city in the rain and in the field a wooden crate and he saw a dog emerge from the crate into the slack and sallow lamplight like a carnival dog forlorn and pick its way brokenly across the rubble of the lot to vanish without fanfare among the darkened buildings" (*ATPH* 255). These qualities are more apparent in both the screenplay and novel versions of *Cities of the Plain*. The older boy (he is nineteen) is still infected by this "cold and soulless" being. He is harder, more easily given to violence. The scar on his face, received during the knife fight in the Saltillo prison, takes on primary significance in *Cities of the Plain*, a mark of his past.[5] It is not surprising when Billy tells him, "More and more you remind me of Boyd" (146), his brother who turned outlaw. John Grady betrays his underlying anger in his reckless and cruel attempts to ride the unbroken horse that has lamed him and in the uncommon brutality with which he kills the wild dogs. He fought in the Saltillo prison to save his life, but he fights Eduardo for revenge and, as Eduardo tells him, to find death. At the end of *All the Pretty Horses*, he tells the judge, "I dont feel justified" about killing his attacker (290). But he feels no remorse for killing Eduardo and tells Billy that "I thought about if I could ask God to forgive me for killin that son of a bitch because you and me both know I aint sorry for it . . ." (*COTP* 259). "There's nothin wrong with you son. I think you'll get it sorted out," the judge tells him in *Horses*. "Yessir. I guess I will. If I live," John Grady answers presciently (293).

On the first page of *Cities of the Plain*, Billy jokingly calls John Grady "the all-american cowboy" (3), an affectionate term he and the others use to show their admiration for the boy. "He's a salty little booger," Troy says. "He's all right. He's just got his own notions about things," Billy replies (20). "John Grady Cole was a rugged old soul . . . . With a buckskin belly and a rubber asshole," Billy later sings (76), comically elevating the boy to folk status, much as his brother Boyd earlier became a figure of peasant story and song. But, as noted above, the John Grady of *Cities of the Plain* is, again like Boyd in *The Crossing*, a troubled character. In an early episode in the book, Billy and Troy visit Troy's brother Elton, and there Billy hears stories about a younger brother Johnny, now dead. Johnny survived the war: "He had whole companies shot out from under him. Never got a scratch. I think it bothered him," Elton says. When Johnny returned from war, he fell in love with a girl who betrayed him. "I told him to his face that he was a damn fool—which he was—and that the worst thing he could do to the old boy was to let him have her. Which it was. . . . I should of just kept out of it. Anybody in the state he was in you cant talk to em noway. No use to try even" (26). Later Troy explains succinctly, "There's a kind of man that when he cant have what he wants he wont take the next best thing but the worst he can find. Elton thinks he was that kind and maybe he was. But I think he loved that girl. I think he knew what she was and he didnt care. I think it was his own self he was blind to. I think he was just lost. This world was never made for him. He'd outlived it before he could walk" (28). In many ways this description fits John Grady. (The blind pianist later says much the same thing about Magdalena: "My belief is that she is at best a visitor. At best. She does not belong here. Among us" [81].)

John Grady believes in the need for a simple equity in the world such as that he attributes to horses: "A good horse will figure things out on his own," he tells Oren. "You can see what's in his heart. He wont do one thing while you're watching him and another when you aint. He's all of a piece. When you've got a horse to that place you cant hardly get him to do somethin he knows is wrong. He'll fight you over it. And if you mistreat him it just about kills him. A good horse has justice in his heart" (53). He tells Billy that he could never lie to a horse, that the horse would instinctively know it (84). Right and wrong are clearly separate entities to the boy: he does not believe in situational ethics. When Mr. McGovern finally beats him at chess, Billy asks John Grady if he "didnt slack up on him just the littlest bit?" and John Grady answers flatly, "No. I dont believe in it" (93).

Eduardo comments on this dichotomous and, to him, adolescent view of the world. He tells Billy:

> Your friend is in the grip of an irrational passion. Nothing you say to him will matter. He has in his head a certain story. Of how things will be. In this story he will be happy. . . . What is wrong with this story is that it is not a true story. Men have in their minds a picture of how the world will be. How they will be in that world. The world may be many different ways for them but there is one world that will never be and that is the world they dream of. [134]

Billy agrees with Eduardo, although "It seems like a betrayal of some kind," he admits. "Anyway, some men get what they want," he suggests. "No man," Eduardo corrects him. "Or perhaps only briefly so as to lose it. Or perhaps only to prove to the dreamer that the world of his longing made real is no longer that world at all" (134–35). Eduardo's words repeat those arguments presented to John Grady by the Dueña Alfonsa in *All the Pretty Horses,* who told the boy, "In the end we all come to be cured of our sentiments. Those whom life does not cure death will. The world is quite ruthless in selecting between the dream and the reality, even where we will not. Between the wish and the thing the world lies waiting" (238).

John Grady argues that he has no options. "There's some things you dont decide," he tells Billy. "Decidin had nothin to do with it" (121). In this belief he is also confirmed by the maestro, whom he asks to be padrino to Magdalena.

> Men speak of blind destiny, a thing without scheme or purpose. But what sort of destiny is that? Each act in this world from which there can be no turning back has before it another, and it another yet. In a vast and endless net. Men imagine that the choices before them are theirs to make. But we are free to act only upon what is given. Choice is lost in the maze of generations and each act in that maze is itself an enslavement for it voids every alternative and binds one ever more tightly into the constraints that make a life. . . . The world takes its form hourly by a weighing of things at hand, and while we may seek to puzzle out that form we have no way to do so. We have only God's law, and the wisdom to follow it if we will. [195]

In this sense, John Grady's eventual fate is inevitable, given the choices he has previously made and therefore is constrained to make. Thus he says to Eduardo, "I come to kill you or be killed" (248), the two choices he sees left to him. Eduardo suggests otherwise. "Before I name you completely to myself I will give you even yet a last chance to save yourself. I will let you walk, suitor. If walk you will" (250). Eduardo in this and other statements already quoted ("Your kind cannot bear that the world be ordinary. That it contain nothing save what stands before one") sounds very much like Judge Holden in *Blood Meridian* ("Your heart's desire is to be told some mystery. The mystery is that there is no mystery" [*BM* 252]). Determined by his sense of justice, his very strict sense of right and wrong, John Grady cannot walk away. In killing Eduardo by stopping his mouth, his talk, his deceit, with his father's hunting knife—"[Eduardo's] mouth was clenched in a grimace. His jaw was nailed to his upper skull and he held the handle in both hands as if he would withdraw it but he did not" (254)—John Grady does what the kid fails to do to the judge. When he prays "Help me . . . . If you think I'm worth it. Amen" (257), he is not asking God to save his life but to let him survive until Billy can arrive and he can settle his accounts, "justify" himself as best he can, before he dies.[6] The kid is devoured in the judge's horrible embrace; John Grady is gathered into Billy's arms and carried back to his own country as Billy cries out for witness: "He was crying and the tears ran on his angry face and he called out to the broken day against them all and he called out to God to see what was before his eyes. Look at this, he called. Do you see? Do you see?" (261).

In carrying John Grady's body back into Texas, Billy is reenacting his earlier effort to return his brother Boyd's remains to their native soil. Although Billy is nomadic, home and family are important to him; indeed, he has spent his entire life looking for that which he lost as a young boy when he left New Mexico to take the wolf back into the Mexican mountains. Just as Billy's story in *The Crossing* repeats in broad outline John Grady's in *All the Pretty Horses,* so does Billy's relationship to John Grady in *Cities of the Plain* bear strong resemblance to that he held with Boyd. What becomes clear in reading the complete trilogy is how thoroughly and complexly McCarthy uses repetition, not simply to retell the same story (for, as his characters so often say, all stories are one) but to create a deep resonance as each parallel story moves towards its inescapable conclusion.

While John Grady Cole can be understood in *Cities of the Plain* without having read *All the Pretty Horses*—indeed, the mystery of his past greatly contributes to his character's status as western loner—we cannot fully appreciate Billy Parham without a knowledge of *The Crossing.* As noted earlier, our first encounter with Billy in *Cities of the Plain* must be disturbing to anyone who has read the earlier book. Rather than the quiet, sad boy we know from *The Crossing,* we at first get a boisterous, coarse cowpoke joking about fucking fat whores. It's a shock, and an unpleasant one. (He has even taken up smoking, something he studiously avoids in *The Crossing.*) In the next scene he blathers and snorts to John Grady about being a cowboy: "I love this life. You love this life, son? I love this life. You do love this life dont you? Cause by god I love it. Just love it" (10). There is obviously an element of self-parody here. Billy reads popular westerns: generic in the screenplay, one book is identified as "Destry" in the novel (59)—most likely *Destry Rides Again* by Max Brand, which tells of a peaceful cowboy who attempts to enforce justice without the use of a gun (James Stewart played the film role in 1939, Audie Murphy in 1955). But we learn quickly that much of Billy is show, bluster, a way to keep more sensitive emotions under wraps.

In quieter moments Billy and John Grady discuss at length the way the country is changing, what is happening to Mr. McGovern and his ranch, to old timers like McGovern's father-in-law, Mr. Johnson, who seems to be creeping into senility. "JC says he aint been right since his daughter died," John Grady says. "Well. There aint no reason why he should be. He thought the world of her," Billy replies (11). Margaret McGovern becomes in the book a primary image of loss, of what was and might have been (although McCarthy constantly warns against "might have been" in his works). "Funny thing, said Billy, is I was fixin to quit about the time she took sick. I was ready to move on. After she died I had a lot less reason to stay on but

I stayed anyways." Speaking of McGovern, he says, "You dont get over a woman like that. . . . Not now, not soon, not never" (12). Near the end of *The Crossing* Billy recalled his own family, all long gone. "I had a younger sister died when I was seven but I remember her just as plain. I went to Fort Sumner to try and find her grave but I couldnt find it. Her name was Margaret. I always liked that name for a girl. If I ever had a girl that's what I'd name her" (*C* 419). And at the end of *Cities* he returns again to De Baca County, his home, searching once more for the grave, and again is unable to find it (289).

Mr. Johnson, Mac McGovern, and Billy all mourn their lost Margarets, and Mr. Johnson especially serves as a clear parallel to Billy now and later. We learn, for example, that Margaret was in fact Mr. Johnson's niece, not his daughter, that he, like Billy, had never married. Mr. Johnson explains to John Grady that there are mysteries—"It's more like just the way things are. If you only knew it"—and "hard lessons" in the world (124, 126), the hardest of which is "that when things are gone they're gone. They aint comin back" (126), words that might easily have been spoken by Billy himself. It is significant that Mr. Johnson illustrates this idea with the example of the eradication of wolves in the country. He tells the boy, "And it had always seemed to me that somethin can live and die but that the kind of thing that they were was always there. I didnt know you could poison that. I aint heard a wolf howl in thirty odd years. I dont know where you'd go to hear one. There may not be any such a place" (126). When Billy, whose attempts to save a wolf set him on his original journey, constantly refers to the old man as "pitiful" and his situation as "awful," he is also reflecting his own personal fears and certainly reveals to us the serious, fatalistic nature beneath his pose.

Billy is in many ways the complete opposite of John Grady, who will not settle for second best. Dianne Luce distinguishes between John Grady as "ardent-hearted" and Billy as "broken-hearted."[7] "When you're a kid you have these notions about how things are goin to be," Billy says. "You get a little older and you pull back some on that. I think you wind up just tryin to minimize the pain" (78). Billy is only twenty-eight, just nine years older than John Grady, but his life has reduced him (Troy tells him he looks "forty-eight" [19]). As he admits to John Grady, he has tried to avoid close relations in order to "minimize the pain," for such relations have always resulted in devastating loss. Thus, he seems to agree with the cynical Eduardo when Eduardo mocks the "love" between John Grady and Magdalena: "Heavens . . . . Do you believe such a thing?" "No," Billy answers (133). Later he crudely and cruelly tells John Grady, "It's just the old story all over again. Losin your head over a piece of tail" (136).

Mr. Johnson, the blind pianist, Mr. McGovern all (based on what they know) support John Grady in his quest for Magdalena. "I think you ought to follow your heart," Mr. Johnson says. "That's all I ever thought about anything" (188); and the maestro tells him, "A man is always right to pursue the thing he loves." "No matter even if it kills him?" John Grady asks. "I think so. Yes. No matter even that," the blind man answers (199). Billy (aside from Eduardo) is the most opposed to this romance, the harshest in his criticism. From his experiences in *The Crossing* and from his awareness of the extreme complications surrounding John Grady's plans, we can understand why. He has lost a brother to such a passion, and he knows that John Grady shares Boyd's incautious ardor and he wishes to save him from it. "You just got a outlaw heart. I've seen it before," he tells John Grady (218).

But Billy is also a decent man: Troy calls him a "Samaritan" when he stops to help the truckload of Mexicans with the flat tire (33), which he does because of the kindness shown to him and his brother years earlier in Mexico. Moreover, he loves John Grady. "I aint jealous you know," he tells him, speaking of John Grady's desire for Magdalena (156), although Oren later says that Billy "might be a little jealous" (202), and of course he is. Nevertheless, once he sees that John Grady is determined to "rescue" Magdalena, he helps him, despite his misgivings, and once more opens his heart to a lost boy and his dream. When it all comes to ruin once again, Billy is allowed a moment of violence, beating Tiburcio senseless, before he is stopped short by Eduardo's words: "You might wish to consider the question of your own implication in this matter" (240). "I should of looked after him better," he tells Mr. McGovern after John Grady's death, echoing his similar statement about his brother Boyd. "We all should of," McGovern answers (263), although we know by now that John Grady was always beyond this type of care. When Billy leaves the ranch, he carries John Grady's puppy "in the bow of the saddle with him" (263), just as he had carried Boyd as a child, the saddle as cradle. And he resumes his wanderings on into the new millennium.

The Fellowship of Men

In a response paper commenting on *All the Pretty Horses,* one of my students wrote that the novel was "a book about masculinity itself . . . a book in which

I see parts of myself as a male and I see them presented in such a way so that they do not seem to be the subject of mockery."[8] Although I have noted that there are conscious masculine exaggerations in *Cities of the Plain,* I think my student's statement nevertheless holds true for this book also. In *Cities* we have two worlds: the McGovern ranch and surrounding countryside are inhabited mostly by men and are ordered according to certain rules of behavior; El Paso and Ciudad Juárez across the bridge are imagined largely in terms of the White Lake and other bordellos, a place in which women are "whores" and men are "pimps" and justice and honor are bought and sold.

The title of the novel alludes to the wicked cities of Sodom and Gomorrah destroyed with "brimstone and fire from the Lord out of heaven" (Genesis 19:24), which McCarthy links to El Paso and Juárez. An urban-rural dichotomy is thus established in the book, but the McGovern ranch and other spreads nearby are themselves threatened by profound changes caused by the post-war society. Fort Bliss is expanding its own boundaries and annexing the property around it. "The army's goin to take this place, but we'll find somethin to do," Mr. McGovern bravely tells Billy as he prepares to leave (264), but the emphasis is on adjustment to a diminished existence, illustrated by the growing number of confined spaces found throughout this novel: barn stalls, hotel and bordello rooms, long dark corridors and back alleys, hospitals and morgue labs, all leading to the packing crate in which John Grady, the all-american man of the west, meets his death.[9] This is certainly the most claustrophobic and the darkest (how many scenes occur at night!) book in the trilogy, and at times it harkens to the hellish netherworld conjured up so expertly in *Outer Dark, Child of God,* and parts of *Suttree.* Eduardo's boast—"And we will devour you, my friend. You and all your pale empire" (lines found in both screenplay and novel)—for all its racist implications also presents a fear that goes beyond simple ethnocentrism, a warning that specific values and ways of behavior are threatened as well. There are honorable people in Juárez—the maestro and the captain of police are two examples, as is Magdalena herself. And there are corrupt men like Wolfenbarger who live across the river. Nevertheless, the moral and sexual typography of this novel distinguishes between the two lands, and the world north of the border in this book is identified primarily as the rural world of men and nature.

This is, however, also an increasingly sterile world. Any reader of McCarthy knows how tentative relationships between men and women are in his books. Few successful marriages are to be found in them, and in the early books especially these relationships are often parodied, sometimes in the grossest manner (the horrifying Rattner husband and wife, Culla and Rinthy Holme as incestuous parents, Lester Ballard and his collection of female corpses, Cornelius Suttree—who is divorced—and the bisexual prostitute Joyce to whom he plays pimp). *Blood Meridian*'s women exist primarily to be raped and/or butchered. Suttree does enjoy a short idyllic romance with the musselharvester's daughter Wanda before she is crushed to death under tons of slate, but even this affair seems on reflection rather ludicrous, and one wonders how seriously McCarthy meant anyone to read it. The Trilogy gives us McCarthy's first extended romances—John Grady and Alejandra, Boyd and the unnamed Mexican girl, John Grady and Magdalena—but the primary love stories in these books are between men and men—John Grady and Rawlins, Billy and Boyd, Billy and John Grady—or men and nature— John Grady and horses, Billy and the wolf. There is also a sampling of good marriages, especially in the western novels—the radio preacher Jimmy Blevins and his wife and the county judge and his at the end of *All the Pretty Horses*; the Parham parents and the blind man and his wife in *The Crossing*; Elton and his wife and Mac and Margaret McGovern in *Cities of the Plain* are examples—but they are the exceptions, and in *Cities of the Plain* (omitting the Epilogue) the suggestion of childlessness, barrenness holds sway. In this world, John Grady's dreams of marriage and domesticity are, as Rawlins and Billy and others try to tell him, unrealistic, especially given his choices of brides, both of whom are, in their own ways, unattainable.

We might, in fact, consider the basis of John Grady's love for Magdalena: to what extent is this relationship a determined attempt to reenact and make right his failed romance with Alejandra (which itself might be seen as a kind of juvenile fantasy)? Magdalena is willing to risk everything in a way Alejandra was not, although, to be sure, Magdalena has much greater reason to take this risk. Moreover, John Grady *needs* to rescue her, and not just for her own sake. We are told that, as a child living in his grandfather's house, he would go to the barn during thunderstorms and comfort his first colt, holding it "with his arms around its neck till it stopped trembling. He would be there all night and he would be there in the morning when Arturo came to the barn to feed." "All his early dreams were the same," we are told. "Something was afraid and he had come to comfort it. He dreamed it yet" (204). We must also remember the guilt he feels for his failure to save Jimmy Blevins: ". . . I stood there and let him walk that boy out in the trees and shoot him and I never said nothin," he confesses to the judge in *All the Pretty Horses*. "Would it have done any good?" the judge asks. "No sir. But that dont make it right," he answers (*ATPH* 293). His actions in *Cities* thus might be seen in part as an attempt to rectify these failures.

Billy's reluctant assistance is also an effort to redeem the past, specifically his inability, as he maintains, to care properly for his brother. Even as an old man Billy will dream of Boyd. "He was the best," he will say. "We run off to Mexico together. . . . We was just kids. He was awful good with horses. I always liked to watch him ride. Liked to watch him around horses. I'd give about anything to see him one more time" (291). Billy could as well be talking about John Grady in this passage, and, indeed, he probably is, for Boyd and John Grady become one in his mind. Billy's most courageous act in *Cities* is to love John Grady, to open his "flawed" heart once again and risk again the pain of loss. The story told by the maestro to John Grady of the man who becomes padrino to the son of his enemy and is ruined by the obligation equally describes Billy's deep affiliation with John Grady. "It was for love of the child that he came to grief, if grief it was," the maestro says but then adds, "I only know that every act which has no heart will be found out in the end. Every gesture" (196). Billy's gestures are pure acts of the heart.

This, then, is primarily a story of male friendship, such as, in fact, are found throughout McCarthy's writings, beginning with his first book *The Orchard Keeper*. Here and in subsequent works the paradigm is the older man or boy who takes on responsibility for a younger, sometimes foolish or simply reckless "outlaw" companion. Such is the case with Marion Sylder (and Arthur Ownby) and John Wesley Rattner, Suttree and Gene Harrogate, Tobin and the kid, John Grady and Jimmy Blevins, Billy and Boyd, and, here, Billy and John Grady. Especially in the trilogy, characters use familial sobriquets like "son" or "brother" or "partner" with great frequency. This is in keeping with western colloquiality, to be sure, but the underlying sense of kinship is always significant. Most of these relationships, however, end badly. Billy's confession that "I should have looked after him better" could be applied to any of these pairs. Nevertheless, the forthright presentation of friendship and affection between heterosexual men is surely one of the reasons McCarthy has earned such a readership for his more recent books. As my student wrote, a work that presents an essentially non-ironic view of masculinity is uncommon enough today to seem quite original.

Which is not to say that the masculine ethos is presented simplistically here or elsewhere in the trilogy. We must acknowledge that Billy's feelings for John Grady run deeper than Billy might admit, and McCarthy, I think, does address the sexual ambivalence that is a part of their relationship. It is reasonable in *Cities of the Plain* to consider Billy's "jealousy" (which he also felt when his brother Boyd "betrayed" him with the Mexican girl), his impassioned violence against the apparently gay Tiburcio (he is stereotypically signed as homosexual in his clothing and physical description), his vocal disgust for "whores" and "pimps," those who make their living sexually, and his apparent discomfort with sexual bonding itself (he seems to limit himself to prostitutes).

All of this suggests that life among men is for Billy cleaner, more orderly, finally more "decent" than life with women (unless they serve the function of mother). Still, it would be a misreading, I think, to argue that Billy is portrayed as homosexual or that his love for John Grady entails overt physical desire, for what McCarthy emphasizes is Billy's removal from emotional commitment and desire in general.[10] Life at the ranch has a monastic propriety about it he enjoys (the only woman there is Socorro, the silent cook), and one that the book implicitly commends in subtle ways. (It is also quasi-military in its structure, its ranking of authority, and one remembers how desperate Billy was to join the services in *The Crossing*: "I dont have any-place to go. I think I need to be in the army" [341].)[11] Oren, for example, ad-monishes John Grady not to read the back of his newspaper while he is reading the front: "It's a bad habit people got. If you want to read a man's paper you ought to ask him" (51). Men eat "slowly and methodically" (135), and when they finish they carry their plates to the sink and put away in the refrigerator whatever is left. There is always a right and a wrong way of doing things, and each man of worth tries very hard to do it the right way.

One might also argue that this is another example of a diminished way of life, a world distinguished by sorrow and loss (Margaret McGovern's death has removed heterosexual love and passion from the place, and this sense of quiet grieving has become the norm). But this kind of rightness, whether in a diminished world or not, translates in McCarthy to a form of humanity, of common decency, and of honor. And this is ultimately, I think, what Mc-Carthy's trilogy is all about.[12] It is what Billy shows in his "Good Samaritan" treatment of other people in need. It is reflected in John Grady's refusal to participate in an underhanded horse transaction ("You wouldnt help a man out though, would you?" "Not that way I wouldnt" [47]) and by his decision to take as his pup the one that has stayed with the dead runt. On the other side of the border, it is shown by the Mexican police captain when he an-swers Billy's angry insult by saying, with dignity, "Mr Parham . . . . Every male in my family for three generations has been killed in defense of this re-public. . . . Any beliefs they may have had now reside in me. Any hopes. This is a sobering thought to me. You understand? I pray to these men. . . . They are my Mexico and I pray to them and I answer to them and to them alone. I do not answer elsewhere. I do not answer to pimps." "If that's true then I take back what I said," Billy responds, acknowledging their shared values (243). Such are the beliefs and actions that this trilogy, and McCarthy's work in general, sanction.

THE EPILOGUE

McCarthy's conclusions are ambiguous and open-ended, mysterious shifts into alternate realities or into parables implying secret truths or gnosis. One immediately thinks of the image that ends *Blood Meridian*, but each novel without exception also fits this description. The almost thirty-page Epilogue to *Cities of the Plain* is the most elaborately conceived of these endings, for it concludes not only the novel but the trilogy itself and, moreover, comments on the totality of McCarthy's work. Like *The Stonemason*, this Epilogue may be read as a deliberate meditation on the nature of artistic creation, the responsibilities and limitations of the creator, and the independent existence of that which is created.

The Epilogue begins three days after John Grady's death as Billy takes leave of the McGovern ranch to continue his wanderings. It then quickly moves through the next decades, years marked at first by the terrific drought, the plague-like desolation that did in truth strike the southwest in the 1950s: "Pasture gates stood open and sand drifted in the roads and after a few years it was rare to see stock of any kind and he rode on. Days of the world. Years of the world. Till he was old" (264). Then, surprisingly, it leaps ahead into the "spring of the second year of the new millennium" (264), 2002 according to Billy's age (he is seventy-eight), a time when the western way of life has finally been reduced to popular entertainment and Billy himself can find work only as a movie extra. (Here, possibly, is a self-reflective joke: *Cities of the Plain* originated as a film screenplay, and with both *All the Pretty Horses* and *Blood Meridian* already sold to Hollywood at the time McCarthy was writing the Epilogue, Billy could possibly be conceived as performing in the filming of one of McCarthy's own works, perhaps even *Cities* itself. It is also true that some actual western figures did portray either themselves or similar character types in the early days of film. Emmett Dalton of the Dalton gang is the best-known example of an outlaw who went on to appear in western films.) Finally evicted from the El Paso hotel (populated by men) where he has lived, Billy leaves without horse or saddle, and even his boots are so "paper thin" (265) that the sole will not hold (some values still exist, however: the cobbler refuses to take money for a useless job). Billy sleeps one night under a concrete overpass in central Arizona (the allusion to *Suttree* is clear: the fourth book of his southern works and the fourth of his western join together here in significant symmetry) and he dreams of his dead sister Margaret. "He woke and lay in the dark and the cold and he thought of her and he thought of his brother dead in Mexico. In everything that he'd ever thought about the world and about his life in it he'd been wrong," we are told one more time (266). Across the highway he spots another figure (his "anti-Billy"?), and he invites this stranger to share his meager food: several packages of crackers. Billy suspects the man might be Death come for him, and he welcomes the arrival. The man denies this identity, but he has a story to tell Billy that ultimately concerns Death, as have so many others during Billy's many years of travel.

There is a strong sense of regret and loss in McCarthy's writing (see the final paragraph of *The Orchard Keeper* for an early example), a realization that nothing lasts except loneliness and pain.[13] Nowhere is the feeling more evident than in this Epilogue. But it is also possible that in reading the many tales and parables in McCarthy's fiction we sometimes approach them with too great a solemnity and miss the understated though intrinsic humor that is woven into the narratives. The three main "parables" in *The Crossing*, for example—the priest's tale, the blind man's story, and the gypsy's allegory— all have quiet comic moments which in no way detract from the seriousness of what they intend. Billy's common-sense questions and responses to the stranger's story in this novel provide a dialogic format for much of the Epilogue, but also create perfect moments of verbal comedy (part Abbott and Costello, part Vladimir and Estragon) that ground the metaphysical aspects of the story and prevent it from drifting into esoteric pretentiousness. As elsewhere in the novel, McCarthy here employs Billy as ballast. For example, the traveler tells Billy that he once drew a path of his life on a map, thinking "that if I could see that pattern and identify the form of it then I would know better how to continue. I would know what my path must be. I would see into the future of my life" (268). The map, he says, turned into a face as he observed it, and then back into the map again. "Did you see it or did you just think you did?" Billy asks. "What would be the difference?" the man replies. The conversation continues:

I dont know. I think there has to be a difference.

So do I. But what is it?

Well. It wouldnt be like a real face.

No. It was a suggestion. Un bosquejo. Un borrador, quizás.

Yes.

In any case it is difficult to stand outside of one's desires and see things of their own volition.

I think you just see whatever's in front of you.

Yes. I dont think that. [269]

The essence of the traveler's story is that we create in retrospect the narrative of our lives; we give shape to the events that have occurred, whether they have inherent connection or not.[14] Billy insists that pictures and dreams are not the same thing as the reality of existence which, he argues, has its own inherent meaning. "But what is your life?" the stranger responds. "Can you see it? It vanishes at its own appearance. Moment by moment. Until it vanishes to appear no more. When you look at the world is there a point in time when the seen becomes the remembered? How are they separate? It is that which we have no way to show" (273). The stranger then goes beyond this distinction between what is experienced and what is remembered. He recounts a lengthy dream he once had in which another traveler, another dreamer, appears, and the stranger then begins to recount that dream, encased within his own dream, as well. Billy questions whether anyone can experience the dream of another dreamer, even if that dreamer appears in the first dreamer's dream, is in effect created by the first dreamer. He then asks if the second dreamer's dream can be said to have a separate existence from the first dream in which it occurs. The stranger is adamant on this point: "But anyway the dreams of this man were his own dreams. They were distinct from my dream" (273). "My own dream is another matter," he later adds. "My traveler sleeps a troubled dream. Shall I wake him? The proprietary claims of the dreamer upon the dreamt have their limits. I cannot rob the traveler of his own autonomy lest he vanish altogether. You see the problem." "I think I'm beginnin to see several problems," Billy wryly answers, providing the reader with a momentary pause. "You may say that he has no substance and therefore no history but my view is that whatever he may be or of whatever made he cannot exist without a history," the stranger then explains. "And the ground of that history is not different from yours or mine for it is the predicate life of men that assures us of our own reality and that of all about us" (274).

This Epilogue is about many things, but chief among them, I think, is the role of the artist, or the dreamer, or the creator, and his responsibilities to the subjects of his dreams. Who has created the story we have just read? We might well suspect that this episode, this stranger himself, are products of Billy's own imagination: he has just awakened, so he thinks, from dreaming of his sister and he has been recalling his brother and his mind is in a state of reverie. But to what extent is the ultimate dreamer revealed in this Epilogue to be McCarthy himself, attempting to explain or justify the story he is now concluding? What, he may be asking, are the storyteller's obligations to his readers? To his characters? Why bring John Grady and Billy to these ends, especially after engaging the reader to them so completely in the two previous books? What is the morality of setting "a snare and a delusion to draw [the reader] in"? Why be bound by a tragic conclusion first conceived in an old screenplay when, as author, he could now revise and manipulate as necessary to avoid these fates? "It was just a dream. You dreamt him. You can make him do whatever you like," Billy insists to the stranger (284). But the traveler demurs, for the dreamer, he insists, cannot alter the story, which has a life and a morality of its own. The author's options are limited, and the tale much stronger than the teller. The same is true of life itself. Although we give personal shape to our existence by the narration we place upon it, the essence of that narrative is not ours to control. "You call forth the world which God has formed and that world only. Nor is this life of yours by which you set such store your doing, however you may choose to tell it" (285), the stranger tells Billy.

"I think you got a habit of makin things a bit more complicated than what they need to be. Why not just tell the story?" Billy asks at one point (278), allowing McCarthy to snatch the rug from under the feet of potential critics. Why indeed does McCarthy resort to such a portentous narrative style time and again? The answer seems to be that a different language is demanded by the subject, and that language, "older than the spoken word" (280–81), can be found only in an alternate way of experiencing and knowing the world. Life is predicated on pain, but pain is necessary for memory, and memory allows us to share the common history of all people.[15] By doing so, we experience the world that is rather than our individual apprehension of it. The "immappable world of our journey" (288) thus refers to the passage taken by all.

The Epilogue reflects once again the pervasive influence in McCarthy's western work of such modern Mexican and Latin American writers as Jorge Luis Borges and Gabriel García Márquez, but it also, I think, is intended to remind us of another work focused on dreams and the artist, another work that is concerned with the passage of time and is concluded by an Epilogue that speaks directly to the reader. "Our revels are now ended. These our actors,/As I foretold you, were all spirits and /Are melted into air, into thin air" Shakespeare writes in *The Tempest* (IV, i, 148–50). The passage continues with the well-known lines, "We are such stuff/As dreams are made on, and our little life/Is rounded with a sleep" (156–58). Such thoughts are clearly applicable to McCarthy's ending, as he, like Prospero, "Untie[s] the spell" (V, i, 254) created through these three books.

Prospero's Epilogue asks his audience to "release me from my bands/With the help of your good hands" (Epilogue, 9–10). What is McCarthy asking of us as he reaches this point in his career? For the first time in years we have no idea what his next work will be. We have come to the end of something, and whatever else McCarthy might do in the future, he has for the moment reached a close. And that thought is sobering, indeed.

THE DEDICATION

Billy ends up in De Baca County, where he lived as a young child and where he once again finds kindness. Like Suttree, he drinks water from a cup and, as in that novel, the act seems a blessing. He comes to reside with a family, and in the company of their affection he waits for his death. After he dreams of Boyd and calls out to him, the woman of the family comes to comfort him, pats his hand: "Gnarled, ropescarred, speckled from the sun and the years of it. The ropy veins that bound them to his heart. There was map enough for men to read. There God's plenty of signs and wonders to make a landscape. To make a world" (291), McCarthy writes, emphasizing the unity, the "matrix," of flesh and earth. Near the end of *All the Pretty Horses*, John Grady Cole tells the judge that "it kindly bothered me in the court what you said. It was like I was in the right about everything and I dont feel that way" (ATPH 290). "I'm not what you think I am. I aint nothin. I dont know why you put up with me," Billy tells the woman. "I know who you are. And I do know why. You go to sleep now. I'll see you in the morning," she answers (292), recalling once again Jesus's parable of the Pharisee and the tax collector (see endnote 6). Thus she acts as mother to the child, and the trilogy ends in the place of lullabies, which takes us back to the title of the first book of the trilogy.

The concluding "Dedication" closes the circle of humanity. "I will be your child to hold/And you be me when I am old," it begins (293). Who speaks in this dedication and what is being dedicated? Who is "I" and who is "you"? The situation describes Billy, to be sure, the old man who has returned to childhood, and McCarthy here takes the tremendous risk of appearing maudlin at the end. But it escapes such sentimentality, I think, because the "Dedication" (of the entire Trilogy, I would assume) speaks to us all. "Every man's death is a standing in for every other," the stranger tells Billy. "And since death comes to all there is no way to abate the fear of it except to love that man who stands for us. . . . That man who is all men and who stands in the dock for us until our own time come and we must stand for him"(288). The "Dedication" thus positions us all with a sweetness and a gentleness that astonishes.

McCarthy's has not mellowed in his view of life. He confirms that "The world grows cold/The heathen rage." But this book, this trilogy, tells us our story, "stands for us" and guides us. "The story's told/Turn the page": surely we wish it might be otherwise.

ACKNOWLEDGEMENTS

I am most grateful to the Southwestern Writers Collection, Albert B. Alkek Library, Southwest Texas State University, San Marcos, TX, for making available to me the unpublished screenplay "Cities of the Plain." This screenplay was essential to the writing of my essay. I would also thank, as always, my co-editor and colleague Dianne C. Luce for all of her careful reading and thoughtful suggestions. I am much indebted to her at every step.

NOTES

[1] This essay was written immediately after *Cities of the Plain* was published in May, 1998. It, of necessity, reflects first thoughts on the novel, some of which will need to be reconsidered, I am certain, after more time has passed. It places this work in the context of the trilogy as a whole and makes initial attempts to deal with certain critical issues in the book and in McCarthy's writing in general.

[2] The unpublished screenplay is 154 pages long, including the title sheet. On this sheet the title is printed in all caps as is the author's name. McCarthy has then signed his name beneath. The pages are numbered in hand also. It is located in the Cormac McCarthy Collection, Southwestern Writers Collection, Albert B. Alkek Library, Southwest Texas State University, San Marcos, Texas.

[3] This is an interesting choice of names for the driver. Ramón A. Gutiérrez is a

noted scholar on Mexico and the Southwest. Among his works are *When Jesus Came, the Corn Maiden Went Away: Marriage, Sexuality, and Power in New Mexico, 1500–1846* (1991) and *Home Altars of Mexico* (1997), both published long after the composition of this screenplay; however, his thesis "Marriage, Sex and the Family: Social Change in Colonial New Mexico: 1690–1846" (University of Wisconsin-Madison) was completed in 1980. His work on Border Theory makes the name especially significant for the man who should bring Magdalena across the border into Texas. This is a curiosity that may be nothing more than coincidence, and it should be noted that the taxi driver goes unnamed in the novel.

⁴The image of Eduardo's passing the knife "back and forth like a shuttle through a loom" is especially significant, given the connection with Melville's "weaver god" in *Moby-Dick*. See Dianne C. Luce's discussion of McCarthy's use of this idea in *The Crossing* in her essay "The Road and the Matrix: The World as Tale in *The Crossing*" in this volume.

⁵This scar is not mentioned in the screenplay, which might suggest that McCarthy at this time had not anticipated John Grady's knife fight in the prison.

⁶The concept of justification is important to John Grady Cole. McCarthy is most likely alluding here to Christ's parable of the Pharisee and the tax collector who enter the temple to pray. The Pharisee thanks God "that I am not as other men are, extortioners, unjust, adulterers, or even as this publican." The publican simply prays "God be merciful to me a sinner." Christ explains, "I tell you, this man went down to his house justified rather than the other: for every one that exalteth himself shall be abased; and he that humbleth himself shall be exalted" (Luke 18:9–14). This parable is also notably quoted in Sam Peckinpah's *Ride the High Country*, in which an old cowboy, Steve Judd (Joel McCrae), maintains a strict moral code and explains to his less-respectable sidekick Gil Westrum (Randolph Scott), "All I want is to enter my house justified." See Michael Bliss, *Justified Lives: Morality and Narrative in the Films of Sam Peckinpah*, 32–58, for a lengthy discussion of this great western, one of the first to view the West in its decline. McCarthy surely knows the film.

⁷See "The Road and the Matrix," 218, n. 17.

⁸Lucas Pasley, "Response Paper to *All the Pretty Horses*," 4 May 1998.

⁹I am thankful to Dianne Luce for this excellent observation, first made at the Round Table Discussion on the Completion of the Border Trilogy, American Literature Association, San Diego, CA, 29 May 1998.

¹⁰Others have argued that *all* westerns are homoerotic in the sense that they celebrate masculinity and the male body. Cowboys are often presented in film and story as objects of desire. In his study *Westerns: Making the Man in Fiction and Film*, Lee Clark Mitchell writes that "No other genre has men bathe as often as Westerns, where they repeatedly strip down to nothing more than an occasional hat, cigar, and bubbles in order to soak the dust away." He argues that these scenes "serve as miniature convalescence sequences in which the hero is reduced to a prone position so that the camera can display him recovering himself. We watch, that is, men becoming

men in the principal way the Western allows, by being restored to their male bodies" (151). Male partnership also operates on a necessarily intimate physical level, given the tasks these men perform and the conditions under which they live and work. McCarthy reflects these realities in his western books. On the other hand, in *All the Pretty Horses,* when the Mexican candelleros offer to buy Jimmy Blevins, their intention seems sexual, which is how John Grady interprets it: "They did not look evil but it was no comfort to him," McCarthy writes (76). There is also the ambiguous prison torture scene in which Rawlins is taken to the shower room and *something* occurs—"He keeps a white coat back there on a hook. He takes it down and puts it on and ties it around his waist with a string," Rawlins tells of the Mexican police captain (169)—but the act itself is left unspecified. There are very few overtly homosexual characters in all of McCarthy's writings, and the ones that do appear are usually presented unsympathetically or, at best, with bemused tolerance, as in *Suttree*. Characters like the monstrous Judge Holden in *Blood Meridian* clearly must be reserved for other classifications altogether.

¹¹This quote also echoes Lester Ballard's plaintive observation when he returns to the hospital in *Child of God*: "I'm supposed to be here, he said" (192).

¹²Jack Schaefer expresses this idea in his novel *Monte Walsh,* whose title character bears similarities to both John Grady Cole and Billy Parham: "Another young one [Walsh] was riding north with a trail herd, with the men and the horses that were taking the Texas longhorn to the farthest shores of the American sea of grass, unthinking, uncaring, unknowing that he and his kind, compound of ignorance and gristle and guts and something of the deep hidden decency of the race, would in time ride straight into the folklore of a weary old world" (29).

¹³None of McCarthy's novels is set in a present time contemporary to the writing (in *Cities of the Plain* the Epilogue's shift to the future adds to its sense of mystery and dream). All of them conjure up a past time, a past life. Although the title to this novel, *Cities of the Plain,* clearly refers to the Biblical cities of Sodom and Gomorrah, it also reflects the fourth volume of Marcel Proust's *Remembrance of Things Past,* which, in the C. K. Scott Moncrieff translation is called *Cities of the Plain* (New York: Random House, 1927). Susan Kollin has further noted that the story of Lot's wife is appropriate to the sense of a lost world: she argues that McCarthy writes against such looking back, that he is essentially anti-nostalgic in the trilogy. Kollin made this argument at the Round Table Discussion on the Completion of the Border Trilogy, held at the American Literature Association meeting, San Diego, CA, 29 May 1998.

¹⁴For a complete discussion of this theme, see Dianne C. Luce. "The Road and the Matrix: The World as Tale in *The Crossing*" in this volume.

¹⁵As the Dueña Alfonsa tells John Grady in *All the Pretty Horses,* "Scars have the strange power to remind us that our past is real. The events that cause them can never be forgotten, can they?" (135).

WORKS CITED

Bliss, Michael. *Justified Lives: Morality & Narrative in the Films of Sam Peckinpah.* Carbondale and Edwardsville: Southern Illinois UP, 1993.

Luce, Dianne C. "The Road and the Matrix: The World as Tale in *The Crossing.*" *Perspectives on Cormac McCarthy.* Revised Edition. Ed. Edwin T. Arnold and Dianne C. Luce. Jackson: UP of Mississippi, 1998. 195–219.

McCarthy, Cormac. *All the Pretty Horses.* New York: Knopf, 1992.

_____. *Blood Meridian or the Evening Redness in the West.* New York: Random House, 1985.

_____. *Child of God.* New York: Vintage, 1973.

_____. *Cities of the Plain.* New York: Knopf, 1998.

_____. "Cities of the Plain." unpublished ts. Cormac McCarthy collection, Southwestern Writers Collection, Albert B. Alkek Library, Southwest Texas State U, San Marcos.

_____. *The Crossing.* New York: Knopf, 1994.

Mitchell, Lee Clark. *Westerns: Making the Man in Fiction and Film.* Chicago & London: University of Chicago Press, 1996.

Schaefer, Jack. *Monte Walsh.* Boston: Houghton Mifflin, 1963.

Shakespeare, William. "The Tempest." *The Complete Works of Shakespeare.* Ed. Hardin Craig. Glenview, IL: Scott, Foresman, 1961. 1247–70.

Woodward, Richard B. "Cormac McCarthy's Venomous Fiction." *New York Times Magazine* (19 April 1992): 28–31+.

Notes on Contributors

Edwin T. Arnold is a professor of English at Appalachian State University in Boone, North Carolina. He has published widely on Erskine Caldwell, William Faulkner, Donald Harington, and Cormac McCarthy. Among his recent works are *Reading Faulkner's* Sanctuary (co-authored with Dawn Trouard) and the introduction to Henry Clay Lewis's *Odd Leaves from the Notebook of a Louisiana Swamp Doctor.*

Leo Daugherty is Professor Emeritus of Literature and Linguistics at the Evergreen State College, where he was founding director of the Center for the Study of Science and Human Values. His short fiction and memoirs have appeared in *Exquisite Corpse, Omni,* and *The Southern Quarterly.* He has also published recent work on Shakespeare and genre theory. He has a new essay on the Elizabethan poet Richard Barnfield in the forthcoming *Richard Barnfield: A Celebration.* He lives in Charlottesville, Virginia.

John M. Grammar teaches English and American literature at the University of the South; his book *Pastoral and Politics in the Old South* was recently published.

Dianne C. Luce chairs the English Department at Midlands Technical College in Columbia, South Carolina. She is the author of *Annotations to William Faulkner's* As I Lay Dying and editor of William Faulkner's *Elmer* and *William Faulkner's* As I Lay Dying: *A Critical Casebook.* She has written several articles on Cormac McCarthy.

Gail Moore Morrison is Director of Academic Affairs at South Carolina's coordinating board, the Commission on Higher Education. She has published essays and delivered papers on a variety of Southern writers including William Faulkner, Cormac McCarthy, Fred Chappell, Joan Williams, Anne Tyler, and Pat Conroy.

David Paul Ragan chairs the English Department at Hammond School in Columbia, South Carolina. He has published two books and several articles on Faulkner and has written on other figures in Southern literature and post-colonial studies. He has been a Fulbright Lecturer in Indonesia and has held fellowships from the Council for Basic Education, the U.S. Department of Education, and the National Endowment for the Humanities.

Steven Shaviro teaches at the University of Washington. He is the author of *Doom Patrols* (Serpent's Tail, 1997) and of *Stranded in the Jungle*, currently being serialized on the World Wide Web. <http://www.dhalgren.com/ Stranded/index.html>

John Sepich lives two miles west and one mile south of Dunlap in rural central Illinois. He has a variety of jobs: in one he works with tractor parts, in another he picks horse stalls, and in yet another he teaches composition.

Thomas D. Young, Jr., who wrote a dissertation on Cormac McCarthy in 1990, is an educational consultant living in Austin, Texas.

Index